AF676806

Handbook of Metallonutraceuticals

Handbook of Metallonutraceuticals

Editor

Jakub Sarto

scitus
academics

Handbook of Metallonutraceuticals
Edited by **Jakub Sarto**

ISBN: 978-1-68117-698-7
Library of Congress Control Number: 2016958858

© 2018 by
SCITUS Academics LLC,
616, Corporate Way, Suite 2, 4766,
Valley Cottage, NY 10989

www.scitusacademics.com

This book contains information obtained from highly regarded resources. Copyright for individual articles remains with the authors as indicated. All chapters are distributed under the terms of the Creative Commons Attribution License, which permits unrestricted use, distribution, and reproduction in any medium, provided the original author and source are credited.

Notice

Reasonable efforts have been made to publish reliable data and views articulated in the chapters are those of the individual contributors, and not necessarily those of the editors or publishers. Editors or publishers are not responsible for the accuracy of the information in the published chapters or consequences of their use. The publisher believes no responsibility for any damage or grievance to the persons or property arising out of the use of any materials, instructions, methods or thoughts in the book. The editors and the publisher have attempted to trace the copyright holders of all material reproduced in this publication and apologize to copyright holders if permission has not been obtained. If any copyright holder has not been acknowledged, please write to us so we may rectify.

Printed in United States of America on Acid Free Paper

Preface

Nutraceuticals is a broad term used to describe a product derived from food sources with additional health benefits besides the basic nutrition found in foods. They can be regarded as non-specific therapies used to promote general well-being, control symptoms and prevent malignancy. The nutraceuticals are usually found in the recommended dose in a medicinal format such as a capsule, powder or tablet. More strictly speaking, nutraceutical means that the extract or food has a physiological benefit or may protect against chronic conditions. Flavonoids antioxidants, alpha linolenic acid from flax seeds, beta carotene from marigold petals, anthocyanins from berries, etc. are other nutraceutical examples. Many botanical and herbal extracts, such as ginseng, oil of garlic, etc. Nutraceuticals are developed. Food and drugs of natural origin play an important role in any nation's public health system. Cooking of terminologies such as nutraceuticals, phytofoods, phytochemicals, dermaceuticals, cosmoceuticals, and functional foods has been caused by the search for specific components of plants, microbials, minerals and animals that are beneficial to our physical and mental health. Handbook of Metallonutraceuticals is intended to explore concepts relating to the nutritional and therapeutic use of metals, product development approaches and concepts that are ready to be realistic for metallonutraceuticals specific to their condition.

The medicinal and nutritional value of metals, such as iron, calcium and zinc, has been known for quite some time in traditional medicine. Some other metals, such as gold and silver, can benefit from cure and health. Ancient psychics found that drugs of different origin (herbal, animal or metal) along with codes of conduct and dietary regulations are appropriate tools to maintain health in diseases that are healthy and eradicating. A special feature of this system is the use of metallic preparations in healthcare. Metals processed such as Mercury, zinc, lead, silver, gold, copper, etc. Psychics were used with great authority in different disease conditions rather often. This book is an immense tool for medical students, health professionals, researchers and professionals.

Table of Contents

Chapter 1

Why Nutraceuticals do not Prevent or Treat Alzheimer's Disease Anna

EO Fisher and Declan P Naughton*

School of Pharmacy and Biomolecular Sciences, University of Brighton, Cockcroft Building, Moulsecoomb, Brighton, UK

ABSTRACT

A great deal of research has pointed to deleterious roles of metal ions in the development of Alzheimer's disease. These include: i) the precipitation and aggregation of amyloid β (Aβ) peptides to form senile plaques and neurofibrillary tangles, and/or ii) the augmentation of oxidative stress by metal ion mediated production and activation of hydrogen peroxide. The growing trend in nutraceutical intake is in part a result of the belief that they postpone the development of dementias such as Alzheimer's disease. However, pathogenic events centred on metal ions are expected to be aggravated by frequent nutraceutical intake. Novel therapeutic approaches centred on chelators with specificity for copper and iron ions should be fully explored.

INTRODUCTION

Dementia currently affects over 750,000 people in the UK, with Alzheimer's disease (AD) accounting for 55 % of those cases. As a result of increasing life expectancy, the number of people predicted to suffer from dementia is expected to rise to over 1.8 million by 2050. Currently there are no known cures for AD. Existing treatments at best only delay the progression of disease and accurate diagnosis can only be made with certainty at autopsy. Hence, there is an urgent need for new therapeutic approaches and for reliable and noninvasive methods to aid in the early diagnosis of AD and to give an indication of disease progression. Advanced AD is evident from the apparent progressive decline in cognitive function as a result of loss of neurons. These are accompanied by pathological changes including extracellular amyloid β plaques and intracellular changes called neurofibrillary tangles, which are abnormal deposits of hyperphosphorylated tau proteins [1].

Recent reports ascribe a major role for the metal ions, iron, copper and zinc in AD. Specifically the redox active metal ions Fe^{2+} and Cu^{+} can generate the highly reactive and oxidizing species, the hydroxyl radical via the Fenton reaction. This species is thought to account for a large proportion of oxidative modifications that are seen in AD brains including lipid peroxidation, nucleic acid oxidation and protein carbonylation. Also metal ions have been shown to be central to Aβ pathogenicity.

The Aβ peptide is a low molecular weight protein consisting of 39–43 amino acids. It has two high affinity binding sites, one specific for copper and one specific for zinc. In the Aβ1–42 peptide (the predominant Aβ species found in amyloid plaques in AD brains) the high affinity binding site binds Cu^{2+} were estimated at log K = 17.2 and 16.3 at pH 7.4 and pH 6.6 respectively, and the low affinity binding site at log K = 8.3 and 7.5 at pH 7.4 and 6.6 respectively [2]. At physiological pH values, soluble Aβ is precipitated by Zn^{2+} *in vitro*. However, at pH levels reflecting physiological acidosis, which is characteristic of AD, *in vitro* precipitation of Aβ is induced by cupric and ferric ions. Cupric ions induce greater precipitation than ferric ions, which is thought to be a result of its higher binding affinity, with Aβ aggregation enhanced to ~85 % [3]. In addition, Cu^{2+} ions are bound at the low affinity site completely displacing the Zn^{2+} ions in physiological acidosis [2]. Levels of copper, iron and zinc have been analyzed in the rims and cores of senile plaques of AD patients and concentrations were found to be highly elevated. Concentrations exhibited in the senile plaques cores were 22.7 ± 6.5, 52.4 ± 14.5 and 67.0 ± 13.0 µg/g for copper, iron and zinc respectively [4]. In addition serum copper levels have been shown to be markedly elevated in AD [5].

The catalytic effects of transition metals on the formation of reactive oxygen species are becoming evident as a major factor in AD. Aβ binds to Cu^{2+} reducing it to Cu^{+}. The Aβ-Cu^{+}complex can then trap dioxygen and reduce it to hydrogen peroxide (H_2O_2). One study demonstrated that 1 µM Cu^{2+} when bound to Aβ could catalytically generate 10 µM H_2O_2, indicating continual redox cycling [6]. In conditions where this reaction is not favorable, biological reducing agents such as vitamin C have been shown to enhance this reaction [7]. The generation of H_2O_2 has been shown to be neurotoxic, which is considered to be a result of its reduction to the hydroxyl radical via Fenton chemistry. Cupric ion binding is dependent on histidine and tyrosine amino acid residues. Upon generation of hydroxyl radicals localized to the Cu^{2+} ion, the tyrosine residues can cross-link to form dityrosine. This further stabilizes the Aβ plaques conferring resistance to proteolysis [8]. Further studies are required to establish if Aβ bound to Cu^{2+} and Zn^{2+} exhibits significant anti-oxidant enzyme activities (superoxide dismutase and catalase activities) in vivo, as many researchers have likened Aβ to the native CuZn superoxide dismutase enzyme in both its conformation and its metal binding affinities [9].

Magnetite and maghemite deposits have been found in brains of patients suffering from AD and studies are underway to correlate enhanced levels with disease progression [10]. However, magnetite detection is only possible after the onset of AD. A comprehensive understanding of the levels and nature of redox-active ferric ions is warranted to assess the mechanisms of magnetite deposition. AD brains exhibit increased levels of oxidatively modified nucleic acids, specifically RNA in vulnerable neurons [11]. Haem oxygenase-1 (HO-1), an enzyme which catalyses the breakdown of haem to biliverdin with release of iron and carbon monoxide, is over-expressed in the brains of AD patients. So it could be postulated that this would be one source of redox-active iron. Immunostaining of neurons demonstrated that HO-1 expression was co-localized to the neurofibrillary tangles [12]. However oxidative damage to nucleic acids was reduced in neurons exhibiting neurofibrillary tangles demonstrating an antioxidant mechanism for HO-1 and an involvement in tau proteins expression. Further studies on the oxidative modifications of RNA in AD demonstrated it to be localized to iron rich lysosomes called lipofuscins originating from the mitochondria. This indicates a disruption in mitochondrial function leading to accumulation of redox-active iron in the neuronal cytoplasm [13] and subsequent reactive oxygen species generation.

Therapeutic Implications

Oxidative stress is one of the key mechanisms of neurotoxicity in AD, and studies have shown that Aβ neurotoxicity can be partially or completely attenuated by the antioxidant enzyme catalase [6, 7]. Plasma levels of antioxidants including vitamin E, uric acid and vitamin C are depleted in AD patients [14]. Therefore, many people have proposed the supplementation of antioxidants such as vitamin E and vitamin C. Several studies have reported that increased intake either through diet or supplementation results in reduced incidence of AD [15, 16, 17]. However, other studies do not report such success [18]. In fact, some studies have shown that vitamin C which can also act as a pro-oxidant can also induce neuronal oxidative stress via its interaction with metal ions [19].

A long-term imbalance in metal ion homeostasis is rarely treatable by alterations in diet. Therefore, research is focusing on the development of new methods for therapeutic intervention, specifically chelators to remove the deleterious metal ions, with concomitant dissolution of the Aβ plaques. *In vitro* studies on the aggregation of Aβ induced by metal ions, showed that this was completely reversible by metal ion chelation [3]. As a result of these observations new chelators are being developed as novel therapies for AD, however many are restricted by their poor target specificity. Clioquinol a Cu/Zn chelator was tested in APP2576 transgenic mice and appeared to selectively bind the Aβ-metal complex resulting in dissolution of Aβ plaques, reducing brain Aβ by 49 % [20]. No neurotoxicity was exhibited. Clioquinol subsequently was tested in a clinical trial with 36 AD patients. It affected a rise in plasma concentrations of zinc, and also decreased plasma concentrations of Aβ 1–42 [21]. However more studies are required to determine its importance in treating AD. Many other metal ion chelators are currently under investigation for treatment of AD [22, 23, 24, 25].

We have developed a series of metal ion chelators for both the study and treatment of metal deposition disorders. These include the development of the first-ever, reactive oxygen and nitrogen species probe for the simultaneous detection of multiple RONS and the role of redox-active metal ions in their generation and suppression [26]. Alteration of the basic structure of these probes affords anti-oxidant enzyme mimics [27]. In addition the chelator EGTA, which has previously been shown to dissolve Aβ plaques [28] was also demonstrated to have substantial superoxide dismutase activity when complexed to redox-active metal ions [29]. Thus, addition of a chelator that generates a superoxide dismutase or catalase mimic could 'dissolve' the magnetite deposits and Aβ plaques and negate oxidative damage arising from them.

CONCLUSION

Metal specific chelators afford a major opportunity for the control of metal ion mediated pathogeneses, which is not currently provided by nutraceuticals. In particular, administration of "prodrug" chelators that mimic anti-oxidant enzymes with high specificity for Cu^{2+} and Fe^{3+} ions will: i) counteract oxidative stress, ii) help to control metal ion deposition and iii) dissolve Aβ plaques and, maghemite and magnetite residues.

ACKNOWLEDGEMENTS

We are grateful to the University of Brighton and the Engineering and Physical Sciences Research Council for financial support.

COMPETING INTERESTS

The author(s) declare that they have no competing interests.

AUTHORS' CONTRIBUTIONS

The authors contributed equally to this work.

REFERENCES

1. Luchsinger JA, Mayeux R: Dietary factors and Alzheimer's disease. Lancet Neurol. 2004, 3: 579-587.

2. Atwood CS, Scarpa RC, Huang X, Moir RD, Jones WD, Fairlie DP, Tanzi RE, Bush AI: Characterization of copper interactions with Alzheimer amyloid β peptides: identification of an attomolar-affinity copper binding site on amyloid β1–42. J Neurochem. 2000, 75: 1219-1233.

3. Atwood CS, Moir RD, Huang X, Scarpa RC, Bacarra NM, Romano DM, Hartshorn MA, Tanzi RE, Bush AI: Dramatic Aggregation of Alzheimer Abeta by Cu(II) Is Induced by Conditions Representing Physiological Acidosis. J Biol Chem. 1998, 273: 12817-12826.

4. Lovell MA, Robertson JD, Teesdale WJ, Campbell JL, Markesbery WR: Copper, iron and zinc in Alzheimer's disease senile plaques. J Neurol Sci. 1998, 158: 47-52.

5. Squitti R, Lupoi D, Pasqualetti P, Dal Forno G, Vernieri F, Chiovenda P, Rossi L, Cortesi M, Cassetta E, Rossini PM: Elevation of serum

copper levels in Alzheimer's disease. Neurology. 2002, 59: 1153-1161.

6. Huang X, Cuajungco MP, Atwood CS, Hartshorn MA, Tyndall JD, Hanson GR, Stokes KC, Leopold M, Multhaup G, Goldstein LE, et al: Cu(II) potentiation of alzheimer Abeta neurotoxicity. Correlation with cell-free hydrogen peroxide production and metal reduction. J Biol Chem. 1999, 274: 37111-37116.

7. Opazo C, Huang X, Cherny RA, Moir RD, Roher AE, White AR, Cappai R, Masters CL, Tanzi RE, Inestrosa NC, et al: Metalloenzyme-like activity of Alzheimer's disease beta-amyloid. Cu-dependent catalytic conversion of dopamine, cholesterol, and biological reducing agents to neurotoxic H_2O_2. J Biol Chem. 2002, 277: 40302-40308.

8. Atwood CS, Perry G, Zeng H, Kato Y, Jones WD, Ling KQ, Huang X, Moir RD, Wang D, Sayre LM, et al: Copper mediates dityrosine cross-linking of Alzheimer's amyloid-beta. Biochemistry. 2004, 43: 560-568.

9. Curtain CC, Ali F, Volitakis I, Cherny RA, Norton RS, Beyreuther K, Barrow CJ, Masters CL, Bush AI, Barnham KJ: Alzheimer's disease amyloid-beta binds copper and zinc to generate an allosterically ordered membrane-penetrating structure containing superoxide dismutase-like subunits. J Biol Chem. 2001, 276: 20466-20473.

10. Dobson J: Nanoscale biogenic iron oxides and neurodegenerative disease. FEBS Lett. 2001, 496: 1-5.

11. Nunomura A, Perry G, Pappolla MA, Wade R, Hirai K, Chiba S, Smith MA: RNA oxidation is a prominent feature of vulnerable neurons in Alzheimer's disease. J Neurosci. 1999, 19: 1959-1964.

12. Schipper HM: Heme oxygenase expression in human central nervous system disorders. Free Radic Biol Med. 2004, 37: 1995-2011.

13. Perry G, Nunomura A, Hirai K, Zhu X, Prez M, Avila J, Castellani RJ, Atwood CS, Aliev G, Sayre LM: Is oxidative damage the fundamental pathogenic mechanism of Alzheimer's and other neurodegenerative diseases?. Free Radic Biol Med. 2002, 33: 1475-1479.

14. Rinaldi P, Polidori MC, Metastasio A, Mariani E, Mattioli P, Cherubini A, Catani M, Cecchetti R, Senin U, Mecocci P, et al: Plasma antioxidants are similarly depleted in mild cognitive impairment and in Alzheimer's disease. Neurobiol Aging. 2003, 24: 915-919.

15. Kontush A, Mann U, Arlt S, Ujeyl A, Luhrs C, Muller-Thomsen T, Beisiegel U: Influence of vitamin E and C supplementation on lipoprotein oxidation in patients with Alzheimer's disease. Free Radic Biol Med. 2001, 31: 345-354.

16. Engelhart MJ, Geerlings MI, Ruitenberg A, van Swieten JC, Hofman A, Witteman JCM, Breteler MMB: Dietary intake of antioxidants and risk of Alzheimer disease. JAMA. 2002, 287: 3223-3229.

17. Morris MC, Evans DA, Bienias JL, Tangney CC, Bennett DA, Aggarwal N, Wilson RS, Scherr PA: Dietary intake of antioxidant nutrients and the risk of incident Alzheimer disease in a biracial community study. J Am Med Assoc. 2002, 287: 3230-3237.

18. Luchsinger JA, Tang MX, Shea S, Mayeux R: Antioxidant vitamin intake and risk of Alzheimer disease. Arch Neurol. 2003, 60: 203-208.

19. White AR, Barnham KJ, Huang X, Voltakis I, Beyreuther K, Masters CL, Cherny RA, Bush AI, Cappai R: Iron inhibits neurotoxicity induced by trace copper and biological reductants. J Biol Inorg Chem. 2004, 9: 269-280.

20. Bush AI: Metal complexing agents as therapies for Alzheimer's disease. Neurobiol Aging. 2002, 23: 1031-1038.

21. Doraiswamy PM, Finefrock AE: Metals in our minds: therapeutic implications for neurodegenerative disorders. Lancet Neurol. 2004, 3: 431-434.

22. Cherny RA, Barnham KJ, Lynch T, Volitakis I, Li QX, McLean CA, Multhaup G, Beyreuther K, Tanzi RE, Masters CL, Bush AI: Chelation and intercalation: complementary properties in a compound for the treatment of Alzheimer's disease. J Struct Biol. 2000, 130: 209-216.

23. Dedeoglu A, Cormier K, Payton S, Tseitlin KA, Kremsky JN, Lai L, Li X, Moir RD, Tanzi RE, Bush AI: Preliminary studies of a novel bifunctional metal chelator targeting Alzheimer's amyloidogenesis. Exp Gerontol. 2004, 39: 1641-1649.

24. Zheng H, Weiner LM, Bar-Am O, Epsztejn S, Cabantchik ZI, Warshawsky A, Youdim MBH, Fridkin M: Design, synthesis, and evaluation of novel bifunctional iron-chelators as potential agents for neuroprotection in Alzheimer's, Parkinson's, and other neurodegenerative diseases. Bioorg Med Chem. 2004

25. Lee JY, Friedman JE, Angel I, Kozak A, Koh JY: The lipophilic metal chelator DP-109 reduces amyloid pathology in brains of human beta-amyloid precursor protein transgenic mice. Neurobiol Aging. 2004, 25: 1315-1321.

26. Fisher AEO, Naughton DP: Novel peptoids for the detection and suppression of reactive oxygen and nitrogen species. Biochem Soc Trans. 2003, 31: 1302-1304.

27. Fisher AEO, Maxwell SC, Naughton DP: Catalase and superoxide dismutase mimics for the treatment of inflammatory diseases. Inorg Chem Comm. 2003, 6: 1205-1208.

28. Maskos Z, Rush JD, Koppenol WH: The hydroxylation of tryptophan. Arch Biochem Biophys. 1992, 296: 514-520.

29. Fisher AEO, Hague TA, Clarke CL, Naughton DP: Catalytic superoxide scavenging by metal complexes of the calcium chelator EGTA and contrast agent EHPG. Biochem Biophys Res Comm. 2004, 323: 163-167.

Chapter 2

Curcumin, Inflammation, Ageing and Age-Related Diseases

E Sikora[1]*, Giovanni Scapagnini[2] , Mario Barbagallo[3]

[1]Laboratory of Molecular Bases of Ageing, Nencki Institute of Experimental Biology, PAS, Warsaw, Poland. 2 Department of Health Sciences, University of Molise, Campobasso, Italy. 3 Geriatric Unit, Dept of Internal Medicine and Emergent Pathologies, University of Palermo, Palermo, Italy.

ABSTRACT

A Symposium regarding the *Pathophysiology of Successful and Unsuccessful Ageing* was held in Palermo, Italy between April 7 and 8th 2009. Here the lecture by Sikora with some input from the chairpersons Scapagnini and Barbagallo is summarized. Ageing is manifested by the decreasing health status and increasing probability to acquire age-related disease such as cancer, Alzheimer's disease, atherosclerosis, metabolic disorders and others. They are likely caused by low grade inflammation driven by oxygen stress and manifested by the increased level of pro-inflammatory cytokines such as IL-1, IL-6 and TNF-α, encoded by genes activated by the transcription factor NF-κB. It is believed that ageing is plastic and can be slowed down by caloric restriction as well as by some nutraceuticals. Accordingly, slowing down ageing and postponing the onset of age-related diseases might be achieved by blocking the NF-κB-dependent inflammation. In this review we consider the possibility of the spice curcumin, a powerful antioxidant and anti-inflammatory agent possibly capable of improving the health status of the elderly.

BACKGROUND

A Symposium regarding the Pathophysiology of Successful and Unsuccessful Ageing was held in Palermo, Italy between April 7-8th 2009. Comments and keynotes by E. Sikora, G. Scapagnini and M. Barbagallo are summarized here.

Ageing and age-related diseases

The ageing process, opposite to longevity, is not genetically programmed. There are no genes that have been selected to actually promote ageing. The theory of evolution assumes that there is a trade-off between body maintenance and investment in reproduction [1]. Lifespan is regulated by genes controlling the activity of metabolism, antioxidant systems, DNA repair, cellular senescence and cell death. Their functions gradually decline due to random errors in DNA replication and damage to macromolecules, what leads to the accumulation of senescent cells and damaged tissue with age. However, diverse tissues building various organs may show different patterns of senescence [2, 3, 4]. The lesions accumulating with age are mainly, but not exclusively, caused by the increasing level of reactive oxygen species (ROS), as originally proposed by Harman [5].

A key in the ageing of an organism is immunosenescence which may play a part in the age-related immunological changes [6]. Lifelong exposure to a plethora of antigens (bacterial, viral, exogenous, auto, which can be considered as stressors) leads to a gradual decline of naive T cells. In turn, there is an accumulation of memory T and effector CD8+CD28- T cells which secrete increased amounts of pro-inflammatory cytokines [7]. Another major consequence of chronic exposure to antigens is the progressive activation of macrophages and related cells in most organs and tissues of the body creating an imbalance between inflammatory and anti-inflammatory networks. This results in the low grade chronic pro-inflammatory status (inflamm-ageing) [6]. Inflamm-ageing can be characterized by an increased level of a variety of pro-inflammatory cytokines in tissues, and other inflammatory markers, such as coagulation cascade components, and the presence of viral infections caused by the following viruses: CMV and Epstein Barr virus (EBV) [8]. Cellular participants in low-grade inflammatory status not only include cells of the immune sytem but also other ones which have undergone genotoxic stress-induced senescence and secrete many inflammatory cytokines, to the so-called senescence-associated secretory phenotype (SASP) [9].

Ageing, although not a disease by itself, makes the organism vulnerable to a plethora of them. Holliday claims that many age-related changes can not be distinguished from age-related diseases [10]. Indeed, it seems that many age-related pathologies share the signalling pathways with the process of ageing. It has been proposed that low-grade inflammation may not be the cause of ageing itself (inflamm-ageing and SASP), but also of many age-related diseases [11, 12,13].

Several lines of evidence have led to the general acceptance of a link between inflammation and cancer. Generally, cancer and inflammation are connected by two pathways: the intrinsic and the extrinsic one. The intrinsic pathway means that oncogene activation induces in transformed cells the production of inflammatory mediators, mainly *via* the activation of the transcription factor NF-κB. Conversely, in the extrinsic pathway inflammatory or infectious conditions augment the risk of cancer development. Epidemiological studies have shown that chronic inflammation predisposes individuals to various types of cancer [14]. Recently inflammation has been proposed as the seventh feature of cancer [15] which should be added to the six canonical previously proposed ones [16].

Inflammation is also considered to be a critical initial step in the development of atherosclerosis [13]. The early phase of atherogenesis is characterized by the attraction/adherence of monocytes to the vascular endothelium and their migration into the vessel wall. The expression of cellular adhesion molecules promotes the adhesion of leukocytes to the vascular endothelium and is induced by inflammatory factors, including IL-1, TNF-a, and CRP. Furthermore, the progressive accumulation of macrophages and their uptake of oxidized LDL ultimately leads to the generation of the so called foam cells and initiation of fatty streaks [12]. It seems that NF-κB is the main mediator of inflammation and endothelial dysfunction in the elderly [17].

An inflammatory state has been documented in senile plaques and surrounding glia with an increased expression of the acute phase protein CRP as well as pro-inflammatory interleukins such as IL-6 and IL-1 in Alzheimer's disease (AD) patients and animal models [18]. The evidence of inflammatory mechanisms being involved in AD is also based on the fact that certain anti-inflammatory drugs could modify the course of the disease [19, 20].

Obesity, insulin resistance and type 2 diabetes are also closely associated with chronic inflammation. Exposure to excess amounts of nutrients and energy can reactivate the ancient inflammatory potential of metabolically important tissues. The adipose tissue of obese individuals has in fact been shown to produce higher levels of the pro-inflammatory cytokines (TNF, IL-6) and other pro-inflammatory factors [21].

The assumption of a link between ageing and age-related diseases raises the pivotal question of whether concentrating the effort on just curing the age-associated diseases is the optimal approach to making our later lives more healthy and comfortable. Indeed, a new strategy hopefully leading to healthy ageing has been proposed. Recently, it has been postulated that interventions aimed at slowing down ageing could offer a much greater benefit than those targeted at individual diseases [22]. The evolutionary theory of disposable soma suggests that ageing is unavoidable but malleable and plastic [23] and perhaps this may be possible by dietary or pharmaceutical intervention or genetic alteration, to extend the lifespan [22].

Curcumin as an anti-inflammatory agent

Nutraceuticals are food ingredients which either have a proven physiological benefit or provide protection against chronic diseases. They may contribute to the prevention of diseases and ageing. Diet has a major role in modulating the risk of development of several diseases and successful ageing. Edible plants, amongst dietary constituents, are important in that they contain phytochemicals which can control biochemical processes at cellular level of animal organism.

Among nutraceuticals, the role of curcumin is supported by a number of scientific evidence that have confirmed its anti-inflammatory and anti-oxidant actions both *in vivo* and *in vitro.*Curcumin is the phytochemical derived from the rhizome of *Curcuma longa*, present in the spice turmeric and it gives Indian curry its yellow color. Curcumin has been used for millennia as a wound-healing agent and for treating a variety of diseases in traditional Indian and Chinese medicine. Recently, it has attracted the attention of researchers as an agent capable of inhibiting the proliferation of cancer cells and/or inducing many signaling pathways leading to various modes of cell death [24, 25]. As a cell death inducer curcumin has gained profound interest as a chemopreventive and anti-cancer agent which found confirmation in many *in vitro*experiments and preclinical studies on animal models.

Furthermore curcumin rises interest as an agent of potential use in therapy of many diseases (not only cancer) with an inflammation constituents including cardiovascular diseases, Alzheimer's disease, rheumatoid arthritis and metabolic syndrome. Although only a few worldwide clinical trials are underway now [26], a plethora of studies using animal and cell line models have been undertaken to elucidate the molecular mechanisms and biological effects of curcumin.

Curcumin has an unprecedented number of molecular targets justifying its chemopreventive, antioxidant and anti-inflammatory activities (reviewed recently in [27, 28]. Briefly, these targets include transcription factors with AP-1 described as the first one, and others such as SP-1, p53, STAT-3, ATF3, Nrf2, PPAR-γ, CHOP, HIF-1α, β-catenin and NF-κB, enzymes such as protein kinases (PKA, PKC, FAK, Src), glutathione S-transferase, DNA topoisomerase-II, telomerase, heme-oxygenase-1, p300 histone acetyltransferase, metaloproteinases, lipoxygenase (5-LOX), cyclooxygenase-2 (COX-2) and others. The most far-reaching physiological consequences seem to stem from the action of curcumin as an inhibitor of the activity of the transcription factor NF-κB. The NF-κB transcription factor is a master regulator of the inflammatory process which activates the expression of many pro-inflammatory cytokines, such as TNF-α, IL-1β and IL-6. Some of the NF-κB-induced proteins, like TNF-α, are also its activators, which is particularly important in the chronic inflammatory state. NF-κB seems to be the culprit of inflammageing, since this signaling system integrates the intracellular regulation of immune responses in both ageing and age-related diseases [29].

Many activities of curcumin can be also explained by its ability to suppress acute and chronic inflammation by scavenging reactive oxygen and reactive nitrogen species and enhancing antioxidant defense (i.e. by increasing glutathione level). However, curcumin is not only a simple antioxidant, but as a electrophilic compound it triggers the Nrf2/ARE signaling pathway which plays a key role in activating antioxidative enzymes, phase 2 enzymes and so - called vitagens (heme oxygenase, Hsp70, thioredoxin reductase and sirtuins), which might have a pivotal role in oxidative stress-induced diseases [30].

The amount of data documenting beneficial effects of curcumin in protecting against different diseases, particularly those which are related to age are increasing. It seems that extraordinary potency of curcumin, which makes it an almost universal remedy, results from the inflammatory origins of many diseases and curcumin's anti-inflammatory activity.

Despite the practical lack of data showing curcumin's influence on ageing and lifespan, there is a strong rational argument suggesting that curcumin can influence the process of senescence and ageing retardation [25].

Curcumin and AD

Recently curcumin has been proposed as a potential remedy against brain ageing and neurodegenerative disorders [31], and it has been evaluated in a pilot clinical trial in AD patients, with encouraging preliminary results [32]. Curcumin is highly lipophilic and might cross the blood-brain barrier (BBB) to reach the brain. Although its bioavailability is very low, since the drug is rapidly metabolized by conjugation, curcumin may reach brain in a sufficient concentration to activate signal transduction events and to decrease Aβ aggregation [33]. Epidemiological studies suggested that curcumin, one of the most prevalent nutritional and medical compounds used by the Indian population, is responsible for the significantly reduced (4.4-fold) prevalence of AD in India compared to United States [34]. Furthermore elderly Singaporeans who ate curry with turmeric had higher Mini-Mental State Examination scores than those who did not [35].

CONCLUSIONS

Curcumin can counteract the pro-inflammatory state which is believed to participate in many age-related diseases. In fact, it seems that curcumin directly affects a few major targets, just like ROS scavenging and production and the NF-κB signaling pathways, which can in turn suppresses the pro-inflammatory state involved in the etiology of ageing and age-related diseases.

The main concern regarding the therapeutic value of curcumin is its poor bioavailability, which, on the other hand, assures lack of toxicity even when consumed in a daily dose of 8 mg. Moreover, the data so far collected, show that curcumin has a very high activity not only in *in vitro* experiments, but also at the organismal level. This could be explained by its hormetic activity [36]. Accordingly, it appears that curcumin is a very safe and beneficial nutraceutical spice which might fend off ageing and age-related diseases. However, at this time there is no data showing that any nutraceutical may influence ageing and lifespan, and complete randomized clinical trials in humans are also needed to confirm the potential use of curcumin in the prevention of diseases with an inflammation constituents, e.g. cardiovascular diseases, AD, cardiometabolic syndrome, and ageing.

ACKNOWLEDGEMENTS

The meeting organizer Prof. C. Caruso is deeply indebted to all the speakers and chairpersons of the meeting who contributed to the scientific success of the symposium. In addition, on the day of the meeting the defense of PhD thesis of students belonging to the Pathobiology PhD course directed by CC were held. Prof. Caruso is proud of the hard and challenging work of his students whose motivation and enthusiasm, with the management of Drs. Giuseppina Candore, Giuseppina Colonna-Romano and Prof. Domenico Lio, have permitted to the whole Immunosenescence Unit to grow in the field of immunosenescence. This work was supported by the Polish Ministry of Science and Higher Education (grant N301 008 32/0549).

COMPETING INTERESTS

The authors declare that they have no competing interests.

AUTHORS' CONTRIBUTIONS

All the Authors drafted the manuscript and approved the final manuscript.

REFERENCES

1. Kirkwood TB: Evolution of ageing. Nature. 1977, 270: 301-304.
2. Holliday R: Aging is no longer an unsolved problem in biology. Ann N Y Acad Sci. 2006, 1067: 1-9.
3. Kirkwood TB: A systematic look at an old problem. Nature. 2008, 451: 644-647.
4. Rattan SI: Increased molecular damage and heterogeneity as the basis of aging. Biol Chem. 2008, 389: 267-272.
5. Harman D: Aging: a theory based on free radical and radiation chemistry. J Gerontol. 1956, 11: 298-300.
6. Franceschi C, Bonafe M, Valensin S, Olivieri F, De Luca M, Ottaviani E, De Benedictis G: Inflamm-aging. An evolutionary perspective on immunosenescence. Ann N Y Acad Sci. 2000, 908: 244-254.
7. Meyer KC: Aging. Proc Am Thorac Soc. 2005, 2: 433-439.
8. Pawelec G, Derhovanessian E, Larbi A, Strindhall J, Wikby A: Cytomegalovirus and human immunosenescence. Rev Med Virol. 2009, 19: 47-56.
9. Coppe JP, Patil CK, Rodier F, Sun Y, Munoz DP, Goldstein J, Nelson PS, Desprez PY, Campisi J: Senescence-associated secretory phenotypes reveal cell-nonautonomous functions of oncogenic RAS and the p53 tumor suppressor. PLoS Biol. 2008, 6: 2853-2868.
10. Holliday R: The close relationship between biological aging and age-associated pathologies in humans. J Gerontol A Biol Sci Med Sci. 2004, 59: B543-546.
11. Chung HY, Sung B, Jung KJ, Zou Y, Yu BP: The molecular inflammatory process in aging. Antioxid Redox Signal. 2006, 8: 572-581.

12. Chung HY, Cesari M, Anton S, Marzetti E, Giovannini S, Seo AY, Carter C, Yu BP, Leeuwenburgh C: Molecular inflammation: underpinnings of aging and age-related diseases. Ageing Res Rev. 2009, 8: 18-30.

13. Vasto S, Candore G, Balistreri CR, Caruso M, Colonna-Romano G, Grimaldi MP, Listi F, Nuzzo D, Lio D, Caruso C: Inflammatory networks in ageing, age-related diseases and longevity. Mech Ageing Dev. 2007, 128: 83-91.

14. Mantovani A, Allavena P, Sica A, Balkwill F: Cancer-related inflammation. Nature. 2008, 454: 436-444.

15. Mantovani A: Cancer: Inflaming metastasis. Nature. 2009, 457: 36-37.

16. Hanahan D, Weinberg RA: The hallmarks of cancer. Cell. 2000, 100: 57-70.

17. Csiszar A, Wang M, Lakatta EG, Ungvari Z: Inflammation and endothelial dysfunction during aging: role of NF-kappaB. J Appl Physiol. 2008, 105: 1333-1341.

18. Finch CE, Morgan TE: Systemic inflammation, infection, ApoE alleles, and Alzheimer disease: a position paper. Curr Alzheimer Res. 2007, 4: 185-189.

19. Gupta A, Pansari K: Inflammation and Alzheimer's disease. Int J Clin Pract. 2003, 57: 36-39.

20. Vasto S, Candore G, Duro G, Lio D, Grimaldi MP, Caruso C: Alzheimer's disease and genetics of inflammation: a pharmacogenomic vision. Pharmacogenomics. 2007, 8: 1735-1745.

21. Hotamisligil GS: Inflammation and metabolic disorders. Nature. 2006, 444: 860-867.

22. Butler RN, Miller RA, Perry D, Carnes BA, Williams TF, Cassel C, Brody J, Bernard MA, Partridge L, Kirkwood T, Martin GM, Olshansky SJ: New model of health promotion and disease prevention for the 21st century. Bmj. 2008, 337: a399-

23. Vijg J, Campisi J: Puzzles, promises and a cure for ageing. Nature. 2008, 454: 1065-1071.

24. Ravindran J, Prasad S, Aggarwal BB: Curcumin and Cancer Cells: How Many Ways Can Curry Kill Tumor Cells Selectively?. Aaps J. 2009, 3: 495-510.

25. Salvioli S, Sikora E, Cooper EL, Franceschi C: Curcumin in Cell Death Processes: A Challenge for CAM of Age-Related Pathologies. Evid Based Complement Alternat Med. 2007, 4: 181-190.

26. Singh S: From exotic spice to modern drug?. Cell. 2007, 130: 765-768.

27. Aggarwal BB, Sundaram C, Malani N, Ichikawa H: Curcumin: the Indian solid gold. Adv Exp Med Biol. 2007, 595: 1-75.

28. Sikora E, Bielak-Zmijewska A, Mosieniak G, Piwocka K: The promise of slow down ageing may come from curcumin. Current Pharmacological Design. 2010,

29. Salminen A, Huuskonen J, Ojala J, Kauppinen A, Kaarniranta K, Suuronen T: Activation of innate immunity system during aging: NF-kB signaling is the molecular culprit of inflamm-aging. Ageing Res Rev. 2008, 7: 83-105.

30. Calabrese V, Bates TE, Mancuso C, Cornelius C, Ventimiglia B, Cambria MT, Di Renzo L, De Lorenzo A, Dinkova-Kostova AT: Curcumin and the cellular stress response in free radical-related diseases. Mol Nutr Food Res. 2008, 52: 1062-1073.

31. Cole GM, Teter B, Frautschy SA: Neuroprotective effects of curcumin. Adv Exp Med Biol. 2007, 595: 197-212.

32. Baum L, Lam CW, Cheung SK, Kwok T, Lui V, Tsoh J, Lam L, Leung V, Hui E, Ng C, Woo J, Chiu HF, Goggins WB, Zee BC, Cheng KF, Fong CY, Wong A, Mok H, Chow MS, Ho PC, Ip SP, Ho CS, Yu XW, Lai CY, Chan MH, Szeto S, Chan IH, Mok V: Six-month randomized, placebo-controlled, double-blind, pilot clinical trial of curcumin in patients with Alzheimer disease. J Clin Psychopharmacol. 2008, 28: 110-113.

33. Yang F, Lim GP, Begum AN, Ubeda OJ, Simmons MR, Ambegaokar SS, Chen PP, Kayed R, Glabe CG, Frautschy SA, Cole GM: Curcumin inhibits formation of amyloid beta oligomers and fibrils, binds plaques, and reduces amyloid in vivo. J Biol Chem. 2005, 280: 5892-5901.

34. Chandra V, Pandav R, Dodge HH, Johnston JM, Belle SH, DeKosky ST, Ganguli M: Incidence of Alzheimer's disease in a rural community in India: the Indo-US study. Neurology. 2001, 57: 985-989.

35. Ng TP, Chiam PC, Lee T, Chua HC, Lim L, Kua EH: Curry consumption and cognitive function in the elderly. Am J Epidemiol. 2006, 164: 898-906.

36. Berge U, Kristensen P, Rattan SI: Hormetic modulation of differentiation of normal human epidermal keratinocytes undergoing replicative senescence in vitro. Exp Gerontol. 2008, 43: 658-662.

Chapter 3

Dietary Polyphenols as Potential Nutraceuticals in Management of Diabetes: A Review

Zahra Bahadoran[1], Parvin Mirmiran[2*] and Fereidoun Azizi[3]

[1]*Nutrition and Endocrine Research Center, and Obesity Research Center, Research Institute for Endocrine Sciences, Shahid Beheshti University of Medical Sciences, No 24 Parvaneh St, Yemen St, Chamran Exp, 19395-4763 Tehran, Iran.*

[2]*Department of Clinical Nutrition and Dietetics, Faculty of Nutrition Sciences and Food Technology, National Nutrition and Food Technology Research Institute, Shahid Beheshti University of Medical Sciences, No 46 Arghavan-e-gharbi St, Farahzadi Blv, Shahrak-e-Ghods, 19395-4741 Tehran, Iran.*

[3]*Endocrine Research Center, Research Institute for Endocrine Sciences, Shahid Beheshti University of Medical Sciences, No 24 Parvaneh St, Yemen St, Chamran Exp, 19395-4763 Tehran, Iran.*

ABSTRACT

In recent years, there is growing evidence that plant-foods polyphenols, due to their biological properties, may be unique nutraceuticals and supplementary treatments for various aspects of type 2 diabetes mellitus. In this article we have reviewed the potential efficacies of polyphenols, including phenolic acids, flavonoids, stilbenes, lignans and polymeric lignans, on metabolic disorders and complications induced by diabetes. Based on several *in vitro*, animal models and some human studies, dietary plant polyphenols and polyphenol-rich products modulate carbohydrate and lipid metabolism, attenuate hyperglycemia, dyslipidemia and insulin resistance, improve adipose tissue metabolism, and alleviate oxidative stress and stress-sensitive signaling pathways and inflammatory processes. Polyphenolic compounds can also prevent the development of long-term diabetes complications including cardiovascular disease, neuropathy, nephropathy and retinopathy. Further investigations as human clinical studies are needed to obtain the optimum dose and duration of supplementation with polyphenolic compounds in diabetic patients.

Keywords : Polyphenols Phenolic acids Flavonoids Stilbenes Lignans Type 2 diabetes Diabetes complications

INTRODUCTION

Type 2 diabetes is a complex metabolic disorder associated with developing insulin resistance, impaired insulin signaling and β-cell dysfunction, abnormal glucose and lipid metabolism, sub-clinical inflammation and increased oxidative stress; these metabolic disorders lead to long-term pathogenic conditions including micro- and macro-vascular complications, neuropathy, retinopathy, nephropathy, and a consequent decrease in quality of life and an increase in the rate of mortality [1, 2, 3]. Among the multiple risk factors underling the incidence and progression of type 2 diabetes, diet is the main modifiable factor. An increasing number of epidemiological investigations show that diet rich in foods with high-content of phytochemicals, high total antioxidant capacity and polyphenolic compounds may be related to lower risk of diabetes and predisposing factors [4, 5, 6, 7, 8, 9].

Based on the current understanding of pathophysiology of insulin resistance and type 2 diabetes, multiple pharmacological and non-pharmacological interventions have been developed with the aim of improving glycemic control and prevention of diabetes complications; in this area, recently the use of functional foods and their bioactive components have been considered as a new approach in the prevention and management of diabetes and its complications [10, 11, 12, 13].

Due to their biological properties, polyphenols may be appropriate nutraceuticals and supplementary treatments for various aspects of diabetes mellitus. Our aim here is to review the current evidences in relation to several potential efficacies of these bioactive components on type 2 diabetes mellitus and related metabolic disorders. We obtained relevant articles, including *in vitro*, animal models and human studies with appropriate design, as well as review articles with good quality, published between 1990 to 2013, through searches of the Medline and PubMed databases. We first describe a brief introduction on dietary polyphenols, food sources and properties, and then summarize the evidence from *in vitro,* animal models and clinical studies.

Dietary polyphenols: food sources, bioavailability and metabolism

Polyphenols are natural phytochemical compounds in plant-based foods, such as fruits, vegetables, whole grains, cereal, legumes, tea, coffee, wine and cocoa; more than 8000 polyphenolic compounds, including phenolic acids, flavonoids, stilbenes, lignans and polymeric lignans have been identified in whole plant foods [5]. These compounds are secondary metabolites of the plants that act as a defense against ultraviolet radiation, oxidants and pathogens [14].

Polyphenols may be classified into several categories based on the number of phenol rings and structural elements that bind these rings to one another [15]. Phenolic acids are approximately a third of the polyphenolic compounds in the diet and include two main classes hydroxybenzoic acid derivatives (protocatechuic acid, gallic acid, *p*-hydroxybenzoic acid) and hydroxycinnamic acid derivatives (caffeic acid, chlorogenic acid, coumaric acid, Ferulic acid, sinapic acid); berry fruits, kiwi, cherry, apple, pear, chicory and coffee are the foods with high content of these phenolic acids [16]. Flavonoids are the most abundant polyphenols in the human diet and more than 4000 types of these compounds have been identified. There are six subclasses of flavonoids including anthocyanins, flavonols, flavanols, flavanones, flavones and isoflavones; anthocyanins (cyanidin, pelargonidin, delphinidin, malvidin) are found in the berries family, red wine, red cabbage, cherry, black grape and strawberry. Flavonols, including quercetin, kampferol and myricetin, have been mainly detected in onion, curly kale, leeks, broccoli and blueberries. Isoflavones are other most important dietary flavonoids that include daidzein, genistein and glycitein; soybeans and soy products are the richest sources of these estrogen-like structure compounds. Lignans, diphenoilc components with phytoesterogenic activity, have been found in high concentrations in linseed and other grains and cereals. Stilbenes occur in the human diet in low quantities; resveratrol, one of the well studied compounds of these groups, is largely detected in grapes and red wine [5, 16, 17].

It is estimated that dietary intake of polyphenols is approximately 1 g/day [18, 19]. Bioavailability of these bioactive components is dependent on food preparation processes, gastrointestinal digestion, absorption and metabolism [20]. During the absorption pathway, dietary polyphenols must be hydrolyzed by the intestinal enzymes or colonic microflora, and then be conjugated in the intestinal cells and later in the liver by methylation, sulfation or glucuronidation [21]. Polyphenols consequently reach and accumulate in the target tissue and induce biological properties; the polyphenol derivates mainly excrete through bile and urine. Several studies showed rapid absorption of the polyphenolic compounds, such as procyanidins, quercetin and flavanols into plasma, with plasma concentrations peaking at 2 or 3 hours after ingestion [16].

Several biological activities and beneficial properties have been documented for dietary polyphenols, and some of the more well known ones include antioxidant, anti-allergic, anti-inflammatory, anti-viral and anti-microbial, anti-proliferative, anti-mutagenic, anti-carcinogenic, free radical scavenging, regulation of cell cycle arrest, apoptosis, and induction of antioxidant enzymes; more interestingly, dietary polyphenols could modulate some important cell signaling pathways such as nuclear factor kappa-B (NF-κB), activator protein-1 DNA binding (AP-1), extracellular signal-regulated protein kinase (ERK), phosphoinositide 3 (PI3) kinase/protein kinase B (Akt), mitogen-activated protein kinases (MAPK), and nuclear factor erythroid 2 related factor 2 (Nrf2) [22].

Anti-hyperglycemic effects of polyphenols with regard to carbohydrate metabolism, β-cell function and insulin resistance

Impaired carbohydrate metabolism and developing insulin resistance is the main metabolic disorder in non-insulin dependent diabetes mellitus leading to hyperglycemia. Altered digestion and absorption of dietary carbohydrate, depletion of glycogen storage, increased gluconeogenesis and over output hepatic glucose, β-cell dysfunction, insulin resistance of peripheral tissue and defect in insulin signaling pathways are more important causes of hyperglycemia [23]. Although the use of oral anti-diabetic drugs including α-glucosidase inhibitors, biguanides, meglitinides, sulfonylureas, thiazolidindiones or insulin therapies are common clinical options in management of type 2 diabetes and hyperglycemia, but traditionally used natural agents have been considered for a long period of time. Among the known natural bioactive components and phytochemicals, recently polyphenols are very popular because of their anti-hyperglycemic effects, safety and non side-effects. Potential efficacy of polyphenols on carbohydrate metabolism and glucose homeostasis has been well investigated in *in vitro*, animal models and some clinical trials [24].

In Figure 1 beneficial effects of polyphenols on management of blood glucose in diabetes are summarized. The hypoglycemic effects of polyphenols are mainly attributed to reduce intestinal absorption of dietary carbohydrate, modulation of the enzymes involved in glucose metabolism, improvement of β-cell function and insulin action, stimulation of insulin secretion, and the antioxidative and anti-inflammatory properties of these components [25, 26, 27].

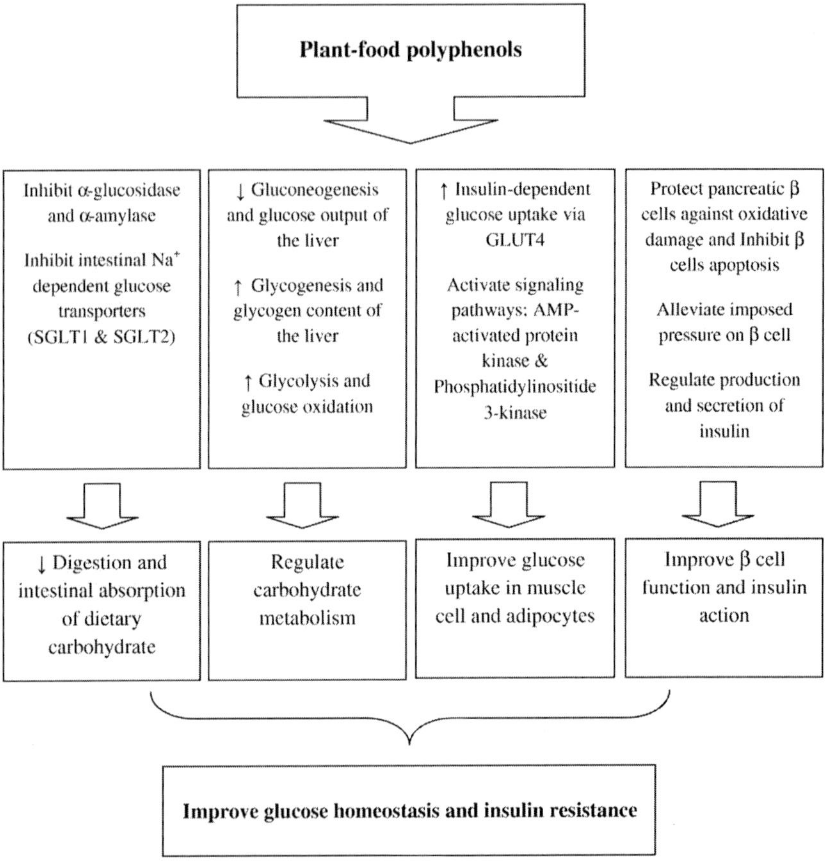

Figure 1. Beneficial effects of polyphenols on management of blood glucose in diabetes. The hypoglycemic effects of polyphenols are mainly attributed to reduce intestinal absorption of dietary carbohydrate, modulation of the enzymes involved in glucose metabolism, improvement of β-cell function and insulin action, and stimulation of insulin secretion.

One of the most well known properties of the polyphenols, especially flavonoids, phenolic acids and tannins, on carbohydrate metabolism is inhibition of α-glucosidase and α-amylase, the key enzymes responsible for digestion of dietary carbohydrates to glucose [26, 28]. Some polyphenols, including green tea catechins and epicatechins, chlorogenic acids, Ferulic acids, caffeic and tannic acids, quercetin and naringenin, could interact with absorption of glucose from intestine via inhibition of Na^+-dependent glucose transporters, SGLT1 and SGLT2 [29, 30]. Some investigations have shown that polyphenolic compounds are also able to regulate postprandial glycemia and inhibit the development of glucose intolerance by a facilitated insulin response and attenuated secretion of glucose-dependent insulinotropic polypeptide (GIP) and glucagon-like polypeptide-1 (GLP-1) [31, 32].

Some polyphenols are able to regulate the key pathways of carbohydrate metabolism and hepatic glucose homeostasis including glycolysis, glycogenesis and gluconeogenesis, usually impaired in diabetes. Ferulic acid, a hydroxycinnamic acid derivate, effectively suppresses blood glucose by elevating glucokinase activity and production of glycogen in the liver and increased plasma insulin levels in diabetic rats [33]. Supplementation of diabetic rats with hesperidin and naringin, two main citrus bioflavonoids, was accompanied with increased hepatic glucokinase activity and glycogen content, attenuated hepatic gluconeogenesis via decrease the activity of glucose-6-phosphatase and phosphoenolpyruvate carboxykinase (PEPCK), and subsequent improvement of glycemic control [34, 35]. Green tea polyphenols, mainly catechins and epicatechins have been shown to attenuate hyperglycemia and hepatic glucose output via downregulation the expression of liver glucokinase and upregulation of PEPCK [36]; in an *in vitro* study, epigallocatechin gallate (EGCG), one of the most abundant catechins in green tea, could activate AMP-activated protein kinase as a required pathway for the inhibition of gluconeogenic enzymes expression [37].

Dietary polyphenols also influence peripheral glucose uptake in both insulin sensitive and non-insulin sensitive tissues; one study showed that phenolic acids stimulated glucose uptake by comparable performance to metformin and thiazolodinedione, main common oral hypoglycemic drugs [38]. The results from the *in vitro* studies showed that some polyphenolic compounds such as quercetin, resveratrol and EGCG improved insulin-dependent glucose uptake in muscle cells and adipocytes by translocation of glucose transporter, GLUT4, to plasma membrane mainly through induction of the AMP-activated protein kinase (AMPK) pathway [39,40]. AMPK, an important sensor of cellular energy status, has a key role in metabolic control; activation of this pathway is considered as a new treatment for obesity, type 2 diabetes, metabolic syndrome and a main target for anti-diabetic drugs including metformin [41, 42]. Interestingly, effect of polyphenols in activation of AMPK has been reported 50-200 times more than metformin [43]. Some polyphenols also have potential to induce phosphatidylinositide 3-kinase (PI3k) as a key signaling pathway for up-regulation of glucose uptake [44].

Isoflavones, particularly genistein, have amazing effects on pancreatic β-cells; Liu et al reported that anti-diabetic effects of genistein are not associated with stimulation of insulin synthesis, expression of glucose tranporter-2 or glycolytic pathway, genistein acts as a novel agonist of cyclic AMP/protein kinas A signaling, an important physiological amplifier of glucose-induced insulin secretion by the pancreatic β-cells [45, 46]. Furthermore, Fu et al indicated that genistein could induce protein expression of cyclin D1, a major cell-cycle regulator of β-cell growth and subsequently improve islet β-cell proliferation, survival and mass [47].

Hyperglycemia-induced oxidative stress in pancreatic β-cells plays a pivotal role in the development of diabetes [48, 49]. Some of the polyphenolic compounds protect β-cells from hyperglycemia-induced and oxidative-induced damage; oral administration of phenolic-rich chestnut extract in STZ-induced diabetic rats had favorable effects on serum glucose and viability of β-cell through attenuation of oxidative stress, enhancing the natural antioxidant system, and inhibition of lipid peroxidation [50]. Another very known phenolic compound, resveratrol (3,4′,5-trihydroxystilbene) found in grapes, wine, grape juice, peanuts, and berries, improve glucose tolerance, attenuate β-cell loss, and reduce oxidative stress in pancreatic islet [51]. Resveratrol also alleviate chronic over stimulation induced-workload and impose pressure on the β-cells, and subsequently delay the degradation of pancreatic islets and progress of type 2 diabetes. This effect appears to be due to the diminished stimulatory effects of hyperglycemia in insulin secretion; some experimental and *in vitro* studies demonstrated that resveratrol has the potential to reduce insulin secretion through induction of metabolic changes in β-cells [51,52].

Some protective effects of polyphenols on β-cells are related to the ability to modulate key cellular signaling pathways; anthocyanins-rich Chinese bayberry extract showed protective effects for pancreatic β cells against oxidative damage through up-regulation of heme oxygenase-1, modulation of ERK1/2 and PI3K/Akt signaling pathway and inhibition of β cells apoptosis [39].

In summary, results of the studies acknowledge that plant polyphenols favorably affect several aspects of diabetes-induced metabolic disorders and modulate carbohydrate metabolism, glucose homeostasis, insulin secretion and insulin resistance.

Cardiovascular protective effects of polyphenols with regard to lipid metabolism, blood pressure, blood coagulation and vascular function

Progressive insulin resistance is mainly accompanied with pro-atherogenic cardiovascular risk profiles and consequently atherosclerotic coronary artery disease and other forms of cardiovascular disease are the major causes of mortality in type 2 diabetic patients [53]. Dyslipidemia, undesirable changes in vascular endothelial and smooth muscle cells, lipid peroxidation especially oxidized low-density lipoprotein particles, oxidative damage and increased inflammatory mediators including chemokines and cytokines, hyper-coagulation and platelet activation have been considered as the main metabolic abnormalities in diabetes mellitus leading to cardiovascular disease [54].

There is growing evidence suggesting that dietary intake of polyphenol-rich foods and supplementation with these bioactive components could have protective effects against diabetes-induced cardiovascular pathogenesis; the mechanisms involved in these properties mainly include regulation of lipid metabolism, attenuation of oxidative damage and scavenging of free radicals, improvement of the endothelial function and vascular tone, enhancement the production of vasodilating factors such as nitric oxide, and inhibition the synthesis of vasoconstrictors such as endothelin-1 in endothelial cells [55, 56, 57].

One of the most important favorable effects of polyphenols on cardiovascular system in diabetes probably is regulation of lipid and lipoprotein metabolism, and improvement of dyslipidemia. Based on research conducted in this area, polyphenolic compounds are capable of reducing digestion and absorption of dietary lipids. Oligomeric procyanidins, contained in apples had inhibitory effects on pancreatic lipase and triglyceride absorption [58]. Apple procyanidins also induce hypolipidemic effects by decreasing of apolipoprotein B synthesis and secretion, inhibition of cholesterol estrification and intestinal lipoprotein production [59]. The hypolipidemic effects of catechins and proanthcyanidins are related to inhibition of key enzymes in lipid biosynthesis pathways, reduce intestinal lipid absorption. Catechins also interact with proteins involved in cholesterol translocation from the enterocyte brush border (ATP-binding cassette proteins, multidrug resistance P-glycoprotein 1, B type1-scavenger receptors, Niemann Pick C-1 like 1 protein), change their function and effectively reduce cholesterol absorption [60]. Administration of tart cherries as medicinal food rich in anthocyanins was accompanied with decrease in hyperlipidemia, hyperinsulinemia, fatty liver and hepatic steatosis through enhanced hepatic PPARα and some target genes including acyl-coenzyme A oxidase [61].

Endothelial dysfunction, proliferation and migration of smooth muscle cells of the vessels are central events in the pathogenesis of diabetes-induced atherosclerosis. Some cardiovascular protective properties of polyphenols are attributed to modulatory effects on the vascular structure and function. Interestingly, some polyphenols inhibit the expression of major proangiogenic, prothrombotic and proatherosclerotic factors such as monocyte chemoattractant protein-1, vascular endothelial growth factor (VEGF) and matrix metalloproteinase-2 (MMP-2) in smooth muscle cells, by redox-sensitive and redox-insensitive mechanisms [62, 63, 64]. Oligomeric proanthcyanidins, found in red apple, cinnamon, cocoa, and grapes have the potential to protect vascular cell against diabetes-induced oxidative stress via increase in activity of superoxide, dismutase inhibition of NADPH oxidase and production of free radicals as well as decrease proliferation of smooth muscle cells [65]. Flanan-3-ols modulate platelet hyperactivity and aggregation, regulate coronary blood flow, reduce endothelial inflammatory cytokines and free radicals, increase production and bioavailability of nitric oxide, and consequently atherosclerosis development [66]. In human trials, consumption of high-polyphenol dark chocolate was accompanied with improvement of endothelial function in individuals with stage 1 hypertension, and attenuation acute transient hyperglycemia-induced endothelial dysfunction and oxidative stress in type 2 diabetic patients [67, 68]. Administration of other polyphenol-rich products such as grape seed extract, cranberry juice, grape and pomegranate juice also had a therapeutic role in decreasing cardiovascular risk factors in patients with type 2 diabetes and metabolic syndrome [69, 70].

Catechins, quercetin and anthocyanins have potent platelet-inhibitory properties and are considered as inhibitors of platelet cell signaling and thrombus formation [71]. As reviewed by Pascul-Tresa, bioactive anthocyanins including delphinidin-3-rotinoside, cyanidin-3-glucoside, cyanidin-3-rutinoside, malvidin-3-glucoside and intestinal metabolites such as dihydroferulic acid and 3- (hydroxyphenyl) propionic acid prevent platelet hyper-activation and aggregation through inhibition of peptides activating thrombin receptor [66].

Undoubtedly, one of the main protective properties of polyphenols in the development of cardiovascular dysfunction in diabetic condition is related to the ability of these bioactive components to prevent lipoproteins oxidation and production of advanced glycation end products. Dietary polyphenolic compounds also protect myocardial tissue against several undesirable changes and diabetic cardiomyopathy. Treatment of diabetic rat models with grape seed proanthcyanidins extracts effectively reduced the receptor of advanced glycation end products (RAGE), nuclear factor-kappaB (NF-kappaB), and transforming growth factor-β (TGF-β) gene expression in myocardial tissue [72].

Human studies have confirmed the benefits of polyphenols on the cardiovascular system; Rizza et al in a randomized cross-over clinical trial shown that oral administration (50 mg/d for 3 week) of hesperidin, a citrus flavonoids, increased flow mediated dilation and reduced circulating inflammatory biomarkers (hs-CRP, serum amyloid A protein, soluble E selectin), decreased adhesion of monocytes, expression of vascular cell adhesion moleculs-1 and generally improved vascular function in patients with metabolic syndrome [73]. Another cross-over trial conducted in postmenopausal type 2 diabetic patients, showed that supplementation with isoflavones from red clover (50 mg/day) after 4 weeks improved endothelial function and decrease systolic and diastolic blood pressure [74].

In summary, results of the studies confirm that polyphenolic compounds attenuate several cardiovascular risk factors in diabetes; dietary polyphenols modulate lipid metabolism and dyslipidemia, improve vascular function, decrease oxidative and inflammatory-induced vascular damage, and regulate blood pressure.

Antioxidative properties of polyphenols

One of the pathogenic mechanisms that explain the development and progression of micro and macro vascular complications in diabetes is oxidative stress; increased generation of free radicals and an impaired antioxidant defense system in diabetic conditions induces imbalance of the oxidant/antioxidant status [2, 75]. Inhibition of these oxidative processes could prevent the onset and development of long-term diabetic complications [76].

Most polyphenolic compounds and their active metabolites have been known as potent antioxidant phytochemicals due to their unique structure. As reviewed by Dembinska-Kiec, these compounds could scavenge free radicals, quench electronically excited compounds, reduce hydroperoxide formation, and attenuate production of reactive oxygen species (ROS) through modulation of several enzymes involved in the development of ROS including xanthine oxidase, cyclooxygenase, lipoxygenase, microsomal monooxygenase, NADH oxidase and mitochondrial succinoxidase [77]. Some experts believe that polyphenols beyond the direct antioxidant capacities in scavenging of free radicals mainly act by direct interactions with important cellular receptors or key signaling pathways, which may result in modification of the redox status of the cell and may trigger a series of redox-dependent reactions [78].

Plant polyphenols can enhance the endogenous antioxidative system, improve oxidant antioxidant balance, and effectively prevent oxidative damage; green tea catechins are the polyphenolic compounds most studied polyphenolic compounds in this area; these bioactive components decreased lipid peroxidation and increased plasma total antioxidant capacity; they also attenuated of stress-sensitive signaling pathways, prooxidant enzymes, and inducted of antioxidant enzymes including superoxide dismutase, catalase and glutathione peroxidase [79].

In summary, polyphenols effectively attenuate oxidative stress, promote endogenous antioxidant defense system, and modulate oxidant/antioxidant balance.

Effects of polyphenols on adipose tissue metabolism

Adipocyte dysfunction is strongly associated with the development of insulin resistance, sub-clinical inflammation, β cell impairment and type

2 diabetes [80]. Polyphenolic compounds have wonderful modulatory effects on many aspects of metabolic, endocrine and cellular signaling transduction of adipose tissue. Some polyphenols such as catechins increase β oxidation in adipocytes, down-regulate the enzymes and genes involved in lipogenesis including lipoprotein lipase, fatty acid synthase complex, peroxisome proliferator-activated receptor γ (PPARγ), CCAAT enhancer-binding protein-α, regulatory element-binding protein 1-c, fatty acid binding protein. Some polyphenols, up-regulate lipolysis pathways via induction of hormone sensitive lipase, adipose tissue lipase, increased gene expression of mitochondrial uncoupling protein 2 (UCP-2) and carnitin palmitoyl transferase-1 (CPT-1) in adipocytes [81, 82].

Anthocyanins, one group of phenolic compounds considered as modulators of adipose tissue metabolism, are bioactive components which improve adipocytes dysfunction and adipocytokines secretion in insulin resistance, increase β oxidation and decrease fat accumulation on adipocytes [83]. Cyanidin and cyanidin-3-glucoside have shown several therapeutic effects on adipocyte dysfunction through decrease in plasminogen activator inhibitor-1 and interleukin-6, induction of mitochondrial uncoupling proteins, acetyl CoA oxidase, perlipin and adiponectin gene expression [84].

Favorable effects of polyphenols in prevention of long-term diabetes complications

One of the most important properties of polyphenols recently identified is its preventive effect against long-term diabetes complications including retinopathy, nephropathy and neuropathy; based on research conducted in this area administration of anthocyanins, flavonoids and other polyphenolic compounds in diabetic conditions may facilitate new approaches for improving the quality of life in diabetic patients.

As reviewed by Ghosh et al, anthocyanins and anthocyanins-rich extracts have the potential to alleviate the developing pathways of some pathologic conditions related to diabetes; anthocyanins facilitate blood flow and prevent diabetes-induced microangiopathy, increase microvascular permeability, decrease leucocytes aggregation in vascular cell wall and improve capillary filtration of albumin [85]. Purple corn extract containing cyanidin 3-glucoside and cyanidin-3-(6″-malonylglucoside) attenuated hyperglycemia-induced mesangial cell proliferation and matrix accumulation, and inhibited over-expression intracellular cell adhesion molecule-1 and monocyte chemoattractant protein-1, as major features of diabetic mesangial fibrosis and glomerulosclerosis [86]. Recently there has been increasing interest in grape seed proanthcyanidin extracts as a natural treatment for some important diabetes complications; proanthcyanidin-rich grape seed extract inhibited the development of retinopathy, nephropathy and neurodegenerative damage in diabetic condition [87, 88].

Flavanols surprisingly have the potential to improve cognitive disorders and cholinergic dysfunction related to diabetes and other secondary consequence of changes in the nervous system induced by hyperglycemia and diabetes oxidative stress; administration of quercetin in diabetic rats improved mental function and memory via inhibition of acetylcholine esterase and attenuation of oxidative damage in nervous system [89].

Green tea catechins including epicatechin, epicatechin-3-gallat, and epigalocatechin gallat decreased the synthesis of thromboxane A2 (TXA2) and increased prostacyclin I2 (PGI2), modulate the impaired balance between these ecosanoids as accelerators of thrombogenesis in the renal tubules, leading consequently improved glomerular filtration and kidney function [90].

CONCLUSION

Type 2 diabetes, a clustering of metabolic disorder, is accompanied with other pathogenic conditions including sub-clinical inflammation and oxidative stress that subsequently leads to insulin resistance and long-term diabetes complications. The rising trend in the prevalence of diabetes complications suggests that current medical treatments for the management of diabetes are not sufficient and use of supplementary treatments, including functional foods and their nutraceuticals, could increase the effectiveness of diabetes management. Plant polyphenols including phenolic acids, flavonoids, stilbenes and lignans, based on *in vitro*studies, animal models and some clinical trials, have been proposed as effective supplements for diabetes management and prevention of its long-term complications. Further investigations using human clinical studies are needed to confirm the beneficial effects of polyphenolic compounds as supplementary treatments for diabetic patients.

ACKNOWLEDGMENTS

This study was funded by the Research Institute of Endocrine Sciences, Shahid Beheshti University of Medical Sciences, Tehran, Iran. The authors express to acknowledge the assistance given by Ms N.Shiva in language editing of the manuscript.

COMPETING INTERESTS

The authors declare that they have no competing interests.

AUTHORS' CONTRIBUTIONS

The study was designed and implemented by ZB and PM. The manuscript was prepared by ZB, PM, and FA. All authors read and approved the final manuscript.

REFERENCES

1. Santaguida PL, Balion C, Hunt D: **Diagnosis, prognosis, and treatment of impaired glucose tolerance and impaired fasting glucose.** *Evid Rep Technol Assess* 2008, **12:** 1–11.

2. Evans JL, Goldfine ID, Maddux BA, Grodsky GM: **Oxidative stress and stress-activated signaling pathways: a unifying hypothesis of type 2 diabetes.** *Endocr Rev* 2002, **23:** 599–622.

3. Spranger J, Kroke A, Möhlig M, Hoffmann K, Bergmann MM, Ristow M, *et al.*: **Inflammatory cytokines and the risk to develop type 2 diabetes: results of the prospective population-based European Prospective Investigation into Cancer and Nutrition (EPIC)-Potsdam Study.** *Diabetes* 2003, **52:** 812–817.

4. Montonen J, Knekt P, Järvinen R, Reunanen A: **Dietary antioxidant intake and risk of type 2 diabetes.***Diabetes Care* 2004, **27:** 362–366.

5. Pandey KB, Rizvi SI: **Plant polyphenols as dietary antioxidants in human health and disease.** *Oxid Med Cell Longev* 2009, **2:** 270–278.

6. Bahadoran Z, Golzarand M, Mirmiran P, Saadati N, Azizi F: **The association of dietary phytochemical index and cardio-metabolic risk factors in adults: Tehran lipid and glucose study.** *J Hum Nutr Diet*2013. In print

7. Bahadoran Z, Golzarand M, Mirmiran P, Shiva N, Azizi F: **Dietary total antioxidant capacity and the occurrence of metabolic syndrome and its components after a 3-year follow-up in adults: Tehran lipid and glucose study.** *Nutr Metab (Lond)* 2012, **9:** 70.

8. Mirmiran P, Bahadoran Z, Golzarand M, Shiva N, Azizi F: **Association between dietary phytochemical index and 3-year changes in weight, waist circumference and body

adiposity index in adults: Tehran lipid and glucose study. *Nutr Metab (Lond)* 2012, **9:** 108.

9. Mirmiran P, Noori N, Zavareh MB, Azizi F: **Fruit and vegetable consumption and risk factors for cardiovascular disease.** *Metabolism* 2009, **58:** 460–468.

10. Perera PK, Li Y: **Functional herbal food ingredients used in type 2 diabetes mellitus.** *Pharmacogn Rev*2012, **6:** 37–45.

11. Bahadoran Z, Mirmiran P, Hosseinpanah F, Hedayati M, Hosseinpour-Niazi S, Azizi F: **Broccoli sprouts reduce oxidative stress in type 2 diabetes: a randomized double-blind clinical trial.** *Eur J Clin Nutr*2011, **65:** 972–977.

12. Bahadoran Z, Mirmiran P, Hosseinpanah F, Asghari G, Rajab A, Azizi F: **Broccoli sprouts Powder could improve serum triglyceride and oxidized LDL/LDL-cholesterol ratio in type 2 diabetic patients: a randomized double-blind placebo-controlled clinical trial.** *Diabetes Res Clin Pract* 2012, **96:** 348–354.

13. Bahadoran Z, Tohidi M, Nazeri P, Mehran M, Azizi F, Mirmiran P: **Effect of broccoli sprouts on insulin resistance in type 2 diabetic patients: a randomized double-blind clinical trial.** *Int J Food Sci Nutr*2012, **63:** 767–771.

14. Beckman CH: **Phenolic-storing cells: keys to programmed cell death and periderm formation in wilt disease resistance and in general defence responses in plants?** *Physiol Mol Plant Pathol* 2000, **57:**101–110.

15. Pietta P, Minoggio M, Bramati L: **Plant polyphenols: structure, occurrence and bioactivity.** *Stud Nat Pro Chem* 2003, **28:** 257–312.

16. Manach C, Scalbert A, Morand C, Rémésy C, Jiménez L: **Polyphenols: food sources and bioavailability.** *Am J Clin Nutr* 2004, **79:** 727–747.

17. Adlercreutz H: **Lignans and human health.** *Crit Rev Clin Lab Sci* 2007, **44:** 483–525.

18. Chun OK, Chung SJ, Song WO: **Estimated dietary flavonoid intake and major food sources of U.S. adults.** *J Nutr* 2007, **137:** 1244–1252.

19. Ovaskainen ML, Törrönen R, Koponen JM, Sinkko H, Hellström J, Reinivuo H, *et al.*: **Dietary intake and major food sources of polyphenols in Finnish adults.** *J Nutr* 2008, **138:** 562–566.

20. Scalbert A, Williamson G: **Dietary intake and bioavailability of polyphenols.** *J Nutr* 2000, **130:** 2073S-2085S.

21. Scalbert A, Morand C, Manach C, Rémésy C: **Absorption and metabolism of polyphenols in the gut and impact on health.** *Biomed Pharmacother* 2002, **56:** 276–282.

22. Han X, Loa T: **Dietary polyphenols and their biological significance.** *Int J Mol Sci* 2007, **8:** 950–988.

23. Dinneen S, Gerich J, Rizza R: **Carbohydrate metabolism in non-insulin-dependent diabetes mellitus.** *N Engl J Med* 1992, **327:** 707–713.

24. Hanhineva K, Törrönen R, Bondia-Pons I, Pekkinen J, Kolehmainen M, Mykkänen H, *et al.*: **Impact of dietary polyphenols on carbohydrate metabolism.** *Int J Mol Sci* 2010, **11:** 1365–1402.

25. Iwai K, Kim MY, Onodera A, Matsue H: **Alpha-glucosidase inhibitory and antihyperglycemic effects of polyphenols in the fruit of Viburnum dilatatum Thunb.** *Agric Food Chem* 2006, **54:** 4588–4592.

26. Iwai K: **Antidiabetic and antioxidant effects of polyphenols in brown alga Ecklonia stolonifera in genetically diabetic KK-A(y) mice.** *Plant Foods Hum Nutr* 2008, **63:** 163–169.

27. Cabrera C, Artacho R, Giménez R: **Beneficial effects of green tea-a review.** *J Am Coll Nutr* 2006, **25:** 79–99.

28. Tadera K, Minami Y, Takamatsu K, Matsuoka T: **Inhibition of alpha-glucosidase and alpha-amylase by flavonoids.** *J Nutr Sci Vitaminol (Tokyo)* 2006, **52:** 149–153.

29. Kobayashi Y, Suzuki M, Satsu H, Arai S, Hara Y, Suzuki K, *et al.*: **Green tea polyphenols inhibit the sodium-dependent glucose transporter of intestinal epithelial cells by a competitive mechanism.** *J Agric Food Chem* 2000, **48:** 5618–5623.

30. Johnston K, Sharp P, Clifford M, Morgan L: **Dietary polyphenols decrease glucose uptake by human intestinal Caco-2 cells.** *FEBS Lett* 2005, **579:** 1653–1657.

31. Johnston KL, Clifford MN, Morgan LM: **Coffee acutely modifies gastrointestinal hormone secretion and glucose tolerance in humans: glycemic effects of chlorogenic acid and caffeine.** *Am J Clin Nutr*2003, **78:** 728–733.

32. Dao TM, Waget A, Klopp P, Serino M, Vachoux C, Pechere L, *et al.*: **Resveratrol increases glucose induced GLP-1 secretion in mice: a mechanism which contributes to the glycemic control.** *PLoS One*2011, **6:** e20700.

33. Jung EH, Kim SR, Hwang IK, Ha TY: **Hypoglycemic effects of a phenolic acid fraction of rice bran and ferulic acid in C57BL/KsJ-db/db mice.** *J Agric Food Chem* 2007, **55:** 9800–9804.

34. Jung UJ, Lee MK, Jeong KS, Choi MS: **The hypoglycemic effects of hesperidin and naringin are partly mediated by hepatic**

glucose-regulating enzymes in C57BL/KsJ-db/db mice. *J Nutr* 2004, **134:** 2499–2503.

35. Jung UJ, Lee MK, Park YB, Kang MA, Choi MS: **Effect of citrus flavonoids on lipid metabolism and glucose-regulating enzyme mRNA levels in type-2 diabetic mice.** *Int J Biochem Cell Biol* 2006, **38:**1134–1145.

36. Waltner-Law ME, Wang XL, Law BK, Hall RK, Nawano M, Granner DK: **Epigallocatechin gallate, a constituent of green tea, represses hepatic glucose production.** *J Biol Chem* 2002, **277:** 34933–34940.

37. Collins QF, Liu HY, Pi J, Liu Z, Quon MJ, Cao W: **Epigallocatechin-3-gallate (EGCG), a green tea polyphenol, suppresses hepatic gluconeogenesis through 5′-AMP-activated protein kinase.** *J Biol Chem* 2007, **282:** 30143–30149. Prabhakar PK, Doble M: **Synergistic effect of phytochemicals in combination with hypoglycemic drugs on glucose uptake in myotubes.** *Phytomedicine* 2009, **16:** 1119–1126.

38. Zhang B, Kang M, Xie Q, Xu B, Sun C, Chen K, Wu Y: **Anthocyanins from Chinese bayberry extract protect β cells from oxidative stress-mediated injury via HO-1 upregulation.** *J Agric Food Chem* 2011,**59:** 537–545.

39. Park CE, Kim MJ, Lee JH, Min BI, Bae H, Choe W, *et al.*: **Resveratrol stimulates glucose transport in C2C12 myotubes by activating AMP-activated protein kinase.** *Mol Med* 2007, **39:** 222–229.

40. Towler MC, Hardie DG: **AMP-activated protein kinase in metabolic control and insulin signaling.** *Circ Res* 2007, **100:** 328–341.

41. Zhou G, Myers R, Li Y, Chen Y, Shen X, Fenyk-Melody J, *et al.*: **Role of AMP-activated protein kinase in mechanism of metformin action.** *J Clin Invest* 2001, **108:** 1167–1174.

42. Zang M, Xu S, Maitland-Toolan KA, Zuccollo A, Hou X, Jiang B, *et al.*: **Polyphenols stimulate AMP-activated protein kinase, lower lipids, and inhibit accelerated atherosclerosis in diabetic LDL receptor-deficient mice.** *Diabetes* 2006, **55:** 2180–2191.

43. Kumar R, Balaji S, Uma TS, Sehgal PK: **Fruit extracts of Momordica charantia potentiate glucose uptake and up-regulate Glut-4, PPAR gamma and PI3K.** *J Ethnopharmacol* 2009, **126:** 533–537.

44. Fu Z, Liu D: **Long-term exposure to genistein improves insulin secretory function of pancreatic beta-cells.** *Eur J Pharmacol* 2009, **616:** 321–327.

45. Liu D, Zhen W, Yang Z, Carter JD, Si H, Reynolds KA: **Genistein acutely stimulates insulin secretion in pancreatic beta-cells through a cAMP-dependent protein kinase pathway.** *Diabetes* 2006, **55:** 1043–1050.

46. Fu Z, Zhang W, Zhen W, Lum H, Nadler J, Bassaganya-Riera J: **Genistein induces pancreatic beta-cell proliferation through activation of multiple signaling pathways and prevents insulin-deficient diabetes in mice.** *Endocrinology* 2010, **151:** 3026–3037.

47. Kajimoto Y, Kaneto H: **Role of oxidative stress in pancreatic beta-cell dysfunction.** *Ann NY Acad Sci*2004, **1011:** 168–176.

48. Drews G, Krippeit-Drews P, Düfer M: **Oxidative stress and beta-cell dysfunction.** *Pflugers Arch* 2010,**460:** 703–718.

49. Yin P, Zhao S, Chen S, Liu J, Shi L, Wang X, Liu Y, Ma C: **Hypoglycemic and hypolipidemic effects of polyphenols from burs of Castanea mollissima Blume.** *Molecules* 2011, **16:** 9764–9774.

50. Szkudelski T, Szkudelska K: **Anti-diabetic effects of resveratrol.** *Ann NY Acad Sci* 2011, **1215:** 34–39.

51. Szkudelski T: **Resveratrol inhibits insulin secretion from rat pancreatic islets.** *Eur J Pharmacol* 2006,**552:** 176–181.

52. Kalofoutis C, Piperi C, Kalofoutis A, Harris F, Phoenix D, Singh J: **Type II diabetes mellitus and cardiovascular risk factors: Current therapeutic approaches.** *Exp Clin Cardiol* 2007, **12:** 17–28.

53. Thomas JE, Foody JM: **The pathophysiology of cardiovascular disease in diabetes mellitus and the future of therapy.** *J Cardiometab Syndr* 2007, **2:** 108–113.

54. Lecour S, Lamont KT: **Natural polyphenols and cardioprotection.** *Mini Rev Med Chem* 2011, **11:** 1191–1199.

55. Schini-Kerth VB, Auger C, Etienne-Selloum N, Chataigneau T: **Polyphenol-induced endothelium-dependent relaxations role of NO and EDHF.** *Adv Pharmacol* 2010, **60:** 133–175.

56. Stoclet JC, Chataigneau T, Ndiaye M, Oak MH, El Bedoui J, Chataigneau M, *et al.*: **Vascular protection by dietary polyphenols.** *Eur J Pharmacol* 2004, **500:** 299–313.

57. Sugiyama H, Akazome Y, Shoji T, Yamaguchi A, Yasue M, Kanda T, *et al.*: **Oligomeric procyanidins in apple polyphenol are main active components for inhibition of pancreatic lipase and triglyceride absorption.** *J Agric Food Chem* 2007, **55:** 4604–4609.

58. Vidal R, Hernandez-Vallejo S, Pauquai T, Texier O, Rousset M, Chambaz J, *et al.*: **Apple procyanidins decrease cholesterol esterification and lipoprotein secretion in Caco-2/TC7 enterocytes.** *J Lipid Res*2005, **46:** 258–268.

59. Koo SI, Noh SK: **Green tea as inhibitor of the intestinal absorption of lipids: potential mechanism for its lipid-lowering effect.** *J Nutr Biochem* 2007, **18:** 179–183.

60. Seymour EM, Singer AA, Kirakosyan A, Urcuyo-Llanes DE, Kaufman PB, Bolling SF: **Altered hyperlipidemia, hepatic steatosis, and hepatic peroxisome proliferator-activated receptors in rats with intake of tart cherry.** *J Med Food* 2008, **11:** 252–259.

61. Oak MH, Chataigneau M, Keravis T, Chataigneau T, Beretz A, Andriantsitohaina R, *et al.*: **Red wine polyphenolic compounds inhibit vascular endothelial growth factor expression in vascular smooth muscle cells by preventing the activation of the p38 mitogen-activated protein kinase pathway.***Arterioscler Thromb Vasc Biol* 2003, **23:** 1001–1007.

62. Oak MH, El Bedoui J, Schini-Kerth VB: **Antiangiogenic properties of natural polyphenols from red wine and green tea.** *J Nutr Biochem* 2005, **16:** 1–8. 1

63. Ndiaye M, Chataigneau T, Chataigneau M, Schini-Kerth VB: **Red wine polyphenols induce EDHF-mediated relaxations in porcine coronary arteries through the redox-sensitive activation of the PI3-kinase/Akt pathway.** *Br J Pharmacol* 2004, **142:** 1131–1136.

64. Wang L, Zhu LH, Jiang H, Tang QZ, Yan L, Wang D, *et al.*: **Grape seed proanthocyanidins attenuate vascular smooth muscle cell proliferation via blocking phosphatidylinositol 3-kinase-dependent signaling pathways.** *J Cell Physiol* 2010, **223:** 713–726.

65. de Pascual-Teresa S, Moreno DA, García-Viguera C: **Flavanols and anthocyanins in cardiovascular health: a review of current evidence.** *Int J Mol Sci* 2010, **11:** 1679–1703.

66. Nogueira Lde P, Knibel MP, Torres MR, Nogueira Neto JF, Sanjuliani AF: **Consumption of high-polyphenol dark chocolate improves endothelial function in individuals with stage 1**

hypertension and excess body weight. *Int J Hypertens* 2012, **2012:** 147321.

67. Mellor DD, Madden LA, Smith KA, Kilpatrick ES, Atkin SL: **High-polyphenol chocolate reduces endothelial dysfunction and oxidative stress during acute transient hyperglycaemia in Type 2 diabetes: a pilot randomized controlled trial.** *Diabet Med* 2012, **30:** 478–483.

68. Kar P, Laight D, Rooprai HK, Shaw KM, Cummings M: **Effects of grape seed extract in Type 2 diabetic subjects at high cardiovascular risk: a double blind randomized placebo controlled trial examining metabolic markers, vascular tone, inflammation, oxidative stress and insulin sensitivity.** *Diabet Med*2009, **26:** 526–531.

69. Shidfar F, Heydari I, Hajimiresmaiel SJ, Hosseini S, Shidfar S, Amiri F: **The effects of cranberry juice on serum glucose, apoB, apoA-I, Lp(a), and Paraoxonase-1 activity in type 2 diabetic male patients.** *J Res Med Sci* 2012, **17:** 355–360.

70. Hubbard GP, Wolffram S, Lovegrove JA, Gibbins JM: **Ingestion of quercetin inhibits platelet aggregation and essential components of the collagen-stimulated platelet activation pathway in humans.** *J Thromb Haemost* 2004, **2:** 2138–2145.

71. Cheng M, Gao HQ, Xu L, Li BY, Zhang H, Li XH: **Cardioprotective effects of grape seed proanthocyanidins extracts in streptozocin induced diabetic rats.** *J Cardiovasc Pharmacol* 2007, **50:**503–509.

72. Rizza S, Muniyappa R, Iantorno M, Kim JA, Chen H, Pullikotil P, *et al*.: **Citrus polyphenol hesperidin stimulates production of nitric oxide in endothelial cells while improving endothelial function and reducing inflammatory markers in patients with metabolic syndrome.** *J Clin Endocrinol Metab* 2011,**96:** E782-E792.

73. Howes JB, Tran D, Brillante D, Howes LG: **Effects of dietary supplementation with isoflavones from red clover on ambulatory blood pressure and endothelial function in postmenopausal type 2 diabetes.***Diabetes Obes Metab* 2003, **5:** 325–332.

74. Goycheva V, Gadjeva BP: **Oxidative stress and its complications in diabetes mellitus.** *Trakia J of Sci*2006, **4:** 1–8.

75. Pérez-Matute P, Zulet MA, Martínez JA: **Reactive species and diabetes: counteracting oxidative stress to improve health.** *Curr Opin Pharmacol* 2009, **9:** 771–779.

76. Dembinska-Kiec A, Mykkänen O, Kiec-Wilk B, Mykkänen H: **Antioxidant phytochemicals against type 2 diabetes.** *Br J Nutr* 2008, **99:** ES109-ES117.

77. Scalbert A, Johnson IT, Saltmarsh M: **Polyphenols: antioxidants and beyond.** *Am J Clin Nutr* 2005, **81:**215S-217S.

78. Crespy V, Williamson G: **A review of the health effects of green tea catechins in in vivo animal models.** *J Nutr* 2004, **134:** 3431S-3440S.

79. Guilherme A, Virbasius JV, Puri V, Czech MP: **Adipocyte dysfunctions linking obesity to insulin resistance and type 2 diabetes.** *Nat Rev Mol Cell Biol* 2008, **9:** 367–377.

80. Nakazato K, Song H, Waga T: **Effects of dietary apple polyphenol on adipose tissues weights in Wistar rats.** *Exp Anim* 2006, **55:** 383–389.

81. Osada K, Suzuki T, Kawakami Y, Senda M, Kasai A, Sami M, *et al.*: **Dose-dependent hypocholesterolemic actions of dietary apple polyphenol in rats fed cholesterol.** *Lipids* 2006, **41:** 133–139.

82. Tsuda T, Horio F, Uchida K, Aoki H, Osawa T: **Dietary cyanidin 3-O-beta-D-glucoside-rich purple corn color prevents obesity and**

ameliorates hyperglycemia in mice. *J Nutr* 2003, **133:** 2125–2130.

83. Tsuda T, Ueno Y, Yoshikawa T, Kojo H, Osawa T: **Microarray profiling of gene expression in human adipocytes in response to anthocyanins.** *Biochem Pharmacol* 2006, **71:** 1184–1197.

84. Ghosh D, Konishi T: **Anthocyanins and anthocyanin-rich extracts: role in diabetes and eye function.***Asia Pac J Clin Nutr* 2007, **16:** 200–208

85. Li J, Lim SS, Lee JY, Kim JK, Kang SW, Kim JL, *et al.*: **Purple corn anthocyanins dampened high-glucose-induced mesangial fibrosis and inflammation: possible renoprotective role in diabetic nephropathy.***J Nutr Biochem* 2012, **23:** 320–331.

86. Li BY, Cheng M, Gao HQ, Ma YB, Xu L, Li XH, *et al.*: **Back-regulation of six oxidative stress proteins with grape seed proanthocyanidin extracts in rat diabetic nephropathy.** *J Cell Biochem* 2008, **104:** 668–679.

87. Cui XP, Li BY, Gao HQ, Wei N, Wang WL, Lu M: **Effects of grape seed proanthocyanidin extracts on peripheral nerves in streptozocin-induced diabetic rats.** *J Nutr Sci Vitaminol (Tokyo)* 2008, **54:** 321–328.

88. Bhutada P, Mundhada Y, Bansod K, Bhutada C, Tawari S, Dixit P, *et al.*: **Ameliorative effect of quercetin on memory dysfunction in streptozotocin-induced diabetic rats.** *Neurobiol Learn Mem* 2010, **94:** 293–302.

89. Rhee SJ, Choi JH, Park MR: **Green tea catechin improves microsomal phospholipase A2 activity and the arachidonic acid cascade system in the kidney of diabetic rats.** *Asia Pac J Clin Nutr* 2002, **11:** 226–231.

Chapter 4

Metal Complexes as Therapeutic Substitute in Tuberculosis Treatment

C Justin Dhanaraj[1*], M Sivasankaran Nair[2]

[1]*Department of Chemistry, University College of Engineering Nagercoil, Anna University, Tirunelveli Region, Tamil Nadu, 629004, India.*

[2] *Department of Chemistry, Manonmaniam Sundaranar Universiy, Tirunelveli, Tamil Nadu, 627012, India*

BACKGROUND

Tuberculosis (TB) is a disease that produces several million deaths annually. With the appearance of multi drug resistant microbial strains of *Mycobacterium tuberculosis*, innovations in TB drug discovery and evolving strategies to bring new agents with best performance is an essential investigation. Taking this into account, there is a pressing need to develop new and more effective anti tubercular agents. The coordination of metal with organic drugs is a promising strategy that has been successful in many cases with different pharmacological activities. The emergence of new cases and the adverse effects of first and second-line antituberculosis drugs have led to renewed research interest in metal drug complexes in the hope of discovering new antituberculosis drugs. The aim of the present study is to assess the antituberculosis activity of Ni (II) and Cu (II) complexes of polymer ligand poly (3-nitrobenzylidene-1-naphthylamine-co-methacrylic acid).

METHODS

Antituberculosis activities of the ligand and its complexes were assessed against *M. tuberculosis*H37 Rv strain by microplate alamar blue assay (MABA) method using pyrazinamide as standard.

RESULTS

The minimum inhibitory concentration values of the ligand and its complexes on comparison with standard (pyrazinamide; 4 µg/mL) indicate that the complexes exhibit promising antituberculosis activity. Cu (II) complex shows more activity (10 µg/ mL) followed by Ni (II) complex (20µg/ mL) and ligand (35 µg/ mL).

CONCLUSION

Among the synthesized compounds, the Cu (II) complex may be used as therapeutic substitute in the treatment of tuberculosis by replacing the routine drugs.

Chapter 5

Nutraceutical Agents with Anti-Inflammatory Properties Prevent Dietary Saturated-Fat Induced Disturbances in Blood–Brain Barrier Function in Wild-Type Mice

Ryusuke Takechi[1,2], Menuka M Pallebage-Gamarallage[1], Virginie Lam[1], Corey Giles[1] and John C Mamo[1,2]

[1]*School of Public Health, Curtin Health Innovation Research Institute, Biosciences Research Precinct, Faculty of Health Sciences, Curtin University, Kent st, Bentley 6102WA, Australia*

[2]*Centre for Metabolic Fitness, Australian Technology Network, GPO Box U1987, Perth 6845WA, Australia*

ABSTRACT

Background

Emerging evidence suggests that disturbances in the blood–brain barrier (BBB) may be pivotal to the pathogenesis and pathology of vascular-based neurodegenerative disorders. Studies suggest that heightened systemic and central inflammations are associated with BBB dysfunction. This study investigated the effect of the anti-inflammatory nutraceuticals garlic extract-aged (GEA), alpha lipoic acid (ALA), niacin, and nicotinamide (NA) in a murine dietary-induced model of BBB dysfunction.

Methods

C57BL/6 mice were fed a diet enriched in saturated fatty acids (SFA, 40% fat of total energy) for nine months to induce systemic inflammation and BBB disturbances. Nutraceutical treatment groups included the provision of either GEA, ALA, niacin or NA in the positive control SFA-group and in low-fat fed controls. Brain parenchymal extravasation of plasma derived immunoglobulin G (IgG) and large macromolecules (apolipoprotein (apo) B lipoproteins) measured by quantitative immunofluorescent microscopy, were used as markers of disturbed BBB integrity. Parenchymal glial fibrillar acidic protein (GFAP) and cyclooxygenase-2 (COX-2) were considered in the context of surrogate markers of neurovascular inflammation and oxidative stress. Total anti-oxidant status and glutathione reductase activity were determined in plasma.

Results

Brain parenchymal abundance of IgG and apoB lipoproteins was markedly exaggerated in mice maintained on the SFA diet concomitant with significantly increased GFAP and COX-2, and reduced systemic anti-oxidative status. The nutraceutical GEA, ALA, niacin, and NA completely prevented the SFA-induced disturbances of BBB and normalized the measures of neurovascular inflammation and oxidative stress.

Conclusions

The anti-inflammatory nutraceutical agents GEA, ALA, niacin, or NA are potent inhibitors of dietary fat-induced disturbances of BBB induced by systemic inflammations.

Keywords : Garlic extract-aged Alpha-lipoic acid Blood–brain barrier Inflammation Neurodegenerative disorders Niacin Nicotinamide Oxidative stress Saturated fatty acids

BACKGROUND

Accumulating evidence suggests that disturbances in cerebral capillary integrity characterized by inflammation, loss of blood–brain barrier (BBB) functions, parenchymal extravasation of plasma proteins, proteinaceous deposits on extracellular matrices, and glial cell activation contribute to the onset or progression of a number of neurodegenerative disorders including vascular dementia, Alzheimer's disease, Parkinson's disease, and multiple sclerosis [1]. Cerebral capillary abnormalities that precede frank pathological or clinical abnormalities include capillary endothelial cell proliferation, perivascular gliosis, and progressive arteriopathy, and thereafter the formation of lacunar lesions [2, 3, 4, 5].

Cerebral capillary dysfunction induced as a consequence of a chronically heightened state of systemic inflammation is positively associated with neurovascular degenerative disorders [6, 7,8, 9]. Comorbidities such as dyslipidemia, hypertension or endocrine disorders, exposure to pollutants such as smoking, alcohol consumption, or atherogenic diets may also increase neurodegenerative disease onset via a cerebral capillary axis [3, 6, 8, 9, 10]. Studies in animal models support the latter. Wild-type mice chronically fed pro-inflammatory diets enriched in saturated fatty acids (SFA) or cholesterol showed hallmark features of BBB dysfunction including cerebral extravasation of large plasma proteins (immunoglobulin G (IgG) and macromolecules (apolipoprotein (apo) B lipoproteins)) concomitant with diminished endothelial tight junction proteins [9, 11, 12, 13].

Several *in vivo* and *in vitro* studies suggest that pharmacological agents with anti-inflammatory or anti-oxidative activity may positively regulate BBB integrity through regulation of systemic inflammatory pathways [14, 15, 16]. The potent antioxidant, probucol, preserved BBB function and profoundly attenuated astroglial cell activation in SFA-fed mice [17]. The cholesterol-lowering 3-hydroxy-methyl-Co-A reductase inhibitor, atorvastatin, prevented BBB disturbances in spontaneously hypertensive rats [18]. Atorvastatin, pravastatin, and the non-selective cyclooxygenase inhibitor, ibuprofen, were shown to also restore BBB function in mice with BBB dysfunction induced by chronic ingestion of a pro-atherogenic diet [18].

Bioactive anti-inflammatories may also confer benefit to cerebral capillary vessels [19, 20]. A bitter melon-attenuated dietary-fat induced BBB disturbances in wild-type mice concomitant with a significant reduction in both central and systemic inflammatory/oxidative stress markers [7]. However, paradoxical observations have been reported in other studies. Provision of omega-3 fatty acids to mice that had been maintained on an SFA enriched diet for twelve weeks, exacerbated measures of BBB dysfunction [11]. A study by Mustata et al. also showed increased glycoxidation in tendon, aorta, and plasma by anti-oxidative green tea and vitamins C and E in a diabetic rat model [21]. Soy isoflavones, such as genistein, inhibit the lipid peroxidation only with super-physiological concentrations due to its poor peroxyl radical scavenging function [22].

In the current study, we investigated the efficacy of selected anti-oxidative nutraceuticals, namely garlic extract-aged (GEA), alpha-lipoic acid (ALA), niacin, and nicotinamide (NA), in an established dietary-induced model of BBB disruption. The GEA contains anti-oxidative phytochemicals including S-allylcysteine, S-allylmercaptocysteine, diallyl sulfide, and allicin, which can scavenge reactive oxygen species. The GEA was shown to inhibit lipid peroxidation and reduce expression of key inflammatory proteins such as nuclear factor-kappa B *in vivo* and*in vitro*[23, 24, 25]. In clinical studies, GEA supplementation was found to reduce measures of oxidative stress and showed therapeutic benefits in subjects with Parkinson's and Alzheimer's disease [26, 27, 28, 29, 30, 31]. ALA is a naturally occurring anti-oxidant that sequesters free radicals. ALA acts indirectly to enhance cellular anti-oxidant status by stimulating uptake of exogenous anti-oxidants and enhancing the production of endogenous anti-oxidant enzymes. ALA also inhibits the production of pro-inflammatory cytokines [32]. In a traumatic brain injury model, Toklu et al. reported that ALA improved BBB function concomitant with attenuated central and systemic inflammation [33]. Niacin and NA are classified within the B3 group of vitamins; however, niacin also has significant lipid-lowering effects [34]. Both niacin and NA can be converted into nicotinamide adenine dinucleotide or nicotinamide adenine dinucleotide phosphate, key mediators in enzymatic anti-oxidative reactions [34]. Morris et al. reported that niacin retards the cognitive decline in Alzheimer's disease and, consistent with those findings, NA was found to delay the cognitive decline in Alzheimer's subjects and reduce amyloid deposition in amyloid transgenic mice [35].

MATERIALS AND METHODS

Animals and diets

Wild-type C57BL/6J female mice were purchased from Animal Resources Centre, WA, Australia. The low-fat (LF) control chow was the maintenance diet (AIN-93M, Specialty Feeds, WA, Australia) containing <4% (w/w) polyunsaturated fats and was free of SFA or dietary cholesterol. Mice with dietary-induced BBB dysfunction were fed a semi-synthetic diet enriched in SFA (SF07-050, Specialty Feeds, WA, Australia) containing 40% energy of fat derived from cocoa butter as previously described (5% w/w palmitic 16:0, 7% stearic 18:0) [17]. The nutraceutical supplements GEA (Kyolic, USA), ALA, niacin, or NA (all Sigma-Aldrich, USA) were incorporated into either the LF or SFA diets at a concentration of 3% (w/w), 0.2% (w/w), 1% (w/w), or 0.3% (w/w), respectively. The dose of nutraceutical ingested relative to weight was within clinical recommendations and similar to previous studies [23, 26, 27, 28, 30, 31, 32, 33, 34, 35]. The components of GEA are standardized by the manufacturer relative to the amount of S-allylcysteine [36]. Animals were kept in individually ventilated cages with 12 h light/dark cycle, under controlled temperature (21°C) and air pressure. All animals had *ad libitum* access to the diets and water. All the procedures described in this study were approved by NHMRC accredited Curtin Animal Ethics Committee (approval no. N34-10).

Dietary/nutraceutical intervention and sample collection

Eight mice were randomly allocated at six weeks of age to dietary or nutraceutical treatment groups of LF control chow; LF diet supplemented with GEA (LF+GEA); LF diet supplemented with ALA (LF+ALA); LF diet supplemented with niacin (LF+Niacin); LF diet supplemented with NA (LF+NA); diet enriched in SFA; SFA diet supplemented with GEA (SFA+GEA); SFA diet supplemented with ALA (SFA+ALA); SFA diet supplemented with niacin (SFA+Niacin); or SFA diet supplemented with NA (SFA+NA). After nine months of dietary/nutraceutical intervention, mice were anesthetized with pentobarbital (45 mg/kg). Blood samples were collected from a cardiac puncture, and plasma was isolated and stored at -80°C until next use. The brain was carefully removed and fixed in 4% paraformaldehyde (w/v in PBS, pH 7.2) for 24 h. Following cryoprotection with 20% sucrose for 72 h at 4°C, the brain tissues were frozen in dry ice/isopentane and stored at -80°C until next use.

Assessment of BBB integrity

The integrity of the cerebrovascular BBB was assessed by an established method of cerebral plasma protein extravasation that indicates the unspecific blood-to-brain leakage of plasma proteins and macromolecules [9, 11, 12, 17, 18, 37, 38]. Briefly, 3-D quantitative immunomicroscopy was used to assess brain parenchymal abundance of IgG (Mw 155 kDa) and of apoB lipoproteins (molecular weight $> 2\times10^7$ kDa). Briefly, 20 µm thick cryosections were prepared from the right hemisphere of frozen brain tissues. After blocking with 10% goat serum for 30 min, the sections were incubated with goat anti-mouse IgG conjugated to Alexa488 (1:200, Invitrogen, US) for 20 h at 4°C. For the immunodetection of apoB, the sections were incubated with rabbit anti-mouse apoB (1:400, Abcam) for 20 h at 4°C, followed by an incubation with anti-rabbit IgG secondary antibody conjugated to Alexa488 (1:200, Invitrogen) for 2 h at 20°C. Following DAPI nuclei counterstaining, the sections were observed under a fluorescent microscope (Axiovert

200M, Zeiss, Germany). A positive control of BBB dysfunction from mice euthanized with carbon dioxide was utilized.

Immunomicroscopic detection of cerebral inflammation

Neuronal inflammation was assessed by determining the abundance of parenchymal glial-fibrillar acidic protein (GFAP) and cyclo-oxygenase-2 (COX-2) using a 3-D quantitative immunofluorescent method previously described [12, 17]. Briefly, 20 μm thick cryosections of the right brain hemisphere were prepared. Non-specific biding sites were blocked with 10% goat serum in PBS for 30 min at 20°C. Either rabbit anti-mouse GFAP (1:200, Abcam, UK) or rabbit anti-mouse COX-2 (1:200, Abcam) was applied to the sections for 20 h at 4°C. The sections were then incubated with goat anti-rabbit IgG conjugated with Alexa488 (1:200, Invitrogen) for 2 h at 20°C. DAPI was used to counterstain the nuclei.

3-D quantitative immunomicroscopy

Immunofluorescent micrographs were quantitatively analyzed in a 3 D context as previously described [12, 17]. One section per animal was used in the estimated stereotaxic areas of 1.7 mm interaural and -2.1 mm Bregma. Immunofluorescent micrographs were captured with mRM digital camera (Zeiss) attached to Axiovert 200M. At a magnification of 200× (20× Zeiss Plan-Neofluar objective with 10× mRM camera), a minimum of five and three 3-D images was captured from randomly selected areas of the cortex and hippocampal formation, respectively, utilizing the AxioVision imaging software (Zeiss). The random images capture process represents approximately half of the cortex and hippocampal formation region of each section. Each 3-D image consisted of 12 Z-stack 2-D images, and the distance between the Z-stack images were 1.225 μm optimized based on Nyquist overlap theory. The voxel intensity of fluorescent dye was then analyzed in 3-D with Volocity 6.2 image analysis software (PerkinElmer, UK). Means of total fluorescent intensities of all the images in cortex and hippocampal formation regions were calculated within each animal, and thereafter compared between the groups.

Plasma oxidative markers

Plasma anti-oxidative status was assessed by determining the plasma concentration of glutathione reductase and plasma total anti-oxidant status (TAS) using commercially available colorimetric assays (Randox, UK). The details are as described in the manufacturer's instructions but with minor modifications. Briefly, for the glutathione reductase assay, 4 μL of plasma sample was mixed with 100 μL of substrate buffer and incubated at 37°C. Exactly at 1, 2, 3, 4, and 5 min after adding 20 μL of NADPH solution, the optical absorbance was read at 340 nm. By plotting the absorbance values, the slope of the linear portion of the curve was determined. The glutathione reductase activity was calculated by determining the reaction rate at 340 nm with the NADPH extinction coefficient of 0.00622/μM/cm.

The TAS assay measures the anti-oxidative status of the samples by measuring the suppression of radical cation 2,2′-azino-di-[3-ethylbenzthiazoline sulphonate] (ABTS) production. Briefly, 2 μL of water, standard or samples were incubated with 100 μL of chromogen solution at 37°C, and the absorbance was read at 600 nm (A1). At exactly 3 min after adding 20 μL of substrate buffer, the absorbance was read at 600 nm (A2). The suppression of ABTS formation (A2 – A1) was determined with the known value of the standard (2.14 mmol/L).

Plasma lipids

Commercially available colorimetric assays were used to measure the concentrations of plasma cholesterol, triglycerides (Randox, UK), and non-esterified fatty acids (NEFA) (WAKO, Japan) according to the manufacturer's instruction with some minor modifications.

Briefly, for cholesterol and triglyceride assays, 2 μL of plasma samples or standards were loaded to a 96-well microplate; 200 μL of reaction solution was then added and incubated for 5 min at 37°C. The optical absorbance was read at 550 nm. For the NEFA assay, 7 μL of plasma samples or standards were loaded to a 96-well microplate; 300 μL of Reagent 1 was added and incubated for 3 min at 37°C, then 150 μL of Reagent 2 was added for 4.5 min at 37°C. The optical absorbance was read at 550 nm.

Statistical analysis

Each dietary and nutraceutical intervention group contained a minimum of eight mice, which was predicted to provide sufficient power based on the coefficient of variation of the key measures previously published [9, 11, 12, 17, 18]. All the statistical analyses were conducted by one-way ANOVA analyses followed by Tukey's post hoc tests. The Pearson's correlation coefficient describing the association between parenchymal protein extravasation (IgG and apoB) and parenchymal inflammatory markers, or plasma oxidative markers was determined. Statistical significance was considered at $P < 0.05$. Data were expressed as means ±SEM.

RESULTS

Mice have similar weight gain pattern and plasma lipids

Animals maintained on the diets enriched in SFA and diets supplemented with nutraceutical agents were well tolerated. The total calories consumed were approximately equivalent for the mice maintained on LF control chow and high SFA diet, and a similar weight gain was recorded in most treatment groups for a nine-month intervention period (Table 1). However, the final mean weight of the SFA+ALA group of mice was less than the SFA group ($P < 0.05$).

Table 1. Mean weight and weight gain

	LF	LF+GEA	LF+ALA	LF+Niacin	LF+NA	SFA	SFA+GEA	SFA+ALA	SFA+Niacin	SFA+NA
Final mean weight (g)	23.36	25.01	21.71	22.81	23.16	23.56	24.95	20.51*	23.16	22.13
SEM	0.3995	0.7448	0.2806	0.6906	0.5106	1.154	0.4088	0.4228	0.2275	0.4956
Mean weight gain (g)	9.05	9.26	5.26	7.78	7.27	8.25	9.76	4.85	7.96	7.29

The mean weights with standard error of mean at the end of nine months dietary intervention are shown in low-fat (LF), saturated fat (SFA) or diets supplemented with nutraceutical aged garlic extract-aged (+GEA), alpha-lipoic acid (+ALA), niacin (+Niacin), or nicotinamide (+NA) groups. The differences of means from the beginning to the end of dietary intervention in each group are also shown. *Indicates the statistical significance at $P < 0.05$ compared to SFA group by using one-way ANOVA followed by Tukey's post hoc test.

The plasma concentration of cholesterol and triglyceride of mice maintained on an SFA diet was not significantly different from that of mice maintained on an LF diet (Figure 1A and B). However, the plasma concentration of NEFA was significantly reduced in SFA fed mice compared to LF fed mice ($P < 0.05$) (Figure 1C). Supplementation of niacin in SFA diet significantly reduced plasma cholesterol, whereas no difference was found in LF+niacin group. Both niacin and NA supplementation significantly lowered the plasma NEFA concentration in the LF mice.

Chronic ingestion of SFA diet causes severe breakdown of BBB, but BBB integrity is restored by nutraceutical agents

We confirm substantial parenchymal perivascular abundance of plasma-derived proteins (IgG) and macromolecules (apoB lipoproteins) in mice maintained on SFA enriched diet for nine months (Figure 2). The 3-D quantitative immunomicroscopy showed that the parenchymal extravasation of IgG and apoB are substantially greater in SFA fed mice compared to mice maintained on LF control chow (Figure 3). However,

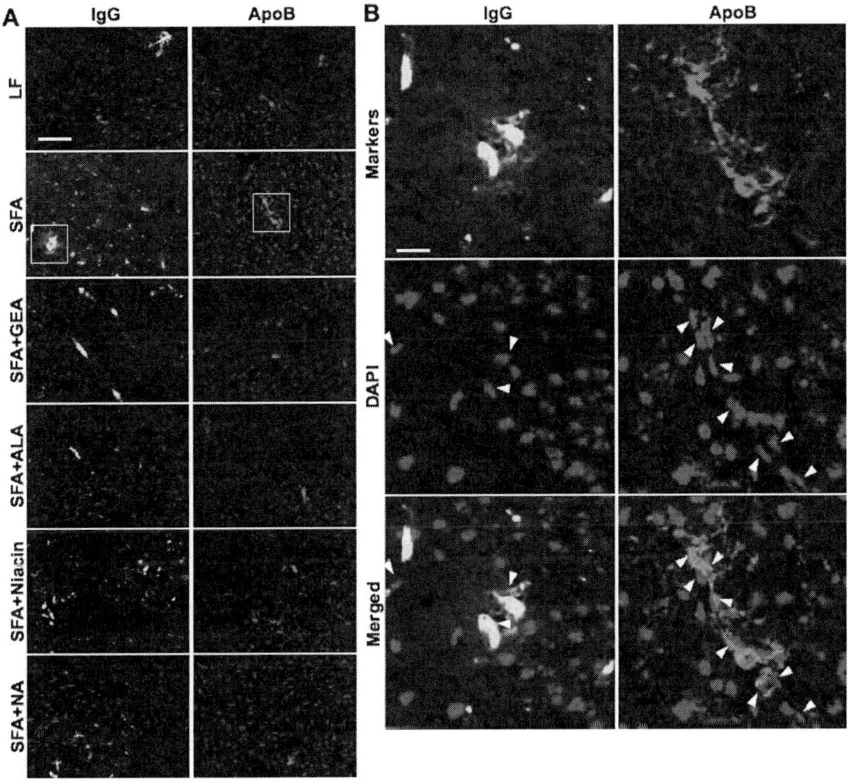

Figure 1. Plasma lipids. The plasma concentrations of cholesterol (**A**), triglyceride (**B**), and non-esterified fatty acid (NEFA) (**C**) were analyzed with commercially available colorimetric kits in mice maintained on low-fat control chow (LF), diet enriched in saturated fat (SFA) or each diet supplemented with nutraceutical garlic extract-aged (+GEA), alpha-lipoic acid (+ALA), niacin (+Niacin) or nicotinamide (+NA) for nine months. One-way ANOVA followed by Tukey's post hoc test was used to analyze the statistical significance at $P < 0.05$. (**a**) Significant difference between LF and SFA; (**b**) Significant difference between LF and each nutraceutical treatment; and (**c**) Significant difference between SFA and each nutraceutical treatment.

provision of GEA, ALA, niacin, or NA with the SFA diet completely ameliorated the BBB damaging effect of dietary-SFA (Figures 2 and 3). The control mice maintained on LF diet for nine months showed some moderate signs of cerebral IgG and apoB lipoprotein extravasation (Figure 2 and 3), however this effect was not attenuated by co-supplementation with GEA, ALA, niacin, or NA.

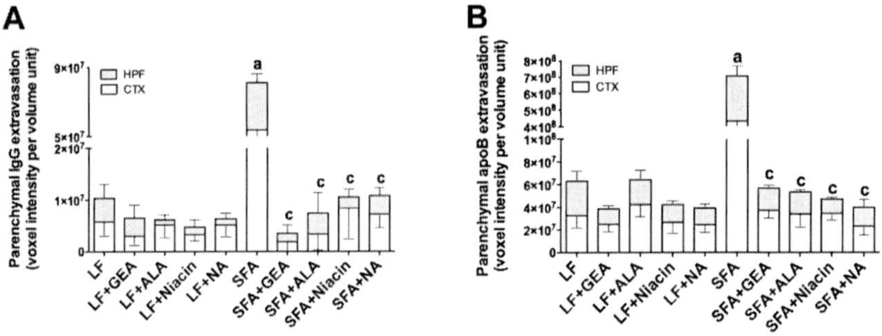

Figure 2. Immunofluorescent micrographs of cerebral extravasations of plasma IgG and apolipoprotein B lipoproteins. The integrity of the BBB was assessed by the detection of brain parenchymal extravasation of plasma derived IgG, and apoB lipoproteins in mice maintained on low-fat control chow (LF), diet enriched in saturated fat (SFA) or each diet supplemented with nutraceutical garlic extract-aged (+GEA), alpha-lipoic acid (+ALA), niacin (+Niacin), or nicotinamide (+NA). (**A**) The representative images of cerebral extravasation of IgG or apoB in the cortex are shown in green or red, respectively. Nuclei are shown in blue. Scale bar indicates 100 μm. (**B**) The magnified images of the regions of interest are indicated by a white rectangle in frame A. Vascular endothelial cells are shown with white arrowheads. Scale bar indicates 12 μm.

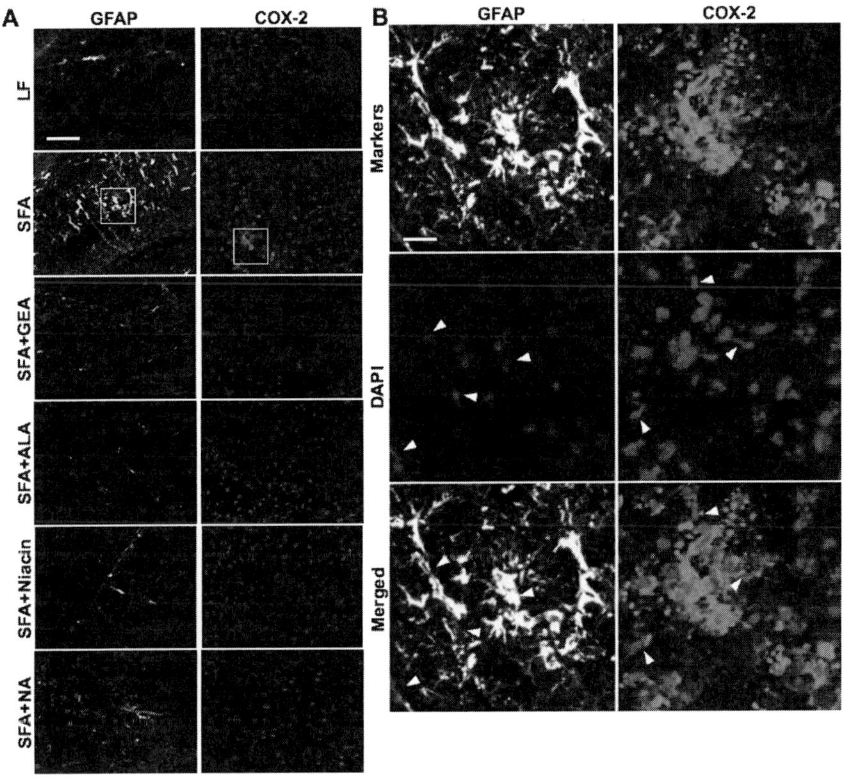

Figure 3. 3-D quantitative analyses of cerebral IgG and apoB extravasation. The optical staining intensities of IgG (**A**) and apoB (**B**) were measured with 3-D image analysis software and shown in the cortex (CTX) and hippocampal formation (HPF) of mice maintained on low-fat control chow (LF), diet enriched in saturated fat (SFA) or each diet supplemented with nutraceutical garlic extract-aged (+GEA), alpha-lipoic acid (+ALA), niacin (+Niacin), or nicotinamide (+NA) for nine months. One-way ANOVA followed by Tukey's post hoc test was used to analyze the statistical significance at $P<0.05$. Data were analyzed in cortex and hippocampal formation separately, however shown as combined since the statistical significance was identical. (**a**) Significant difference between LF and SFA; (**c**) Significant difference between SFA and each nutraceutical treatment.

Parenchymal inflammations occur following the BBB disruption

Evidence of significant neurovascular inflammation and oxidative stress was concomitant with compromised BBB integrity in mice maintained on an SFA enriched diet for nine months. Cerebral parenchymal abundance of GFAP was elevated 3-fold in SFA mice compared to LF-fed mice at nine-months (Figure 4). Similarly, COX-2 expression was substantially increased because of chronic ingestion of the SFA-enriched chow (Figure 4). Consistent with the suppression of parenchymal plasma protein extravasation in SFA mice, provision of either GEA, ALA, niacin, or NA, completely suppressed the SFA-induced expression of GFAP and COX-2 (Figures 4 and 5A,D). A heightened state of neurovascular inflammation was not indicated by GFAP and COX-2 in mice maintained on the LF-diet for nine months (Figures 4 and 5A,D). A causal association between inflammation (indicated by GFAP and COX-2 abundance) and BBB-dysfunction (parenchymal IgG and apoB lipoprotein abundance) is suggested by Pearson's correlation analysis (Figure 5B,C,E,F).

Nutraceutical agents restore the systemic oxidative status

Plasma total anti-oxidative status was expressed relative to *in vitro* suppression of enzymatic genesis of a cation radical. Plasma TAS was significantly less in SFA fed mice compared to the LF fed control (Figure 6A). In contrast, mice supplemented with either GEA, ALA, niacin, or NA in the SFA treatment groups had a plasma TAS similar to age-matched low-fat controls. Pearson's correlation analysis showed that the plasma TAS was negatively associated with parenchymal IgG and apoB lipoprotein extravasation in mice (Figure 6B,C). Glutathione reductase activity was not reduced in SFA mice compared to controls and provision of nutraceuticals had no significant effect (Figure 6D). Glutathione reductase activity was not associated with cerebral IgG or apoB-lipoprotein extravasation (Figure 6E,F).

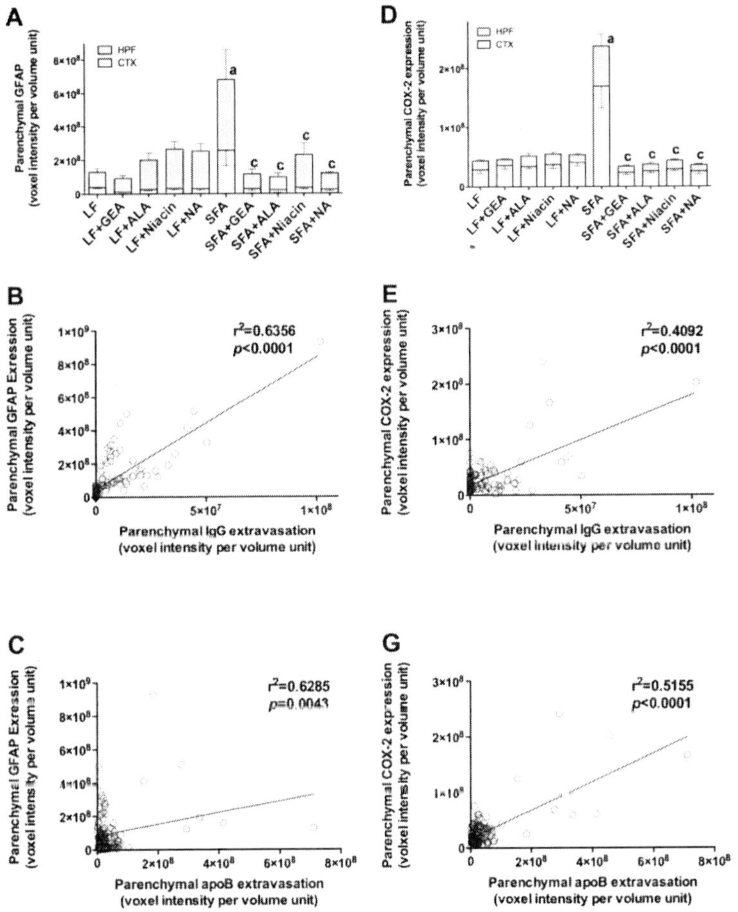

Figure 4. Immunofluorescent micrographs of cerebral inflammation (GFAP) and oxidative stress (COX-2). Cerebral astrocytic activation and oxidative stress were analyzed by the detection of parenchymal GFAP and COX-2 expression after nine months of dietary intervention with low-fat control chow (LF), a diet enriched in saturated fat (SFA) or LF/SFA diet supplemented with nutraceutical garlic extract-aged (+GEA), alpha-lipoic acid (+ALA), niacin (+Niacin), or nicotinamide (+NA). (**A**) The representative staining of GFAP in the hippocampus and COX-2 in the cortex are shown in yellow and cyan, respectively. Nuclei are shown in blue. The scale bar indicates 100 μm. (**B**) The magnified images of the regions of interest are indicated by a white rectangle in frame A. Vascular endothelial cells are shown with white arrowheads. The scale bar indicates 12 μm.

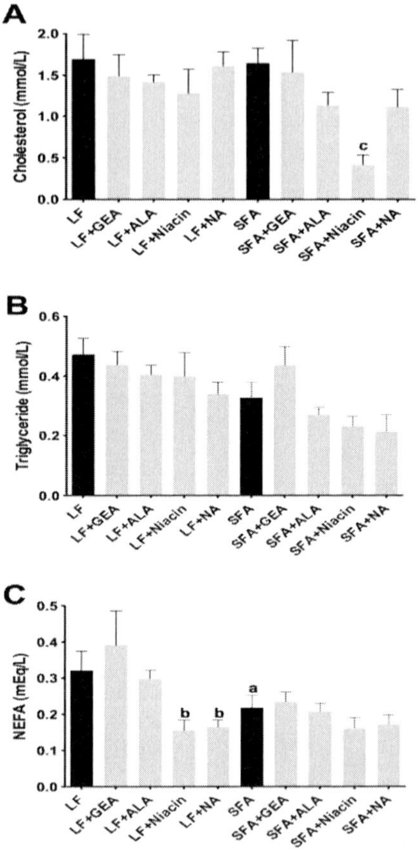

Figure 5. 3-D quantitative analyses of cerebral GFAP and COX-2 expressions. The optical staining intensities of GFAP (**A**) and COX-2 (**D**) were measured with 3-D image analysis software and shown in the cortex (CTX) and hippocampal formation (HPF) of mice maintained on low-fat control chow (LF), diet enriched in saturated fat (SFA) or each diet supplemented with nutraceutical garlic extract-aged (+GEA), alpha-lipoic acid (+ALA), niacin (+Niacin) or nicotinamide (+NA) for nine months. One-way ANOVA followed by Tukey's post hoc test was used to analyze the statistical significance at P <0.05. Data were analyzed in the cortex and hippocampal formation separately, however they are shown as combined since the statistical significance was identical. (**a**) Significant difference between LF and SFA; (**c**) Significant difference between SFA and each nutraceutical treatment. (**B** and **E**) show the correlation between parenchymal IgG extravasation and GFAP or COX-2 expression in all groups. Pearson's correlation coefficient is indicated. For GFAP and parenchymal abundance of plasma proteins (**B** and **E**) and for COX-2 versus IgG and apoB (**C** and **G**).

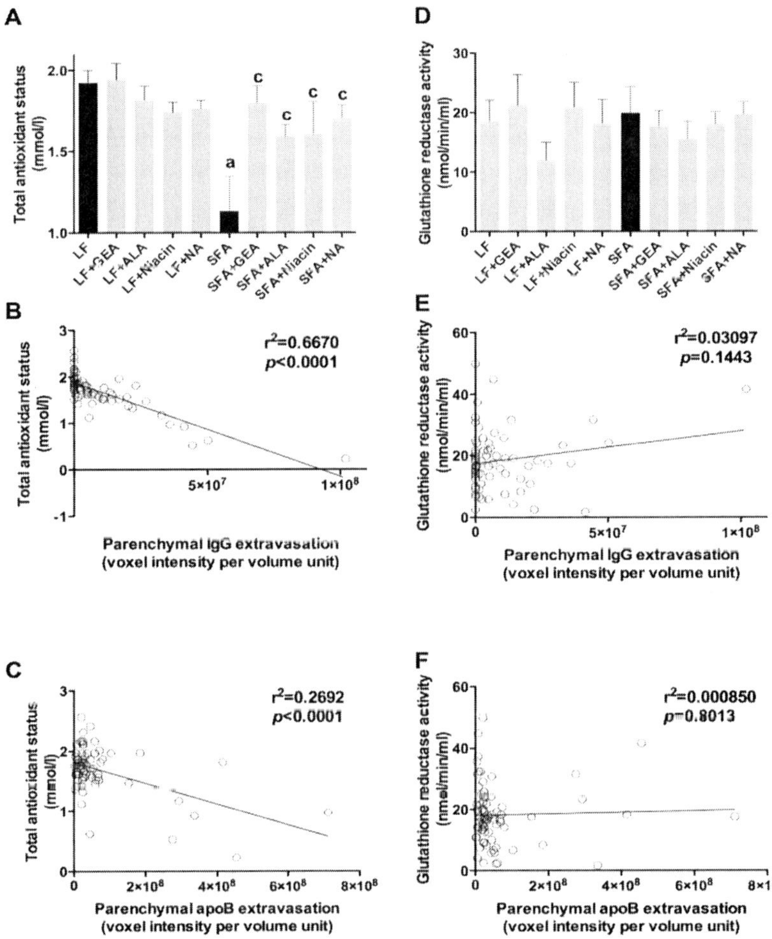

Figure 6. Plasma anti-oxidant status. The plasma total anti-oxidant status (**A**) and activity of glutathione reductase (**D**) were measured with commercially available colorimetric kits in mice maintained on low-fat control chow (LF), diet enriched in saturated fat (SFA), or each diet supplemented with nutraceutical garlic extract-aged (+GEA), alpha-lipoic acid (+ALA), niacin (+Niacin), or nicotinamide (+NA) for nine months. One-way ANOVA followed by Tukey's post hoc test was used to analyze the statistical significance at $P < 0.05$. (**a**) Significant difference between LF and SFA; (**c**) Significant difference between SFA and each nutraceutical treatment. (**B** and **E**) show the correlation between parenchymal IgG extravasation and total anti-oxidative status or glutathione reductase activity in all groups. The correlation coefficient was analyzed by Pearson's analysis. Similarly, (**C** and **F**) show Pearson's correlation coefficient between parenchymal apoB extravasation and total anti-oxidative status or glutathione reductase activity in all groups.

DISCUSSION

The present study investigated the efficacy of the anti-oxidant nutraceuticals GEA, ALA, niacin, and NA in preventing BBB disruption in genetically unmanipulated mice maintained on a pro-inflammatory diet enriched in SFA. Consistent with previous studies showing progressive deterioration of BBB commensurate with the duration of feeding [7, 9, 11, 12, 17, 18], in this study mice maintained on the SFA diet for nine months had substantial breakdown of BBB function. Compromised BBB integrity was indicated by established methodologies which considered the parenchymal abundance of plasma derived IgG, and also by the extravasation of larger macromolecules (apoB triglyceride rich lipoprotein) [9, 11, 12, 17, 18, 37, 38]. Quantitative 3-D immunohistochemical microscopy indicated that cerebral extravasation of IgG and apoB were substantially greater in the mice maintained on the SFA diet for nine months compared to the control LF-fed mice. Moreover, the dietary SFA-induced blood-to-brain kinetics and retention of plasma proteins and macromolecules occurred concomitant with evidence of heightened state of inflammation (GFAP and COX-2). Indeed, the correlation analyses showed an association between inflammation and parenchymal IgG and apoB abundance. In addition, our recent study showed the colocalization of parenchymal IgG extravasation and increased GFAP abundance in the same SFA-fed mouse model [12]. Interestingly, provision of the anti-oxidants GEA, ALA, niacin, or NA showed similar effects and completely suppressed SFA-induced BBB dysfunction. The prevention of BBB disruption by the indicated nutraceuticals occurred concomitant with the suppression of inflammation (GFAP and COX-2) and restoration of plasma total anti-oxidative status.

Earlier studies suggested that dyslipidemia might be central to brain capillary disturbances in this established model of BBB dysfunction [9, 39, 40]. In the present study, SFA feeding for nine months had no significant effect on the plasma concentration of cholesterol, triglycerides, or NEFA. Cell culture studies suggest several mechanisms by which dietary cholesterol may be pro-inflammatory and some of these appear to be analogous to the effects of dietary SFA. Yao and colleagues reported that excess cholesterol causes ER and mitochondrial stress that can lead to apoptosis [41]. Central to the latter, may be regulatory processes via altered ceramide/sphingosine-1-phosphate homeostasis [42]. Interestingly, Myriocin, an inhibitor of ceramide biosynthesis was effective in ameliorating ceramide accumulation in animals fed diets enriched in SFA [43, 44]. Other mechanisms for SFA-induced alterations in the BBB functions include stimulation of NADPH-oxidase derived reactive oxygen species generated by activated microglial cells [45]. Substantially increased parenchymal COX-2 activity and diminished anti-oxidant status are consistent with exaggerated oxidative metabolism. COX-2 is an inducible enzyme most commonly associated with activated macrophages [46]. Increased abundance of COX-2 in SFA mice is consistent with the pro-inflammatory effects of SFA reported in many other studies [47, 48]. Whilst not directly explored in this study, COX-2 may be associated with activated glial cells in mice fed SFA. Moreover, GFAP, a hallmark feature of activated glial cells, was markedly greater in the SFA treatment group suggesting the heightened cerebrovascular inflammation. In addition, our previous study also showed elevated peri-cerebrovascular CD68 immunoreactivity in SFA-fed mice [39]. Although markers of systemic inflammation were not measured in the present study, glutathione reductase, which serves to recycle glutathione by reducing its oxidized form (glutathione disulfide), was not significantly different in SFA mice, suggesting that this pathway for minimizing oxidative stress was not compromised in SFA-fed mice [49]. Many studies provide evidence that redox (reduction-oxidation) homeostasis is associated with vascular integrity via an axis of exposure to potentially toxic peroxides and free radicals [50, 51, 52]. Relevant to the findings described, a study by Kumar et al. reported that elevated plasma malondialdehyde and nitrate/nitrite were positively associated with increased BBB permeability in subjects with perinatal asphyxia [50]. A recent study reported that a high-fat diet (58% fat of total energy) significantly increased BBB permeability concomitant with compromised anti-oxidative status [7].

A clinical study by Williams et al. showed that GEA improved endothelial function in subjects with cardiovascular disease without altering plasma lipid homeostasis [53]. In insulin resistant subjects, ALA reduced the systemic oxidative stress and improved vascular endothelial function whilst having no effect on plasma lipids or lipoproteins [54]. ALA is transported through the BBB and reported to suppress cerebral and peripheral inflammation and oxidative stress [55]. Animal studies report that GEA attenuates systemic and central inflammation through increased hemoxygenase-1 activity and superoxide scavenging, and through decreased superoxide production both *in vivo* and *in vitro*[56, 57]. In rats with subarachnoid hemorrhage, ALA supplementation completely suppressed the BBB disturbances, reduced parenchymal neuroinflammation, and increased plasma anti-oxidative status [58]. In three alternate animal models of systemic inflammation, ALA was shown to reduce cerebral reactive oxygen species and GFAP expression via increased cerebral superoxide dismutase, glutathione, and glutathione peroxidase activity [59, 60, 61]. Collectively, the studies suggest that GEA and ALA are likely to protect BBB function by suppressing systemic and central oxidative stress and inflammatory pathways.

In this study, supplementation of niacin or NA significantly reduced plasma cholesterol concentration in SFA-fed mice. These two agents also reduced the plasma concentration of NEFA in the LF-control group. Maintenance of BBB function in mice given niacin or NA may have in part reflected diminished vascular exposure to plasma lipids; however, this is unlikely given that the SFA fed group of mice were normolipidemic. Both niacin and NA at the dose rates indicated were equipotent to GEA and ALA in suppressing cerebral neuroinflammation (GFAP and COX-2) and oxidative homeostasis (plasma oxidative status). Ganji et al. showed in vascular endothelial cells *in vitro*, that niacin significantly increased cellular NADPH and glutathione levels, and reduced reactive oxygen species production and low-density lipoprotein oxidation [62].

A modest increase in cerebral extravasation of plasma IgG and apoB was observed in the LF-treatment group at nine months. The findings are consistent with an aging effect on BBB function recently reported in the same model, commencing at 30 weeks of age [12]. We extend on those findings and show that the supplementation of anti-oxidative nutraceutical agents did not prevent these aging-related alterations to BBB function. This finding is perhaps not unexpected in the context that TAS was similar to the LF control group. The findings suggest that the aging-related alterations in BBB function may occur independent of oxidative stress pathways [63, 64, 65].

CONCLUSIONS

The primary findings of this study showed that compromised systemic anti-oxidative status induced by chronic SFA diet ingestion was associated with BBB dysfunction and neurovascular inflammatory responses. The provision of the anti-oxidants GEA, ALA, niacin, and NA prevents disruption of the BBB in high SFA-fed mice, concomitant with an improved redox state. However, the indicated nutraceuticals had no beneficial effects on aging-related disturbance in BBB function.

AUTHOR'S INFORMATION

RT is a Research Fellow of the National Health and Medical Research Council of Australia and of School of Public Health, Faculty of Health Sciences, Curtin University. MMPG, VL, and CG are PhD candidates of the School of Public Health, Faculty of Health Sciences, Curtin University, supervised by RT and JCM. MMPG, VL, and CG are supported by the Australian Postgraduate Awards scholarship. JCM is a Professor of Faculty of Health Sciences, Curtin University, and a Director of Centre for Metabolic Fitness, Australian Technology Network.

ACKNOWLEDGEMENTS

The authors would like to acknowledge Professor Satvinder Dhaliwal (Biostatistician, School of Public Health, Curtin University) for his assistance in statistical analyses. This project was financially supported by an NHMRC Project Grant.

COMPETING INTERESTS

The authors declare that they have no competing interests.

AUTHORS' CONTRIBUTIONS

RT conceived and designed the study and was involved in sample and data collection, data interpretation, and manuscript preparation. MMPG, VL, and CG were involved in sample and data collection. JCM was responsible for the supervision of the entire project and was involved in the study design, data interpretation, manuscript preparation, and funding. All authors read and approved the final manuscript.

REFERENCES

1. Zlokovic BV: The blood–brain barrier in health and chronic neurodegenerative disorders. Neuron. 2008, 57: 178-201.

2. Kalaria RN: Vascular basis for brain degeneration: faltering controls and risk factors for dementia. Nutr Rev. 2010, 68 (Suppl 2): S74-S87.

3. Dickstein DL, Walsh J, Brautigam H, Stockton SD, Gandy S, Hof PR: Role of vascular risk factors and vascular dysfunction in Alzheimer's disease. Mt Sinai J Med N Y. 2010, 77: 82-102.

4. Miyakawa T: Vascular pathology in Alzheimer's disease. Psychogeriat. 2010,

5. Fisher CM: The arterial lesions underlying lacunes. Acta Neuropathol. 1968, 12: 1-15.

6. Stolp HB, Johansson PA, Habgood MD, Dziegielewska KM, Saunders NR, Ek CJ: Effects of neonatal systemic inflammation on blood–brain barrier permeability and behaviour in juvenile and adult rats. Cardiovasc Psychiatry Neurol. 2011, 2011: 469046.

7. Nerurkar PV, Johns LM, Buesa LM, Kipyakwai G, Volper E, Sato R, Shah P, Feher D, Williams PG, Nerurkar VR: Momordica charantia (bitter melon) attenuates high-fat diet-associated oxidative stress and neuroinflammation. J Neuroinflam. 2011, 8: 64

8. Drake C, Boutin H, Jones MS, Denes A, McColl BW, Selvarajah JR, Hulme S, Georgiou RF, Hinz R, Gerhard A, Vail A, Prenant C, Julyan P, Maroy R, Brown G, Smigova A, Herholz K, Kassiou M, Crossman D, Francis S, Proctor SD, Russell JC, Hopkins SJ, Tyrrell PJ, Rothwell NJ, Allan SM: Brain inflammation is induced by co-morbidities and risk factors for stroke. Brain Behav Immun. 2011, 25: 1113-1122.

9. Takechi R, Galloway S, Pallebage-Gamarallage MM, Wellington CL, Johnsen RD, Dhaliwal SS, Mamo JC: Differential effects of dietary fatty acids on the cerebral distribution of plasma-derived apo B lipoproteins with amyloid-beta. Br J Nutr. 2010, 103: 652-662.

10. Takechi R, Galloway S, Pallebage-Gamarallage MM, Lam V, Mamo JC: Dietary fats, cerebrovasculature integrity and Alzheimer's disease risk. Prog Lipid Res. 2010, 49: 159-170.

11. Pallebage-Gamarallage MM, Lam V, Takechi R, Galloway S, Mamo JC: A diet enriched in docosahexanoic Acid exacerbates

brain parenchymal extravasation of apo B lipoproteins induced by chronic ingestion of saturated fats. Int J Vasc Med. 2012, 2012: 647689.

12. Takechi R, Pallebage-Gamarallage MM, Lam V, Giles C, Mamo JC: Aging-related changes in blood–brain barrier integrity and the effect of dietary fat. Neurodegen Dis. 2012

13. Takechi R, Galloway S, Pallebage-Gamarallage MM, Mamo JC: Chylomicron amyloid-beta in the aetiology of Alzheimer's disease. Atheroscler Suppl. 2008, 9: 19-25.

14. Ifergan I, Wosik K, Cayrol R, Kebir H, Auger C, Bernard M, Bouthillier A, Moumdjian R, Duquette P, Prat A: Statins reduce human blood–brain barrier permeability and restrict leukocyte migration: relevance to multiple sclerosis. Ann Neurol. 2006, 60: 45-55.

15. Kalayci R, Kaya M, Elmas I, Arican N, Ahishali B, Uzun H, Bilgic B, Kucuk M, Kudat H: Effects of atorvastatin on blood–brain barrier permeability during L-NAME hypertension followed by angiotensin-II in rats. Brain Res. 2005, 1042: 184-193.

16. Pallebage-Gamarallage MM, Takechi R, Lam V, Galloway S, Dhaliwal S, Mamo JC: Post-prandial lipid metabolism, lipid-modulating agents and cerebrovascular integrity: implications for dementia risk. Atheroscler Suppl. 2010, 11: 49-54.

17. Takechi R, Galloway S, Pallebage-Gamarallage MM, Lam V, Dhaliwal SS, Mamo JC: Probucol prevents blood–brain barrier dysfunction in wild-type mice induced by saturated fat or cholesterol feeding. Clin Exp Pharmacol Physiol. 2013, 40: 45-52.

18. Pallebage-Gamarallage M, Lam V, Takechi R, Galloway S, Clark K, Mamo J: Restoration of dietary-fat induced blood–brain barrier dysfunction by anti-inflammatory lipid-modulating agents. Lipids Health Dis. 2012, 11: 117

19. Chen X, Ghribi O, Geiger JD: Caffeine protects against disruptions of the blood–brain barrier in animal models of Alzheimer's and Parkinson's diseases. J Alzheimer Dis. 2010, 20 (Suppl 1): S127-S141.

20. Chen X, Gawryluk JW, Wagener JF, Ghribi O, Geiger JD: Caffeine blocks disruption of blood brain barrier in a rabbit model of Alzheimer's disease. J Neuroinflam. 2008, 5: 12

21. Mustata GT, Rosca M, Biemel KM, Reihl O, Smith MA, Viswanathan A, Strauch C, Du Y, Tang J, Kern TS, Lederer MO, Brownlee M, Weiss MF, Monnier VM: Paradoxical effects of green tea (Camellia sinensis) and antioxidant vitamins in diabetic rats: improved retinopathy and renal mitochondrial defects but deterioration of collagen matrix glycoxidation and cross-linking. Diabetes. 2005, 54: 517-526.

22. Patel RP, Boersma BJ, Crawford JH, Hogg N, Kirk M, Kalyanaraman B, Parks DA, Barnes S, Darley-Usmar V: Antioxidant mechanisms of isoflavones in lipid systems: paradoxical effects of peroxyl radical scavenging. Free Radic Biol Med. 2001, 31: 1570-1581.

23. Geng Z, Rong Y, Lau BH: S-allyl cysteine inhibits activation of nuclear factor kappa B in human T cells. Free Radic Biol Med. 1997, 23: 345-350.

24. Kim HK, Choi YW, Lee EN, Park JK, Kim SG, Park DJ, Kim BS, Lim YT, Yoon S: 5-Hydroxymethylfurfural from black garlic extract prevents TNF alpha-induced monocytic cell adhesion to HUVECs by suppression of vascular cell adhesion molecule-1 expression, reactive oxygen species generation and NF-kappaB activation. Phytother Res. 2011, 25: 965-974.

25. Ban JO, Oh JH, Kim TM, Kim DJ, Jeong HS, Han SB, Hong JT: Anti-inflammatory and arthritic effects of thiacremonone, a

novel sulfur compound isolated from garlic via inhibition of NF-kappaB. Arthritis Res Ther. 2009, 11:

26. Rojas P, Serrano-Garcia N, Medina-Campos ON, Pedraza-Chaverri J, Maldonado PD, Ruiz-Sanchez E: S-Allylcysteine, a garlic compound, protects against oxidative stress in 1-methyl-4-phenylpyridinium-induced parkinsonism in mice. J Nutr Biochem. 2011, 22: 937-944. Chauhan NB, Sandoval J: Amelioration of early cognitive deficits by aged garlic extract in Alzheimer's transgenic mice. Phytother Res. 2007, 21: 629-640.

27. Chauhan NB: Effect of aged garlic extract on APP processing and tau phosphorylation in Alzheimer's transgenic model Tg2576. J Ethnopharmacol. 2006, 108: 385-394.

28. Pasinetti GM, Eberstein JA: Metabolic syndrome and the role of dietary lifestyles in Alzheimer's disease. J Neurochem. 2008, 106: 1503-1514.

29. Ray B, Chauhan NB, Lahiri DK: Oxidative insults to neurons and synapse are prevented by aged garlic extract and S-allyl-L-cysteine treatment in the neuronal culture and APP-Tg mouse model. J Neurochem. 2011, 117: 388-402.

30. Gupta VB, Indi SS, Rao KS: Garlic extract exhibits antiamyloidogenic activity on amyloid-beta fibrillogenesis: relevance to Alzheimer's disease. Phytother Res. 2009, 23: 111-115.

31. Maczurek A, Hager K, Kenklies M, Sharman M, Martins R, Engel J, Carlson DA, Munch G: Lipoic acid as an anti-inflammatory and neuroprotective treatment for Alzheimer's disease. Adv Drug Deliv Rev. 2008, 60: 1463-1470.

32. Toklu HZ, Hakan T, Biber N, Solakoglu S, Ogunc AV, Sener G: The protective effect of alpha lipoic acid against traumatic brain injury in rats. Free Rad Res. 2009, 43: 658-667.

33. MacKay D, Hathcock J, Guarneri E: Niacin: chemical forms, bioavailability, and health effects. Nutr Rev. 2012, 70: 357-366.

34. Morris MC, Evans DA, Bienias JL, Scherr PA, Tangney CC, Hebert LE, Bennett DA, Wilson RS, Aggarwal N: Dietary niacin and the risk of incident Alzheimer's disease and of cognitive decline. J Neurol Neurosurg Psychiatry. 2004, 75: 1093-1099.

35. Lawson LD, Gardner CD: Composition, stability, and bioavailability of garlic products used in a clinical trial. J Agric Food Chem. 2005, 53: 6254-6261.

36. Van Broeck B, Van Broeckhoven C, Kumar-Singh S: Current insights into molecular mechanisms of Alzheimer disease and their implications for therapeutic approaches. Neurodegener Dis. 2007, 4: 349-365.

37. Kumar-Singh S, Pirici D, McGowan E, Serneels S, Ceuterick C, Hardy J, Duff K, Dickson D, Van Broeckhoven C: Dense-core plaques in Tg2576 and PSAPP mouse models of Alzheimer's disease are centered on vessel walls. Am J Pathol. 2005, 167: 527-543.

38. Bowman GL, Kaye JA, Quinn JF: Dyslipidemia and blood–brain barrier integrity in Alzheimer's disease. Curr Gerontol Geriatr Res. 2012, 2012: 184042.

39. Burgess BL, McIsaac SA, Naus KE, Chan JY, Tansley GH, Yang J, Miao F, Ross CJ, van Eck M, Hayden MR, van Nostrand W, St George-Hyslop P, Westaway D, Wellington CL: Elevated plasma triglyceride levels precede amyloid deposition in Alzheimer's disease mouse models with abundant A beta in plasma. Neurobiol Dis. 2006, 24: 114-127.

40. Yao PM, Tabas I: Free cholesterol loading of macrophages is associated with widespread mitochondrial dysfunction and activation of the mitochondrial apoptosis pathway. J Biol Chem. 2001, 276: 42468-42476.

41. Messmer TO, Wang E, Stevens VL, Merrill AH: Sphingolipid biosynthesis by rat liver cells: effects of serine, fatty acids and lipoproteins. J Nutr. 1989, 119: 534-538.

42. Ussher JR, Koves TR, Cadete VJ, Zhang L, Jaswal JS, Swyrd SJ, Lopaschuk DG, Proctor SD, Keung W, Muoio DM, Lopaschuk GD: Inhibition of de novo ceramide synthesis reverses diet-induced insulin resistance and enhances whole-body oxygen consumption. Diabetes. 2010, 59: 2453-2464.

43. Holland WL, Brozinick JT, Wang LP, Hawkins ED, Sargent KM, Liu Y, Narra K, Hoehn KL, Knotts TA, Siesky A, Nelson DH, Karathanasis SK, Fontenot GK, Birnbaum MJ, Summers S: Inhibition of ceramide synthesis ameliorates glucocorticoid-, saturated-fat-, and obesity-induced insulin resistance. Cell Metab. 2007, 5: 167-179.

44. Choi SH, Aid S, Kim HW, Jackson SH, Bosetti F: Inhibition of NADPH oxidase promotes alternative and anti-inflammatory microglial activation during neuroinflammation. J Neurochem. 2012, 120: 292-301.

45. Tzeng SF, Hsiao HY, Mak OT: Prostaglandins and cyclooxygenases in glial cells during brain inflammation. Curr Drug Targets Inflamm Allergy. 2005, 4: 335-340.

46. Kadotani A, Tsuchiya Y, Hatakeyama H, Katagiri H, Kanzaki M: Different impacts of saturated and unsaturated free fatty acids on COX-2 expression in C(2)C(12) myotubes. Am J Physiol Endocrinol Metab. 2009, 297: E1291-E1303.

47. Lee JY, Sohn KH, Rhee SH, Hwang D: Saturated fatty acids, but not unsaturated fatty acids, induce the expression of cyclooxygenase-2 mediated through Toll-like receptor 4. J Biol Chem. 2001, 276: 16683-16689.

48. Meister A: Glutathione metabolism and its selective modification. J Biol Chem. 1988, 263: 17205-17208.

49. Kumar A, Mittal R, Khanna HD, Basu S: Free radical injury and blood–brain barrier permeability in hypoxic-ischemic encephalopathy. Pediatrics. 2008, 122: e722-e727.

50. Lehner C, Gehwolf R, Tempfer H, Krizbai I, Hennig B, Bauer HC, Bauer H: Oxidative stress and blood–brain barrier dysfunction under particular consideration of matrix metalloproteinases. Antioxid Redox Signal. 2011, 15: 1305-1323.

51. Potenza MA, Gagliardi S, De Benedictis L, Zigrino A, Tiravanti E, Colantuono G, Federici A, Lorusso L, Benagiano V, Quon MJ, Montagnani M: Treatment of spontaneously hypertensive rats with rosiglitazone ameliorates cardiovascular pathophysiology via antioxidant mechanisms in the vasculature. Am J Physiol Endocrinol Metab. 2009, 297: E685-E694.

52. Williams MJ, Sutherland WH, McCormick MP, Yeoman DJ, de Jong SA: Aged garlic extract improves endothelial function in men with coronary artery disease. Phytother Res. 2005, 19: 314-319.

53. Xiang G, Pu J, Yue L, Hou J, Sun H: Alpha-lipoic acid can improve endothelial dysfunction in subjects with impaired fasting glucose. Metabolism. 2011, 60: 480-485.

54. Chng HT, New LS, Neo AH, Goh CW, Browne ER, Chan EC: Distribution study of orally administered lipoic acid in rat brain tissues. Brain Res. 2009, 1251: 80-86.

55. Park HJ, Jeon BT, Kim HC, Roh GS, Shin JH, Sung NJ, Han J, Kang D: Aged red garlic extract reduces lipopolysaccharide-induced nitric oxide production in RAW 264.7 macrophages and acute pulmonary inflammation through haeme oxygenase-1 induction. Acta Physiol (Oxf). 2012, 205: 61-70.

56. Morihara N, Hayama M, Fujii H: Aged garlic extract scavenges superoxide radicals. Plant Foods Hum Nutr. 2011, 66: 17-21. 10.1007/s11130-011-0216-6.

57. Ersahin M, Toklu HZ, Cetinel S, Yuksel M, Erzik C, Berkman MZ, Yegen BC, Sener G: Alpha lipoic acid alleviates oxidative stress and preserves blood brain permeability in rats with subarachnoid hemorrhage. Neurochem Res. 2010, 35: 418-428.

58. Martins RR, de Oliveira Macedo UB, Leite LD, Rezende AA, Brandao-Neto J, Almeida M: Lipoic acid and moderate swimming improves the estrous cycle and oxidative stress in Wistar rats. Appl Physiol Nutr Metab. 2011, 36: 693-697.

59. Jesudason EP, Masilamoni JG, Jebaraj CE, Paul SF, Jayakumar R: Efficacy of DL-alpha lipoic acid against systemic inflammation-induced mice: antioxidant defense system. Mol Cell Biochem. 2008, 313: 113-123.

60. Skibska B, Jozefowicz-Okonkwo G, Goraca A: Protective effects of early administration of alpha-lipoic acid against lipopolysaccharide-induced plasma lipid peroxidation. Pharmacol Rep. 2006, 58: 399-404.

61. Ganji SH, Qin S, Zhang L, Kamanna VS, Kashyap ML: Niacin inhibits vascular oxidative stress, redox-sensitive genes, and monocyte adhesion to human aortic endothelial cells. Atherosclerosis. 2009, 202: 68-75.

62. Black JE, Polinsky M, Greenough WT: Progressive failure of cerebral angiogenesis supporting neural plasticity in aging rats. Neurobiol Aging. 1989, 10: 353-358.

63. Chavez JC, LaManna JC: Hypoxia-inducible factor-1alpha accumulation in the rat brain in response to hypoxia and ischemia is attenuated during aging. Ad Exp Med Biol. 2003, 510: 337-341. 10.1007/978-1-4615-0205-0_55.

64. Rapino C, Bianchi G, Di Giulio C, Centurione L, Cacchio M, Antonucci A, Cataldi A: HIF-1alpha cytoplasmic accumulation is associated with cell death in old rat cerebral cortex exposed to intermittent hypoxia. Aging Cell. 2005, 4: 177-185.

Chapter 6

Nutraceutical Effects of Table Green Olives: A Pilot Study with Nocellara Del Belice Olives

Giulia Accardi[1*] , Anna Aiello[1*] , Valeria Gargano2 , Caterina Maria Gambino[1] , Santo Caracappa[2] , Sandra Marineo[2] , Gesualdo Vesco[2] , Ciriaco Carru[3] , Angelo Zinellu[3] , Maurizio Zarcone[4] , Calogero Caruso[1] and Giuseppina Candore[1]

[1] *Sezione di Patologia generale del Dipartimento di Biopatologia e Biotecnologie Mediche (DIBIMED), Università di Palermo, Corso Tukory 211, 90134 Palermo, Italy.*

[2] *Istituto Zooprofilattico Sperimentale della Sicilia, Via Gino Marinuzzi 3, 90129 Palermo, Italy.*

[3] *Dipartimento di Scienze Biomediche, Università di Sassari, Viale San Pietro 43/b, 07100 Sassari, Italy.*

[4] *UOC Epidemiologia Clinica con registro tumori di Palermo e provincia, AOUP "Paolo Giaccone", Palermo, c/o Dipartimento di Scienze per la promozione della salute e materno infantile "G. D'Alessandro", Università di Palermo, Via del Vespro 133, 90131 Palermo, Italy.*

ABSTRACT

Background

The aim of this study was to analyse the nutraceutical properties of table green olives *Nocellara del Belice*, a traditional Mediterranean food. The Mediterranean Diet has as key elements olives and extra virgin olive oil, common to all Mediterranean countries. Olive oil is the main source of fat and can modulate oxidative stress and inflammation, whereas little is known about the role of olives. Moreover, emerging evidences underline the association between gut microbiota and food as the basis of many phenomena that affect health and delay or avoid the onset of some age-related chronic diseases.

Methods

In order to show if table green olives have nutraceutical properties and/or probiotic effect, we performed a nutritional intervention, administering to 25 healthy subjects (mean age 38,3), 12 table green olives/day for 30 days. We carried out anthropometric, biochemical, oxidative stress and cytokines analyses at the beginning of the study and at the end. Moreover, we also collected fecal samples to investigate about the possible variation of concentration of*Lactobacilli*, after the olives consumption.

Result

Our results showed a significant variation of one molecule related to oxidative stress, malondialdehyde, confirming that *Nocellara del Belice* green olives could have an anti-oxidant effect. In addition, the level of interleukin-6 decreased significantly, demonstrating how this food could be able to modulate the inflammatory response. Moreover, it is noteworthy the reduction of fat mass with an increase of muscle mass, suggesting a possible effect on long time assumption of table olives on body mass variation. No statistically significant differences were observed in the amount of *Lactobacilli*, although a trend towards an increased concentration of them at the end of the intervention could be related to the nutraceutical effects of olives.

Conclusion

These preliminary results suggest a possible nutraceutical effect of daily consumption of green table olives *Nocellara del Belice*. To best of our knowledge, this is the first study performed to assess nutraceutical properties of this food. Of course, it is necessary to verify the data in a larger sample of individuals to confirm their role as nutraceuticals.

Keywords : Table green olives Mediterranean Diet Nutraceuticals Dietary intervention Oxidative stress Inflammatory status

BACKGROUND

Nowadays, ageing process and the related diseases constitute one of the bigger challenges in Western countries. The general increase of lifespan does not go, hand in hand, with the increase of healthy lifespan, the so-called "healthspan". This constitutes a worldwide problem, in particular due to age-related chronic diseases [1].

It is well known that the pathogenesis of age-related diseases is characterized by a low-grade inflammation. In particular, the visceral adipose tissue is a source of inflammatory mediators produced by adipocytes and infiltrating monocytes [2].

Abdominal obesity with dyslipidaemia, elevated blood pressure and impaired glucose tolerance characterizes metabolic syndrome (MS) that predisposes to the onset of age-related diseases. As many studies demonstrate, a dietary Mediterranean regimen can positively influence these parameters. Large intervention trials showed, in fact, that Mediterranean Diet (MedDiet) could prevent and or delay the onset of age-related diseases with a great implication in the health social system [3, 4, 5, 6, 7].

The traditional MedDiet is a common dietary pattern, adopted by inhabitants of countries within Mediterranean basin where the olive tree, *Olea europaea*, is widely cultivated for the production of table olives and oil. They are the essential components of the MedDiet with a very significant economic value. Besides of the economical contribution to national economies, these are important in terms of nutritional value. Extra virgin olive oil (EVOO) has been claimed to play a key role in the prevention of age-related diseases and in the attainment of longevity. This is due to the high levels of monounsaturated fatty acids, likely responsible for the decreased low density lipoprotein levels, and phenolic compounds claimed to play a role as antioxidants and anti-inflammatories [6, 8, 9].

Foods with bioactive molecules can be considered "nutraceuticals", defined as "Naturally derived bioactive compounds that are found in foods, dietary supplements and herbal products, and have health promoting, disease preventing, or medicinal properties". The term was coined in 1989 by Stephen De Felice and was born from the conjunction between nutrition and pharmaceutics [10].

As reported in a recent review, table olives are extremely rich sources of polyphenols, especially oleuropein and hydroxytyrosol, comprising 1–3 % of the fresh pulp weight. Despite the high levels of hydroxytyrosol in both table olives and EVOO, in humans its bioavailability was proved only in oil. Accordingly, to the best of our knowledge, there are no human studies on health effects of table olives [11]. However, the amount of polyphenols is strongly influenced by the variety and the geographical origin. *Greek Koroneiki* have a very high level of them, while the polypenol content of the *Spanish Arbequina* is low and that of *Sicilian Nocellara* is medium-high [12]. So, a possible anti-inflammatory and anti-oxidant effect of these Sicilian olives is conceivable.

The development of strategies aimed at counterbalancing the frailty in the elderly is a major challenge for the medicine of 21st century [1]. As recently reviewed, ageing affects the gut microbiota composition and its influence in immune response. Age-related gut microbiota changes are associated with immunosenescence and inflamm-ageing. Hence, the gut ecosystem shows the potential to become a promising target for strategies able to contribute to the health status of elderly. In this context, the consumption of pro/prebiotics may be useful in both prevention and treatment of age-related pathophysiological conditions, favouring the attainment of longevity [13].

Probiotics are defined as "Live microorganisms which when administered in adequate amounts confer a health benefit on the host". *Lactobacilli* (*L.*) and *Bifidobacteria* are the most commonly used bacterial probiotics [14]. Nutritional supplementation in aged people might help to maintain good immune-inflammatory responses by re-equilibrating the gut microbiota.

Fermentation is one of the oldest methods to preserve olives. It has applied worldwide for thousands of years. The microbiota of olives during fermentation, that varies somewhat from*cultivar* to *cultivar*, has been recently reviewed, showing that *L.* are the major constituents of*Nocellara del Belice* olives microbiota [15, 16]. So, a possible probiotic-like effect of these olives is feasible.

The aim of this pilot study was to evaluate the effect of green table olives *Nocellara del Belice* on clinical and biological parameters of healthy individuals at baseline (T0) and after the assumption of 12 olives/day for 30 days (T1) (this amount was chosen to assure the administration of $2x10^7$ *L.*/die, see below).

RESULTS AND DISCUSSION

Hematochemical tests

At the end of the intervention, all hematochemical parameters did not experienced variations, with the exception of alkaline phosphatase that significantly increased (Table 1).

However, the increased values were in normal range. This means that a regular consumption of 12 green olives/day for 30 days does not have a detrimental effect on liver and kidney function and on lipid values.

Table 1. The Table shows the arithmetic average values at T0 and T1, the p-value and the variation in percentage (+ indicates an increase of the variable at T1; - a decrease at T1)

Variable	T0 ± SD	T1 ± SD	p-value	%
Alkaline phosphate (IU/L)	49.95 ± 13.26	53.73 ± 16.81	0.022	+7.57
Fat mass%	29.70 ± 7.92	28 ± 7.24	0.004	−5.72
Muscle mass %	66.97 ± 7.62	68.36 ± 6.85	0.003	+2.09
IL-6 (FI)	31.52 ± 29.37	20.89 ± 11.93	0.027	−33.73
MDA (μmol/L)	2.72 ± 0.64	2.33 ± 0.49	0.005	−14.24
Weight (Kg)	70.44 ± 14.07	69.93 ± 13.77	0.08	−0.72
BMI (Kg/m^2)	24.37 ± 4.19	24.24 ± 4.16	0.22	−0.53

T0 baseline, *T1* the end of the nutritional intervention (30 days), *BMI* Body Mass Index, *IL-6* interleukin-6, *IF* indirect fluorescence, *MDA* malondialdehyde, *SD* standard deviation

Anthropometric measurements

At T1, in analysed subjects the fat mass significantly decreased together to an increase of muscle mass (Table 1). The possible explanation could be linked to the capacity of conjugated linoleic acid (CLA) to reduce the body fat levels [17]. This molecule is present both in EVOO and table olives, and can also be produced during their digestion. In experimental models, acting as signalling mediators, CLAs inhibit lipogenesis, increase fat oxidation, and reduce adipocytes size [18, 19].

Cytokines analyses

The serological analysis of the levels of the main pro and anti-inflammatory cytokines was conducted. Although it was not possible to evaluate the absolute concentration of interleukin (IL)-6 because it is too low, a significant variation was measured in the indirect fluorescence (IF). In fact, its levels significantly decreased at the end of the dietary intervention (Table 1).

IL-6 is a pleiotropic cytokine capable of regulating proliferation, differentiation and activity in a variety of cell types. In particular, it plays a pivotal role in acute phase responses and in the balancing of the pro and anti-inflammatory pathways. It is involved in impaired lipid metabolism and in the production of triglycerides. Moreover, it decreases lipoprotein lipase activity and monomeric lipoprotein lipase levels in plasma which contributes to increased macrophage uptake of lipids [20]. This datum suggests that a regular consumption of green olives can have anti-inflammatory effects linked to polyphenols, known to have anti-inflammatory properties [6].

Oxidative stress analyses

At the end of intervention, the values of malondialdehyde (MDA) significantly decreased (Table 1), while paraoxonase (PON) plasma levels and reduced glutathione in the red blood cells were not changed (data not shown). MDA is the main product of the polyunsaturated fatty acids peroxidation and is an important index of oxidative stress [21]. So, its reduction should be linked to the increased assumption of mono-unsatured oleic acid by olives.

Microbiological analyses on feces

The amount of *L.*/g of feces was quantified before and after the intervention. No statistically significant differences were observed, although a trend towards an increased amount of *L.* was highlighted in some subjects at T1 (data not shown). Thus, we can speculate that a more durable dietary intervention and a bigger sample of people could give more interesting results.

CONCLUSIONS

The traditional MedDiet is a common dietary pattern that identify a lifestyle and a culture. It was proven that it contributes to better health and quality of life. Concerning its healthy effects, low content of animal protein and low glycaemic index may directly modulate the insulin/insulin-like growth factor-1 and the mammalian target of rapamycin pathways, known to be involved in ageing, age-related diseases and longevity. In addition to the influence on nutrient sensing pathways, many single components of MedDiet are known to have positive effects on health, reducing inflammation, oxidative stress and other important risk factors of age-related diseases [6].

This pilot study demonstrates an anti-inflammatory and anti-oxidant effect of daily consumption of green table olives *Nocellara del Belice*. Moreover, it is noteworthy the reduction of fat mass with an increase of muscle mass. Although no statistically significant probiotic effect was observed, the positive trend related to *L.* amount at T1 could represent a starting point for further studies.

It is to note that the study presents limitations. One is strictly related to the intrinsic complexity of human as study model and to the inter/intra-individual variability. These features are more evident in ageing than in younger people. This is the reason why we chose middle age people. So, our choice represented the second limitation of the study because we did not analyze the effects of the intervention in elderly. Thirdly, it is necessary to verify these data in a larger sample of individuals to confirm the role of table green olives as nutraceutical foods. Also the duration of the intervention could be inadequate. In fact, we developed a short-term dietary regimen (30 days). This is a good choice in terms of compliance to the study because the more is the time of intervention the more is the drop out effect. But, a long-term dietary intervention could be stronger in terms of variation of analyzed parameters (e.g., *L.* amount in feces).

However, these new knowledges give an important achievement for the food and farming industry, especially in Sicily, where the olives represent a great potential resource. No approved healthy property and claim exist for them. Therefore, adding such a common product to the class of nutraceuticals could represent a big deal.

In the era of many expansive and mysterious longevity elixirs, the olives could represent a traditional, cheap and accessible to everyone "healthy food".

METHODS

Study design

The trial consisted in the assumption of 12 olives/day for 30 days. They belonging to the variety*Nocellara del Belice*, were processed in salt solution without any chemical additives.

See Fig. 1 for the flow chart of the study design.

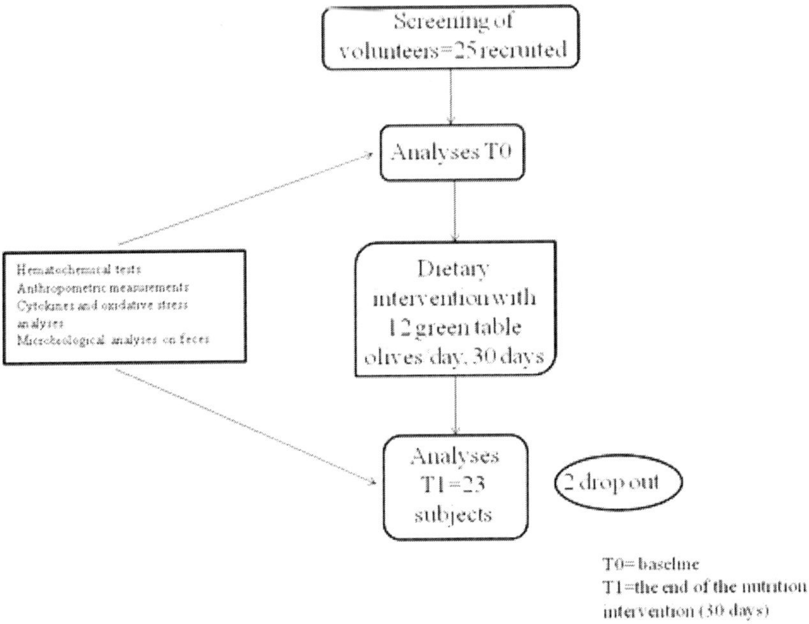

Figure 1. The figure shows the flow chart of the study design

Study population

Twenty-five randomized volunteers (mean age 38,3), both men and women, were recruited from April 2015 to July 2015. The subjects included were: healthy, with age between 18 and 65 years and Caucasian. The exclusion criteria provided: a history of the absence of pathologies (obesity, MS); a history of use of any pre or probiotics as dietary supplements within 3 months prior to the study; a history of treatment with statins or similar and with lyposoluble drugs; the onset of gastrointestinal disorders or the use of antibiotics during the nutritional intervention. No restriction related to sex was considered. Two subjects dropped out of the trial. All participants signed an informed consent before the enrolment. To respect the privacy, everyone was identified with an alphanumeric code. Height and weight were measured wearing light clothes and barefoot. The body composition was registered using specific hardware and software. Body mass index was calculated as weight (in kilos) over height squared (in square metre) (Table 1). Dietary habits were assessed through a food frequency questionnaire, officially validate by the EPIC study. Blood tests, oxidative stress and cytokines analyses were carried out for all subjects at T0 and T1. Molecular analyses were conducted on *L.* DNA obtained from fecal samples to measure the variation of its amount. A database was created to insert all participants' data and to handle the collected information.

Hematochemical tests

The recruited people underwent to venipuncture at T0 and at T1. Blood samples were collected in specific blood collection tubes containing ethylenediaminetetraacetic acid (EDTA) for plasma analyses and in serum tubes with no additives. Plasma and sera were separated from whole blood by low-speed centrifugation at 2,500 rpm for 15′ at 4 °C. After separation, the samples were stored at −80 °C for further tests. We also obtained gruel of red blood cells from blood collected in tubes with EDTA through three washes with physiological solution (centrifugation at 2,500 rpm for 15′ at 4 °C).

Evaluation of parameters of oxidative stress

These analyses were conducted in collaboration with the University of Sassari. Thiobarbituric acid reactive substances (TBARS) were determined according to the method described by Esterbauer and Cheeseman [22]. TBARS methodology measures MDA and other aldehydes produced by lipid peroxidation induced by hydroxyl free radicals. For the measurements, plasma was mixed with 10 % trichloroacetic acid and 0.67 % thiobarbituric acid and heated at 95 °C in thermoblock heater for 25′. TBARS were determined by measuring the absorbance at 535 nm. A calibration curve was obtained using standard MDA and each curve point was subjected to the same treatment as that of the samples.

PON activity was determined by measuring the increase in absorbance at 412 nm (formation of 4-nitrophenol), using paraoxon (O, O diethyl-O-p-nitrophenyl phosphate) as a substrate [22]. The enzyme activity was calculated by using the molar extinction coefficient of 17,100 $M^{-1}cm^{-1}$and one unit of PON activity was defined as 1 nanomole of 4-nitrophenol formed per minute. For red blood cell glutathione quantification, 200 µl (µL) of thawed packed cells were lysed by adding 600 µL of cold water and keeping the samples at 4 °C for 15′. 200 µL of lysed samples were deproteinized by adding 200 µL acetonitrile and centrifuged at 2,000 × g for 5′. Samples were then derivatized by mixing 100 µL of supernatant with 100 µL of sodium phosphate buffer (60 µmol (mmol)/L, pH 12.5), and 25 µL of 5-Iodoacetamidofluorescein (4.1 mmol/L). After vortex mixing, samples were incubated for 15′ at room temperature. Derivatized samples were diluted 100-fold in water and analysed by capillary electrophoresis with laser induced fluorescence detection [23].

Pro and anti-inflammatory cytokines analyses

These analyses were conducted using Luminex assays, coupled to Bio-Plex Manager software.

Data obtained have been checked by technical department and quality control parameters. Values of the standard curve were compared to the values provided by the manufacturer of the kits used and must not exceed a CV of 15 %. All of above parameters were applied on, at least, the 90 % of the standard curve values.

Microbiological and molecular analyses of *Lactobacilli*

In order to quantify the amount of *L.* in each olive, 1 g of pulp was suspended in phosphate-buffered saline solution (1 mL), homogenized for 2′ at maximum speed, and then serially diluted. Decimal dilutions were plated and incubated on *de Man, Rogosa and Sharp*e at 30 °C for 48 h to observe the *L.* growth. The colonies' count was performed in triplicate and the *L.* DNA was extracted from them to perform molecular analyses. Moroever, colony suspension were used as a template for Real Time PCR. The primers and probes used to detect *L. species* (*spp*) were based on 16S rRNA gene sequences retrieved from the NCBI databases (Table 2). The amplification reactions were carried out in a total volume of 25 ml containing 1X SSoFast Probe mix (BIORAD), primers (each at 200 nM concentration), 100 nM TaqMan MGB probe, 60 ng purified target DNA. Amplification (1 cycle of 5′ at 95 °C, 45 cycles of 15″ at 95 °C and 1 cycle of 1′ at 60 °C) and detection were carried out on a CFX Real Time system (BIORAD).

Fluorescent probe was labeled at 5′ end with the reporter dye 6-carboxyfluorescein and at 3′ end with a quencher dye. A negative and a positive control were included on the reaction plate.

Table 2. Primer and probe sequences for analyses of *L. spp* in Real Time PCR

	Oligonucleotide sequence 5'-3'
Primer Forward	GAGGCAGCAGTAGGGAATCTTC
Primer Reverse	GGCCAGTTACTACCTCTATCCTTCTTC
Probe	FAM-ATGGAGCAACGCCGC-QUENCER

In order to perform the quantification of *L.* in each feces sample, the QIAamp DNA Stool Minikit (Qiagen) was used to extract DNA from an appropriate amount of frozen stool sample, according to the manufacturer's instructions. The Real Time PCR was performed as previous described and the cycle threshold of each sample was compared to a standard curve made by diluting genomic DNA (10-fold serial dilution) from cultures of known concentrations of *L.*(10^6 CFU/ml).

Statistical analyses

The paired comparisons were performed with the Student's *t*-test or the Wilcoxon signed rank test, according to the normality of samples. Statistical analyses were performed with the IDE RStudio for the R (version 3.2.2) software [24, 25].

ACKNOWLEDGMENTS

This work was supported by PON DIMESA (Programma Operativo Nazionale Ricerca e Competitività 2007/2013 - Progetto "DI.ME.Sa." PON02_00451_3361785. Valorisation of typical products of the Mediterranean diet and their nutraceutical use to improve health) to CC. GA is a Post Doc at DiBiMed. AA and CMG are students of the PhD course directed by CC.

We are grateful to Dr. Nicola Locorotondo for his continuous enthusiastic support.

COMPETING INTERESTS

The authors declare that they have no competing interest.

AUTHORS' CONTRIBUTION

GA, AA, VG, and CC* conceived and designed the study; GA, AA, CMG, VG, SM, SC, GV, AZ, CC* and CC** performed or supervised experiments. MZ executed statistical analysis. GA, AA, VG, CC*, and CC** analyzed and interpreted data; GA and AA drafted the paper. GC, CC* and CC** made critical revisions to the draft. All authors read and approved the final manuscript. CC*: Calogero Caruso. CC**: Ciriaco Carru

REFERENCES

1. Longo VD, Antebi A, Bartke A, Barzilai N, Brown-Borg HM, Caruso C, Curiel TJ, de Cabo R, Franceschi C, Gems D, Ingram DK, Johnson TE, Kennedy BK, Kenyon C, Klein S, Kopchick JJ, Lepperdinger G, Madeo F, Mirisola MG, Mitchell JR, Passarino G, Rudolph KL, Sedivy JM, Shadel GS, Sinclair DA, Spindler SR, Suh Y, Vijg J, Vinciguerra M, Fontana L. Interventions to Slow Aging in Humans: Are We Ready? Aging Cell. 2015;14:497–510.

2. Balistreri CR, Caruso C, Candore G. The role of adipose tissue and adipokines in obesity-related inflammatory diseases. Mediators Inflamm. 2010.

3. Estruch R, Martínez-González MA, Corella D, Salas-Salvadó J, Ruiz-Gutiérrez V, Covas MI, Fiol M, Gómez-Gracia E, López-Sabater MC, Vinyoles E, Arós F, Conde M, Lahoz C, Lapetra J,

Sáez G, Ros E; PREDIMED Study Investigators. Effects of a Mediterranean-style diet on cardiovascular risk factors: a randomized trial. Ann Intern Med. 2006;145:1–11.

4. Fitó M, Guxens M, Corella D, Sáez G, Estruch R, de la Torre R, Francés F, Cabezas C, López-Sabater Mdel C, Marrugat J, García-Arellano A, Arós F, Ruiz-Gutierrez V, Ros E, Salas-Salvadó J, Fiol M, Solá R, Covas MI; PREDIMED Study Investigators. Effect of a traditional Mediterranean diet on lipoprotein oxidation: a randomized controlled trial. Arch Intern Med. 2007;167:1195–203.

5. Casas R, Sacanella E, Estruch R. The immune protective effect of the Mediterranean diet against chronic low-grade inflammatory diseases. Endocr Metab Immune Disord Drug Targets. 2014;14:245–54.

6. Vasto S, Buscemi S, Barera A, Di Carlo M, Accardi G, Caruso C. Mediterranean diet and healthy ageing: a Sicilian perspective. Gerontology. 2014;60:508–18.

7. Kastorini CM, Milionis HJ, Esposito K, Giugliano D, Goudevenos JA, Panagiotakos DB. The effect of Mediterranean diet on metabolic syndrome and its components: a meta-analysis of 50 studies and 534,906 individuals. J Am Coll Cardiol. 2011;57:1299–313.

8. Uylaşer V, Yildiz G. The historical development and nutritional importance of olive and olive oil constituted an important part of the Mediterranean diet. Crit Rev Food Sci Nutr. 2014;54:1092–101.

9. Vasto S, Rizzo C, Caruso C. Centenarians and diet: what they eat in the Western part of Sicily. Immun Ageing. 2012;9:10.

10. DeFelice SL. FIM, Rationale and Proposed Guidelines for the Nutraceutical Research & Education Act NREA, Foundation for Innovation in Medicine.

2002.http://www.fimdefelice.org/archives/arc.researchact.html archact.html. Accessed 10 Nov 2002.

11. Hoffman R, Gerber M. Food Processing and the Mediterranean Diet. Nutrients. 2015;7:7925–64.

12. Aiello A, Guccione GD, Accardi G, Caruso C. What olive oil for healthy ageing? Maturitas. 2015;80:117–8.

13. Biagi E, Candela M, Turroni S, Garagnani P, Franceschi C, Brigidi P. Ageing and gut microbes: perspectives for health maintenance and longevity. Pharmacol Res. 2013;69:11–20.

14. Lefevre M, Racedo SM, Ripert G, Housez B, Cazaubiel M, Maudet C, Jüsten P, Marteau P, Urdaci MC. Probiotic strain Bacillus subtilis CU1 stimulates immune system of elderly during common infectious disease period: a randomized, double-blind placebo-controlled study. Immun Ageing. 2015;12:24.

15. Heperkan D. Microbiota of table olive fermentations and criteria of selection for their use as starters. Front Microbiol. 2013;4:143.

16. Aponte M, Ventorino V, Blaiotta G, Volpe G, Farina V, Avellone G, Lanza CM, Moschetti G. Study of green Sicilian table olive fermentations through microbiological, chemical and sensory analyses. Food Microbiol. 2010;27:162–70.

17. Lehnen TE, da Silva MR, Camacho A, Marcadenti A, Lehnen AM. A review on effects of conjugated linoleic fatty acid (CLA) upon body composition and energetic metabolism. J Int Soc Sports Nutr. 2015;12:36.

18. Fazzari M, Trostchansky A, Schopfer FJ, Salvatore SR, Sánchez-Calvo B, Vitturi D, Valderrama R, Barroso JB, Radi R, Freeman BA, Rubbo H. Olives and olive oil are sources of electrophilic fatty acid nitroalkenes. PLoS One. 2014;14(9):e84884.

19. Wang Y, Jones PJ. Dietary conjugated linoleic acid and body composition. Am J Clin Nutr. 2004;6 Suppl 79:1153S–8S.

20. Ershler WB, Keller ET. Age-associated increased interleukin-6 gene expression, late-life diseases, and frailty. Annu Rev Med. 2000;51:245–70.

21. Czerska M, Mikołajewska K, Zieliński M, Gromadzińska J, Wąsowicz W. Today's oxidative stress markers. Med Pr. 2015;66:393–405.

22. Gan KN, Smolen A, Eckerson HW, La Du BN. Purification of human serum paraoxonase/arylesterase. Evidence for one esterase catalyzing both activities. Drug Metab Dispos. 1991;19:100–6.

23. Zinellu A, Sotgia S, Usai MF, Chessa R, Deiana L, Carru C. Thiol redox status evaluation in red blood cells by capillary electrophoresis-laser induced fluorescence detection. Electrophoresis. 2005;26:1963–8.

24. RStudio Team. RStudio: Integrated Development for R. Boston, MA: RStudio, Inc.; 2015.http://www.rstudio.com/.

25. R Core Team. R. A language and environment for statistical computing. Vienna, Austria: R Foundation for Statistical Computing; 2015. https://www.R-project.org/

Chapter 7

Nutrigerontology: A Key for Achieving Successful Ageing and Longevity

Anna Aiello[1] , Giulia Accardi[1] , Giuseppina Candore[1] , Giuseppe Carruba[2] , Sergio Davinelli[3] , Giuseppe Passarino[4] , Giovanni Scapagnini[3] , Sonya Vasto[5] and Calogero Caruso[1*]

[1]*Department of Pathobiology and Medical Biotechnologies, University of Palermo, Palermo, Italy.*

[2]*Division of Research and Internationalization, ARNAS-Civico Di Cristina e Benfratelli, Palermo, Italy.*

[3]*Department of Medicine and Health Sciences, School of Medicine, University of Molise, Campobasso 86100, Italy.*

[4]*Department of Biology, Ecology and Earth Science, University of Calabria, Rende (CS) 87036, Italy.*

[5]*Department of Biological Chemical and Pharmaceutical Sciences and Technologies (STEBICEF), University of Palermo, Palermo, Italy and Institute of biomedicine and molecular immunology "Alberto Monroy" CNR, Palermo, Italy*

ABSTRACT

During the last two centuries the average lifespan has increased at a rate of approximately 3 months/year in both sexes, hence oldest old people are becoming the population with the fastest growth in Western World. Although the average life expectancy is increasing dramatically, the healthy lifespan is not going at the same pace. This underscores the importance of studies on the prevention of age-related diseases, in order to satisfactorily decrease the medical, economic and social problems associated to advancing age, related to an increased number of individuals not autonomous and affected by invalidating pathologies. In particular, data from experimental studies in model organisms have consistently shown that nutrient signalling pathways are involved in longevity, affecting the prevalence of age-related loss of function, including age-related diseases. Accordingly, nutrigerontology is defined as the scientific discipline that studies the impact of nutrients, foods, macronutrient ratios, and diets on lifespan, ageing process, and age-related diseases. To discuss the potential relevance of this new science in the attainment of successful ageing and longevity, three original studies performed in Sicily with local foods and two reviews have been assembled in this series. Data clearly demonstrate the positive effects of nutraceuticals, functional foods and Mediterranean Diet on several biological parameters. In fact, they could represent a prevention for many age-related diseases, and, although not a solution for this social plague, at least a remedy to alleviate it. Thus, the possibility to create a dietary pattern, based on the combined strategy of the use of both nutraceuticals and functional foods should permit to create a new therapeutic strategy, based not only on a specific bioactive molecule or on a specific food but on a integrated approach that, starting from the local dietary habits, can be led to a "nutrafunctional diet" applicable worldwide.

Keywords: Ageing Longevity Mediterranean Diet Nutraceuticals Nutrigerontology Phytochemicals

BACKGROUND

Nutrigerontology is defined as the scientific discipline that studies the impact of nutrients, foods, macronutrient ratios, and diets on lifespan, ageing process, and age-related diseases. Its goal is to investigate about compounds, foods, and diets that can reduce the risk of ageing-related diseases and increase the healthy lifespan, so achieving successful ageing and longevity [1].

Many definitions of longevity and successful ageing have been proposed but none has been accepted yet. In May 2012, a group of scientists and clinicians met in Athens (Greece) to consider the relevance of ageing, longevity, exceptional longevity and related genetic and non genetic markers. The workshop led to the creation of a consensus statement to highlight the importance of a common view related to these processes, since they represent phenotypes that are rapidly spreading worldwide [2].

As reported in this panel: "Successful ageing involves avoidance (or late onset) of age-related diseases including cardiovascular disease which is the main cause of death, and other organ specific diseases, disability, preservation of desirable cognitive and physical function and social activities throughout the lifespan". Moreover, it proposes the definition of exceptional longevity in relative and absolute terms, on the basis of demographic data. It quotes that: ""Relative" suggests that longevity is concept country/population specific and must take into consideration the life expectancy of the different populations/countries, which show great variability owing to historical, anthropological and socio-economic differences. In "absolute" terms longevity could be defined according to the maximum lifespan attained and scientifically validated by human beings in the planet" [2].

Also, the statement reported the main genes related to longevity and ageing. Such genes and their encoded proteins are included in a variety of signalling pathways, i.e., the nutrient sensing insulin/insulin-like growth factor-1 (IGF-1) or mammalian target of rapamicin (mTOR), the oxidative stress and anti-oxidant ones and that involved in the control of immune-inflammatory responses [2].

In addition, it is becoming clear that epigenetic changes linked to environmental/life style factors (such as physical activity, diet and emotional stress) play a role in longevity attainment [2, 3].

In particular, a nutrient-sensing pathway is activated by nutrients that trigger signals that lead to a downstream activation of genes involved in ageing processes. The complex relationship among nutrition and healthy ageing is not fully understood, but evidences have already demonstrated that both in animal models and humans, dietary intervention can positively modulate ageing process, preventing or decreasing various age-related diseases and their generalized pro-inflammatory status, the inflammageing [4, 5]. So, healthy diets that not overstimulate mTOR and insulin/IGF-1 pathways because poor in refined sugars and animal proteins can substantially reduce the risk of age-related diseases, hence favouring successful ageing and longevity [6, 7]. On the contrary, a bad dietary lifestyle accelerates the ageing process, activating the pathways with nutrients, growth factors and mitogenic stimuli, so accelerating ageing phenotype [1].

Mediterranean Diet (MedDiet) is one of the most studied healthy dietary patterns. It is an alimentary regimen with low-glycaemic index and low animal protein intake that contains phytochemical compounds found in vegetables, fruits, red wine, olive oil or nuts, with anti-inflammatory and anti-oxidant effects. This pattern, that more than a diet could be defined a lifestyle, owes its health properties also to the nutraceuticals [1, 8, 9, 10, 11], defined as "naturally derived bioactive compounds that are found in foods, dietary supplements and herbal products, and have health promoting, disease preventing, or medicinal properties". The term, coming from the conjunction among nutrition and pharmaceutics, was coined in 1989 by Stephen De Felice [12].

Dietary phytochemicals belong to this group. They are non-nutrients compounds from a wide range of plant-derived foods. Despite the translational gap among basic and clinical research, the current understanding of the molecular interactions between phytochemicals and immune-inflammatory and oxidative stress pathways could help in designing effective nutritional strategies to delay ageing and age-related diseases. In particular, it has been claimed that dietary phytochemicals trigger a condition defined hormesis [1, 8, 13, 14]. This process is due to low-doses of bioactive compounds that act as mild stressors to induce adaptive expression of stress-protective genes and enhance resistance to mechanisms that determine ageing. The signal passes through the modulation of kinases, leading to the activation of downstream targets, among which FoxO3A and sirtuins. In this last case, it is to note the known effect of resveratrol, phytochemical contained in the grape, that, downstream, inhibits the NF-kB pathway, with interesting anti-inflammatory effects, although it is not totally clear and contrasting results exist [15]. *In vitro* and *in vivo* evidences suggested that many phytochemicals can affect the expression of numerous genes encoding pro-survival proteins, including antioxidant enzymes, neurotrophic or anti-apoptotic factors [1, 8].

Extra-virgin olive oil (EVOO) is full of these compounds, such as hydroxytyrosol, tyrosol and secoiridoids. It is extracted from olive fruits of *Olea Europea* and its health beneficial effects are well established. An extensive literature demonstrated that they can be attributed to many different substances belonging to the phenolic fraction of EVOO. However, the concentration of these molecules is strongly affected by belonging to a particular *cultivar*, by agronomic and environmental factors, and by the extraction and storage conditions [8, 16, 17].

Interestingly, experimental evidence suggests that hydroxytyrosol is not only effective in removing reactive oxygen species generated by impaired redox balance but it may also be a potent inducer of phase II detoxifying enzymes and an enhancer of mitochondrial biogenesis. Indeed, its effect is mostly observed at the transcriptional level through modulation of the redox-sensitive nuclear factor-E_2-related factor 2 (Nrf2), which regulates gene expression of several phase II detoxifying enzymes and supports the structural and functional integrity of the mitochondria. For instance, in a study performed on rats, hydroxytyrosol supplementation improves neurogenesis and cognitive function through increased activity of the transcription factors FoxO1 and FoxO3, as well as Nrf2, resulting in decreased oxidative stress and increased mitochondrial function [18].

Several health claims for EVOO and its derivatives have been assessed in recent years but only one was authorized in Europe. It relates the impact of olive phenolic compounds on the protection of blood lipids from oxidative stress: "A daily intake of 20 g of olive oil, which contains at least 5 mg of hydroxytyrosol and its derivatives (e.g., oleuropein and tyrosol) provides the expected beneficial effects" [19].

Phytochemicals are also ingredients of many dietary supplements commercially available to prevent or ameliorate specific diseases, including age-related ones. The majority of these products are not substantiated by solid scientific evidences and have not been approved yet by the EFSA and/or FDA. Beyond them, functional foods are widely used, especially in Japan and in USA. Although a universal definition of them does not exist, they are often considered as foods with healthy properties that contain bioactive compounds naturally or added to obtain processed foods.

However, further observational studies and dietary intervention trials in large cohorts of healthy subjects are essential to evaluate whether these foods and compounds can help to prevent age-related disorders.

The series

To discuss the potential relevance of nutrigerontology in the attainment of successful ageing and longevity, three scientific studies and two reviews have been assembled in this series.

As discussed by Passarino et al., on the whole, although the genetic factors account for only 25 % of human lifespan, the knowledge of the genetic basis of longevity may give significant hints on modulating lifestyle, in order to extend health span. That is, a few subjects can attain successful ageing and longevity thanks to a lucky combination of polymorphisms, which allow them to have an efficient metabolism or an efficient response to different types of stress. Most of the others can reach similar results by targeting the same pathways with appropriate lifestyle or interventions to slow ageing. In this context, the importance of epigenetic factors, both as biomarkers of ageing and target of interventions will certainly grow in the forthcoming studies [20].

The aim of the study of Accardi et al., was to analyse the nutraceutical properties of table green olives *Nocellara del Belice*, a traditional Mediterranean food, since little is known about the role of olives as nutraceutics. After the intake of 12 olives a day for 30 days, a significant decrease of malondialdehyde, a molecule related to oxidative stress, was observed. In addition, the level of interleukin-6 (IL-6) underwent a significant reduction, demonstrating how this food could be able to modulate the inflammatory response. Moreover, it was noteworthy the reduction of fat mass with an increase of muscle mass, suggesting a possible effect on long time assumption of table olives on body mass variation [9].

In Barera et al. study, the authors considered the nutraceutical effects of β-glucans, alimentary fibers, added to pasta, in order to produce a functional food. After 30 days of pasta intake, they obtained encouraging results with a significant decrease of low-density lipoprotein cholesterol, IL-6 and advanced glycation end-product levels. In fact, MedDiet is also characterized by a large intake of fibers, which contribute to lowering cholesterol and are positively associated with colon cancer prevention. However, in Mediterranean towns most people do not have a close adherence to MedDiet, hence adding fibers to pasta would achieve the same effects [21].

Data from dietary intervention studies of Carruba et al. underlined some interesting aspects related to mechanisms underpinning both biological and clinical effects of nutrition and specific activities of Mediterranean food components. In particular, the authors provided evidence that MedDiet may regulate oestrogen metabolism in postmenopausal women. In fact, it seems that the formation of potentially harmful genotoxic oestrogen compounds is remarkably reduced by the adoption of a traditional Mediterranean dietary model, while the levels of parent hormone estradiol become slightly increased. So, this result would imply that traditional Mediterranean food reduce the risk of developing breast cancer, while limiting the side effects of oestrogen withdrawal in menopause. Technological innovation and prototypical industrialization of either, processes or products, could be used to obtain traditional Mediterranean food with high health potential and market capacities. Precisely, the production of monocultivar EVOOs revealed that they may have differential activity on cellular and metabolic processes, eventually leading to produce highly characterized EVOOs with a preferential use for the prevention and care of various chronic diseases [22].

The review of Davinelli et al., attempted to summarise recent evidences about phytochemicals as anti-oxidants and anti-inflammatories. In fact, as previous mentioned, they may act as positive modulators of inflammation and oxidation by attenuating pro-inflammatory signalling associated with the redox imbalance that occurs in brain ageing. They also discussed the need to initiate long-term nutritional intervention studies in healthy subjects. In fact, their manuscript highlighted crucial aspects but that require further studies to determine the effective physiological concentrations and to explore the real impact of dietary phytochemicals in preserving brain health before the onset of symptoms leading to cognitive decline and inflammatory neurodegeneration [23].

DISCUSSION

As stated by Kolovou et al. [3] during the last two centuries the average lifespan has increased at a rate of approximately 3 months/year in both sexes. The most important steps in prolonging human lifespan were the decrease of child and maternal deaths, the lowering of infant and juvenile mortality rate due to, respectively, vaccination and treatment of infectious diseases. Moreover, in the last decades, the survival of elderly people improved thanks to secondary and primary prevention of ageing-related diseases and, particularly, coronary heart one [3].

So, all the factors above mentioned contribute to the fact that oldest old people are becoming the population with the fastest growth in Western World. Although the average life expectancy is increasing dramatically, the healthy lifespan is not going at the same pace. Hence, ageing and age-associated diseases are emerging as among the greatest challenges and financial burdens, faced by developed and developing countries [7].

Data from experimental studies in model organisms have consistently shown that both chronic dietary restriction, affecting nutrient signalling pathways, and mutations in nutrient and growth signalling pathways can extend longevity by 30–50 % [6, 7]. Also, they can lower the prevalence of age-related loss of function, including immunosenescence and multiple diseases, such as cancer, cardiovascular disease, and neurodegeneration [6, 7, 24].

In addition, several experimental data clearly demonstrate the hormetic effects of phytochemicals by inducing cellular stress resistance mechanisms [1, 8]. In designing human intervention studies to provide high-quality evidence for their health benefits, the following factors have to be considered: 1) the phytochemicals need to be sufficiently characterised, as well as its optimal physiologic dose, 2) the characteristics of targeted populations including their nutritional status, health condition, and genetic background have to be taken into account, 3) clinically relevant, sensitive, reproducible, and feasible endpoints have to be identified, 4) length of the intervention have to be commonly agreed [24, 25, 26]. However, even though experimental data have not always translated to a definitive clinical effect, the antioxidant and anti-inflammatory properties of phytochemicals have been widely accepted.

CONCLUSION

The new findings presented in the experimental studies of the series give a great achievement for the food and farming industry, especially in

Sicily, where local products represent a great potential resource. No approved healthy property and claim exist for them. Therefore, adding such products to the class of "healthy food" could represent a big deal. In the era of many expansive and mysterious longevity elixirs, they could represent a traditional, cheap and accessible "healthy food" to everyone. But more than for the single food, the Accardi's study [9] highlights the importance to analyse local products that are traditional and easy to find. So, in Italy one should find phytochemicals in table green olives, in China in the Goji berries. In fact, the key is not a specific molecule in a specific food but its beneficial effect and the possibility for everyone to benefit.

The interesting effects of nutraceuticals and functional foods could represent a prevention for many age-related diseases, and, if not a total solution, at least a piece of their puzzle.

So, the possibility to create a dietary pattern, based on the combined strategy of the use of both nutraceuticals and functional foods, should permit to create a new therapeutic strategy based not only on a specific bioactive molecule or on a specific food but on a integrated approach that, starting from the local dietary habits, can be led to a "nutrafunctional diet" applicable worldwide.

Additional longitudinal observations on community-based cohorts are needed to confirm these data and investigate the biological mechanisms, including epigenetic ones, through which effects are induced, and to fully explore their therapeutic potential.

Nevertheless, nutrigerontology, putting together branches strictly related to ageing process, as biogerontology, medicine and nutrition, should be the key for achieving successful ageing and longevity.

ACKNOWLEDGEMENTS

Original work was supported by PON DI.ME.SA. (Programma Operativo Nazionale Ricerca e Competitività 2007/2013 - Progetto "DI.ME.SA."

PON02_00451_3361785. Valorisation of typical products of the Mediterranean diet and their nutraceutical use to improve health) to CC, SV and GC, that are grateful to Ing. Antonio Giallanza, Project Manager, for his valued professional work. AA is a student of the PhD course directed by CC.

Provenance and peer review

Commissioned; not externally peer reviewed.

Open Access This article is distributed under the terms of the Creative Commons Attribution 4.0 International License (http://creativecommons.org/licenses/by/4.0/), which permits unrestricted use, distribution, and reproduction in any medium, provided you give appropriate credit to the original author(s) and the source, provide a link to the Creative Commons license, and indicate if changes were made. The Creative Commons Public Domain Dedication waiver (http://creativecommons.org/publicdomain/zero/1.0/) applies to the data made available in this article, unless otherwise stated.

COMPETING INTEREST

The authors declare no conflict of interest.

AUTHORS' CONTRIBUTIONS

CC wrote the paper. All authors edited the paper and approved its final version.

REFERENCES

1. Verburgh K. Nutrigerontology: why we need a new scientific discipline to develop diets and guidelines to reduce the risk of aging-related diseases. Aging Cell. 2015;14(1):17–24.

2. Avery P, Barzilai N, Benetos A, Bilianou H, Capri M, Caruso C, Franceschi C, Katsiki N, Mikhailidis DP, Panotopoulos G, Sikora E, Tzanetakou IP, Kolovou G. Ageing, longevity, exceptional longevity and related genetic and non genetics markers: panel statement. Curr Vasc Pharmacol. 2014;12(5):659–61.

3. Kolovou G, Barzilai N, Caruso C, Sikora E, Capri M, Tzanetakou IP, Bilianou H, Avery P, Katsiki N, Panotopoulos G, Franceschi C, Benetos A, Mikhailidis DP. The challenges in moving from ageing to successful longevity. Curr Vasc Pharmacol. 2014;12(5):662–73.

4. Fontana L, Partridge L. Promoting health and longevity through diet: from model organisms to humans. Cell. 2015;161:106–18.

5. Santoro A, Pini E, Scurti M, Palmas G, Berendsen A, Brzozowska A, Pietruszka B, Szczecinska A, Cano N, Meunier N, de Groot CP, Feskens E, Fairweather-Tait S, Salvioli S, Capri M, Brigidi P, Franceschi C; NU-AGE Consortium. Combating inflammaging through a Mediterranean whole diet approach: the NU-AGE project's conceptual framework and design. Mech Ageing Dev. 2014;136–137:3–13.

6. Fontana L, Partridge L, Longo VD. Extending healthy life span--from yeast to humans. Science. 2010;328(5976):321–6.

7. Longo VD, Antebi A, Bartke A, Barzilai N, Brown-Borg HM, Caruso C, Curiel TJ, de Cabo R, Franceschi C, Gems D, Ingram DK, Johnson TE, Kennedy BK, Kenyon C, Klein S, Kopchick JJ, Lepperdinger G, Madeo F, Mirisola MG, Mitchell JR, Passarino G, Rudolph KL, Sedivy JM, Shadel GS, Sinclair DA, Spindler SR, Suh

Y, Vijg J, Vinciguerra M, Fontana L. Interventions to Slow Aging in Humans: Are We Ready? Aging Cell. 2015;14(4):497–510.

8. Vasto S, Buscemi S, Barera A, Di Carlo M, Accardi G, Caruso C. Mediterranean diet and healthy ageing: a Sicilian perspective. Gerontology. 2014;60(6):508–18.

9. Accardi G, Aiello A, Gargano V, Gambino CM, Caracappa S, Marineo S, Vesco G, Carru C, Zinellu A, Zarcone M, Caruso C, Candore G. Nutraceutical effects of table green olives: a pilot study with Nocellara del Belice olives. Immun Ageing. 2016;13:11.

10. Accardi G, Aiello A, Gambino CM, Virruso C, Caruso C, Candore G. Mediterranean nutraceutical foods: Strategy to improve vascular ageing. Mech Ageing Dev. 2016 (16)30011–2.

11. Vasto S, Barera A, Rizzo C, Di Carlo M, Caruso C, Panotopoulos G. Mediterranean diet and longevity: an example of nutraceuticals? Curr Vasc Pharmacol. 2014;12(5):735–8.

12. Gupta S, Chauhan D, Mehla K, Sood P, Nair A. An overview of nutraceuticals: current scenario. J Basic Clin Pharm. 2010;1(2):55–62.

13. Calabrese EJ, Iavicoli I, Calabrese V. Hormesis: its impact on medicine and health. Hum Exp Toxicol. 2013;32(2):120–52. d

14. Chirumbolo S. Possible role of NF-κB in hormesis during ageing. Biogerontology. 2012;13(6):637–46.

15. Zhang C, Lin G, Wan W, Li X, Zeng B, Yang B, Huang C. Resveratrol, a polyphenol phytoalexin, protects cardiomyocytes against anoxia/reoxygenation injury via the TLR4/NF-κB signaling pathway. Int J Mol Med. 2012;29:557–63.

16. Aiello A, Dara Guccione G, Accardi G, Caruso C. What olive oil for healthy ageing? Maturitas. 2015;80(2):117–8. d

17. Virruso C, Accardi G, Colonna-Romano G, Candore G, Vasto S, Caruso C. Nutraceutical properties of extra-virgin olive oil: a natural remedy for age-related disease? Rejuvenation Res. 2014;17(2):217–20.

18. Zheng A, Li H, Cao K, Xu J, Zou X, Li Y, Chen C, Liu J, Feng Z. Maternal hydroxytyrosol administration improves neurogenesis and cognitive function in prenatally stressed offspring. J Nutr Biochem. 2015;26(2):190–9.

19. European Community. Council Regulation No. 432/2012 of 16 May 2012 establishing a list of permitted health claims made on foods, other than those referring to the reduction of disease risk, to children's development, health. Off J Eur Union. 2012;L136:1–40.

20. Passarino G, De Rango F, Montesanto A. Human longevity: Genetics or Lifestyle? It takes two to tango. Immun Ageing. 13:12.

21. Barera A, Buscemi S, Monastero R, Caruso C, Caldarella R, Ciaccio M, Vasto S. β-Glucans: *ex vivo*inflammatory and oxidative stress results after pasta intake. Immun Ageing. 13:14.

22. Carruba G, Cocciadiferro L, Di Cristina A, Granata OM, Dolcemascolo C, Campisi I, Zarcone M, Cinquegrani M, Traina A. Nutrition, aging and cancer: lessons from dietary intervention studies. Immun Ageing. 13:13.

23. Davinelli S, Maes M, Corbi G, Zarrelli A, Willcox DC, Scapagnini G. Dietary Phytochemicals and Neuro-inflammaging: From Mechanistic Insights to Translational Challenges. Immun Ageing. 13:16.

24. Pae M, Meydani SN, Wu D. The role of nutrition in enhancing immunity in aging. Aging Dis. 2012;3(1):91–129.

25. Albers R, Bourdet-Sicard R, Braun D, Calder PC, Herz U, Lambert C, Lenoir-Wijnkoop I, Méheust A, Ouwehand A, Phothirath P, Sako T, Salminen S, Siemensma A, van Loveren H, Sack U. Monitoring immune modulation by nutrition in the general population: identifying and substantiating effects on human health. Br J Nutr. 2013;110:S1–30.

26. Navas-Carretero S, Martinez JA. Cause-effect relationships in nutritional intervention studies for health claims substantiation: guidance for trial design. Int J Food Sci Nutr. 2015;66 Suppl 1:S53–61.

Chapter 8

Gold Nanoparticle and Berberine Entrapped into Hydrogel Matrix as Drug Delivery System

Camila Rufino Souza[1], Henrique R. Oliveira[1], Wagner M. Pinheiro[2], Lubhandwa S. Biswaro[2], Ricardo B. Azevedo[2], Anderson J. Gomes[1*], Claure N. Lunardi[1*]

[1]*Laboratory of Nanobiotechnology, Faculty of Ceilandia, University of Brasilia, Brasilia, Brazil*

[2]*Institute of Biological Sciences, University of Brasilia, Brasilia, Brazil*

ABSTRACT

In this study the novel hydrogel loaded with gold nanoparticle (AuNP) enhanced the berberine (BS) release when compared with other formulations of hydrogel. Hydrogels are hydrophilic polymer networks having the capacity to absorb water, ranging from about twenty to thousand times their dry weight. BS is a natural product, a quaternary ammonium salt from the group of isoquinoline alkaloids found in medicinal plants as Berberis Vulgaris. BS has some activity against dysentery, hypertension, inflammation, and liver disease in China and Japan. In this work, BS was used as a model drug to study its association with different types of hydrogel composites of polyvinyl alcohol (BS-PVA 10%); gellan gum (BS-GG 2%), gellan gum-PVA crosslinked with cysteine (cys) (BSGG2%PVA2%cys) and gellan gum-PVA cosslinked with cysteine associated with gold nanoparticles (AuNP-BSGG2%PVA2%cys). Several parameters such as fraction of retained water (Wf), hydration percentage (%H), Swelling (DSw) and time course profile (t = 100%) (TC) were evaluated for all preparations. The results showed that the AuNP-BS-GG2%PVA2%cys was able to retain more water and swelling than the other preparations. The time course of release of the BS to the medium was greater for AuNP-BS-GG2%PVA2%cys making it a candidate to drug delivery studies in biological assays. Also Scanning Electron Microscopy (SEM) images of the surface of these hydrogel were performed. Furthermore, crosslink of the resulting hydrogels were investigated by Fourier Transform Infrared Spectroscopy (FTIR) and differential scanning calorimetry (DSC) and thermogravimetric analysis (TGA). Thus, briefly, the aim of this work was to study three composition of hydrogel loaded with BS and its composition in relation to addition to AuNP and evaluate its profile for further drug delivery application using the Surface Plasmonic Resonance (SPR) as a tool improving the drug release in the new hydrogel.

Keywords: Hydrogel, Berberine, Drug Delivery, AuNPs

1. INTRODUCTION

Berberine (BS) is a natural product, a quaternary ammonium salt from the group of isoquinoline alkaloids, belongsto structural class of protoberberine, which positively-charged ion turns it hydro soluble. It is found in medicinal plants as Berberis Vulgaris [1] -[3] and the salts are derived of ammoniac form, solid, nonvolatile, crystallizable and inodorous when it is oxygenized. Due to its yellow color and characteristics the BS is applied with basic nature pigment [4] . The most interesting aspect of BS is related to its pharmacological properties been reported in the treatment of illness, such as: dysentery, hypertension, diabetes, inflammation, and also cancer [5] - [12] .

Hydrogel is report itself as polymeric network (reticulated structure), which has the feature to swell with water or biological fluids. Moreover, hydrogel storage a large amount of these fluids in its structure without dissolves itself [13] [14] . Besides, it exhibits some particular characteristics, such as hydrophilic behavior, insoluble in water, floppy, elastic and in contact with water, its volume increases considerably, without lose its shape, until achieve physic-chemical equilibrium. Hydrogels are able to mimic nature tissue, being biocompatibility [15] [16] . This feature leads to the amount of storage a large amount of water and special surface property. Hence, in this background, synthetics hydrogels are awaken interest at tissue engineering, cell encapsulate and drug delivery [17] . Another type of nanomaterial that have attracted increasing attention due to their unique properties in multidisciplinary research fields are gold nanoparticles (AuNPs) [2] [3] . The gold core is inert and essentially non-toxic to cells [18] . The particles absorb and resonantly scatter visible and near-infrared light upon excitation of their surface plasmon oscillation (SPR).

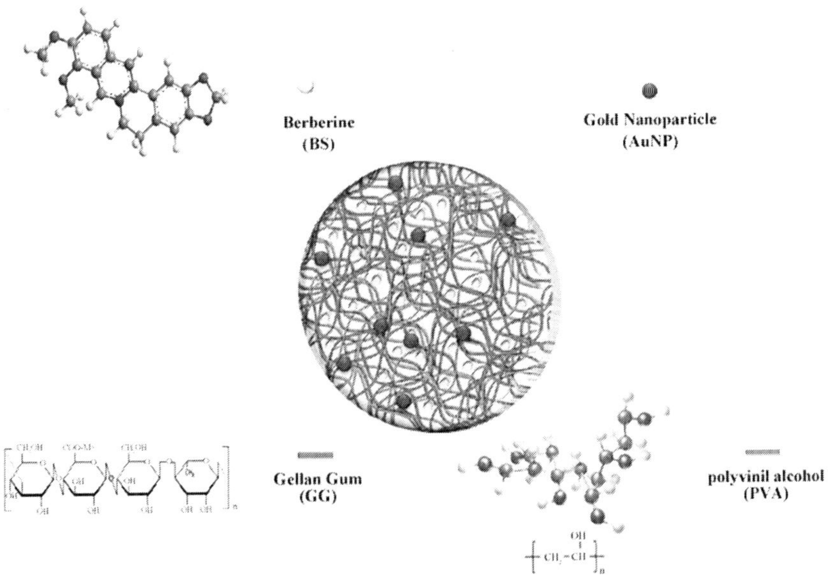

Figure 1. Schematic illustration of possible interaction of BS-GG2%PVA2%cys and AuNPs into the composite.

Gold nanoparticles associated to hydrogels are based on the behavior of AuNPs properties like the SPR band leading to evaluation of parameters like size among others [19] . Another important characteristic of AuNPs is the ability of dissipating heat when absorbing light, being an interest approach for thermal therapy as a trigger to release of encapsulated drugs from thermosensitive hydrogels [9] [17] . Moreover, there are no reports on the use of BS for preparing crosslinked AuNPs hydrogel nanocomposites, despite its relevance in the context of new formulations for biocompatible hydrogels. The aim of this article was to study the different types of hydrogelbiodegradable composites and the inclusion of gold nanoparticles to this system, evaluating parameters of surface and it's correlation to release time course profile of BS improving the efficiency and versatility to be used in existing therapies.

2. EXPERIMENTAL

2.1. Materials

Berberine (BS from Sigma Chem. Co.); polyvinil alcohol (88% PVA from Sigma Chem. Co.); Deacylated gellan gum GG-LA (Kelcogel from Cpkelco); chloridric acid (from Akros Chem); Au(III) solution (1%) was prepared with HAuCl4, citric acid (from Sigma Chem. Co.); HEPES buffer (from Sigma Chem. Co.); Cisteyne (CYS). Double distilled water was used for the preparation of all solutions.

2.2. Preparation of Hydrogel Composites

PVA 10%. Hydrogel composites were prepared with 10% PVA solution, 7.5% citric acid solution in distilled water,BS was and used as received. All the reagents were of analytical grade. The preparation of the hydrogel has been described elsewhere [20] . In short, 100 mL of a 10% aqueous solution of PVA and citric acid solution and concentrated hydrochloric acid (HCl, 0.05 mL) were mixed, and the resulting dispersion was stirred (using a overhead stirrer at 100 ± 5 rpm) at 70°C for a half-hour to carry out the crosslinked PVA hydrogel production. The thick dispersion so obtained was converted into a membrane by the conventional solution casting method. The resultant membrane was washed thoroughly with distilled water to remove the HCl and was stored in a desiccators at 37°C. The empty hydrogel was designated PVA 10% and the berberine loaded was designated BS- PVA10%.

Gellan Gum. The gellan gum (GG) hydrogel composite were prepared using HEPES (50 mM, pH = 4), following proportion: 2% of GG-LA (89.1 COOH) [21] [22] . In short, 6 mL of HEPES and 20µM of solution CYS and GG-LA were mixed, and the resulting dispersion was stirred (using a overhead stirrer at 100 ± 5 rpm) at 80°C for ten minutes to carry out the crosslinked kelcogell hydrogel production. The thick dispersion so obtained was converted into a membrane by the conventional solution casting method. The empty hydrogel was designated GG2% and the berberine loaded was designated BS-GG2%.

PVA 2% plus Gellan Gum 2%. The hydrogel composite were prepared using HEPES 50 mM, pH = 4), following proportion: 2% of GG-LA (89.1 COOH) and 2% of PVA. In short, 6 mL of HEPES, 20 µM of solution CYS, GG-LA and PVA were mixed, and the resulting dispersion was stirred (using a overhead stirrer at 100 ± 5 rpm) at 80°C for ten minutes to carry out the crosslinked kelcogell hydrogel production. The thick dispersion so obtained was converted into a membrane by the conventional solution casting method. The empty hydrogel was designated GG2%PVA2%cys and the berberine loaded was designated BS-GG2%PVA2%cys.

The BS in micromolar range (10-6M) concentration was added before stirring time to produce hydrogels composites. AuNPs: Gold nanoparticle was prepared by modified sodium citrate reduction method by Turkevich [23] . Placed 0.70 mL of 0.1% HAuCl4 into a 150 mL beaker, then added water to near 60 mL and the solution was heated to boiling. An amount of 2 mL of 1% sodium citrate solution was added dropwhise into beaker solution. The solution became rubbish during stirring for 30 minutes. This solution is called naked AuNPs.

AuNPs-PVA 2% plus Gellan Gum 2%. The nanocomposites were prepared by blending the Au NPs with the PVA 2% plus Gellan Gum 2%. The colloidal AuNPs was added to the BS in micromolar range (10-6 M) concentration was added before stirring time to produce hydrogels composites in the same procedure as described before.

2.3. In Vitro Stability and Swelling of Biodegradable Hydrogel Composite

Approximately 30 mg of each type of composites loaded with 465 µM of BS was deposited into pre-weighed polypropylene sample tubes, weighed, warmed to 37 ˚C, and combined with 1000 µL of warm HEPES solution at pH 7.4. Samples were incubated at 37˚C on a rotary shaker and the HEPPES buffer sampled with total replacement after: 30, 60,120 minutes and daily during 8 days showing stable weight. Recovered buffer was sonicated to disrupt residual hydrogel before Uv-vis analysis (Uv-vis Hitachi U-3900). The swelling ratio, DSw, of each type of composite were determined by accurately weighing each gel sample in the stability study after the HEPES buffer had been removed, correcting for residual buffer, and dividing by the original hydrated sample mass [24] -[26] . To compare the degradation of composites with different swelling characteristics, normalized DSw was defined as:

$$DSw = \frac{m}{m^{*}} \tag{1}$$

where m and m^{*} are the weight of hydrated composite and dried composite respectively.

2.4. Drug Release from Biodegradable Hydrogel Composite

Release profiles of each loaded drug composite were obtained by depositing approximately 30 mg of drug loaded dry hydrogel and adding 1000 µL of HEPES buffer into polypropylene sample tubes, warming to 37°C. Samples were incubated at 37°C on a rotary shaker and the HEPPES buffer sampled with total replacement after 15, 30, 60, 120, 360 minutes and 24 h and daily during 90 days for each preparation. All samples were fresh analyzed by UV-vis measurements were performed on Hitachi U-3900H UV-Vis Spectrophotometer in the wavelength interval of 200 - 800 nm at 37°C using HEPES buffer as blank. The measurements were accomplished when the values of absorbance of BS in the medium in each sample reached the plateau. These values were transformed to percentage of release (100%) and correlated to time (hours) and displayed as time course profile (TC). The fraction of retained water (Wf); hydration percentage (%H); Swelling (DSw) and time course profile (t = 100%) (TC) were evaluated for all hydrogel composite as described in Equations (2)-(4):

$$Wf = \frac{(m - m^*)}{1} \tag{2}$$

$$EWC = Wf \times 100 \tag{3}$$

$$H = 100 \times \frac{(m - m^*)}{m^*} \tag{4}$$

where m and m^* are the weight of hydrated composite and dried composite respectively.

2.5. Fourier Transform Infrared (FTIR) Spectroscopy of Biodegradable Hydrogel Composite

The chemical structure of the biodegradable composite materials and the composite itself (unloaded and loaded with BS) were analyzed by FTIR (IR Prestige-21 FRIT-8400S, Shimadzu, Japan) in transmission mode. For that, each composite (1.0 mg) were mixed with KBr (40.0 mg) and then formed into a disc in a manual press. Transmission spectra were recorded using at least 32 scans with 4.0 cm^{-1} resolution, in the spectral range 4000 - 400 cm^{-1}.

2.6. Differential Scanning Calorimetry (DSC) Biodegradable Hydrogel Composite

Thermal characterization of biodegradable hydrogel composite was performed with a Shimadzu DSC-60A. The equipment was calibrated with indium. The sample (approximately 3.0 mg) was heated twice from 25°C to 400°C at 20°C/min in a nitrogen atmosphere (flow rate 30 mL/min). The melting temperature (Tm) was determined from the endothermic peak of the DSC curve recorded in the first heating scan.

2.7. Thermogravimetric Analyses (TGA) of Biodegradable Hydrogel Composite

The composites and its material were analyses. The samples weighting about 3 mg heated from 25°C to 400°C in a platinum pan rate 20°C/min in the nitrogen atmosphere at flow of 30 mL/min. The glass transition temperature (Tg) was determined from the DSC curve recorded in the second heating scan.

2.8. Scanning Electron Microscopy Measurements (SEM)

Scanning electron microscopy (SEM) was used to evaluate the surface of biodegradable composite hydrogel. Samples containing biodegradable composite hydrogel were mounted on aluminum stubs and due to their lack of electrical conductivity they were coated with 50 nm gold coating under an argon atmosphere. The composites were examined and photographed by a Jeol 840 A (Tokyo, Japan) Scanning Electron Microscope operating at 20 kV in the traditional mode (SE1 detector). SEM images were obtained to characterize the surface of the BS-PVA 10%, BS-GG2%cys, BS-GG2%PVA2%cys and AuNPs-BS-GG2%PVA2%cys hydrogel films.

2.9. Statistical Analysis

Experiments were performed in triplicate using freshly prepared samples. Statistical analysis data are expressed as means± standard deviation unless otherwise noted. Comparisons of groups of means were determined by ANOVA and pairs of mean by Student's t-test where appropriate. Significance was assigned at $p < 0.05$.

3. RESULTS AND DISCUSSION

3.1. Hydrogel Composite Preparation

The first attempt to production of biodegradable hydrogel composite with PVA was done in 7.5% w/w however, this hydrogel type dissolved when added to solution of HEPES. As alternative, the concentration was increased to 10%. In this way, we characterized the hydrogel in terms of thickness as displayed for GG2% hydrogel preparation in dried and swollen form (Figure 2) by using a pachymeter. The values obtained for each preparation were GG2% 0.4 mm for dry and 3.1 mm for swollen. Also for PVA10% were 0.2 mm dry and 2.0 swollen; GG2%PVA2%cys were 0.2 dry and 4.0 mm swollen and AuNP-GG2%PVA2%cys were 0.2 dry and 3.5 mm swollen.

3.2. Water Content Parameters and Time Course Release of BS

Water content in the hydrogel composite was affected by the concentration of gellan gum and also by the cysteine content. The values of the fraction of retained water (Wf); hydration percentage (%H); Swelling (DSw) is displayed in Table 1. The hydrogel of BS-PVA10% showed the lower values for all the parameters assayed. Only the time course (TC) of the BS release was higher and this might be due the rigid network during gel formation. Also the others hydrogel composite BS-GG 2%, BS-GG2%PVA2%cys and AuNP-GG2%PVA2%cys preparations showed increased values of water parameters with a faster time course of BS release. This results could be explained by the characteristics of GG, a well known polysaccharide manufactured by microbial fermentation of the Sphingomonas paucimobilis microorganism, that can be dissolved in water, and when heated and mixed with mono or divalent cations its forms gels [13] ; this behavior associated with PVA and cross-linked with cysteine, turned it in the most suitable composite from the preparations evaluated. These features indicate

Figure 2. The pachymeter for determining the thickness of GG2% hydrogel in dried and swollen form.

Table 1. Biodegradable hydrogel composite: swelling feature and time course release using BS [465 μM].

Hydrogel composite/ [BS] = 465 μM	Hydrogel properties			
	Wf	%H	DSw	TC (hs)
BS-PVA 10%	0.4962 ± 0.005	96.9 ± 2.06	1.82 ± 0.22	72 ± 3.90
BS-GG 2%	0.6747 ± 0.438	211.74 ± 40.0	3.1174 ± 0.40	22 ± 0.04
BS-GG 2%PVA2%cys	0.9184 ± 0.013	1150.87 ± 186.1	12.508 ± 1.84	22 ± 0.15
AuNP-BS-GG2% PVA2%cys	0.9623 ± 0.021	1450.87 ± 100.2	8.41 ± 1.105	14 ± 0.50

Wf (fraction of retained water); %H (hydration percentage); DSw (Swelling); TC (Time course).

that this preparation is suitable for a drug delivery system for BS in biological systems with high content of water. The citrate-capped AuNPs decreases the intensity of the crosslinking reaction between the PVA/GGcys and BS showing a less cross-linked hydrogels, with reduced swollen profile when compared with BS-GG2%PVA 2%cys.

3.3. SEM Measurements of Hydrogel Composites

In Figure 3 are displayed the SEM of the hydrogels surface of BS-PVA 10%, BS-GG2%, and BS-GG2%PVA2%cys hydrogel films respectively, of dried hydrogels films. The flat and featureless images indicate that the films have a condensed structure and clearly show the appearance of a smooth or fibrous structure. The soft and stiff surface of PVA 10% can explain the lower time course release of the BS from matrix. However, the porous and fibrous like surface of BS-GG2%, and BS-GG2%PVA2%cys could explain the faster BS release and the increased values of physical chemistry parameters analyzed. In addition, 10%PVA hydrogel are less able to hydrate than the types with GG2% explaining its lower time course profile. In these words, GG2% hydrogels com- posite and associated with PVA are capable of storage a large amount of BS and maintain longer time at thera- peutic line. Both images from Figures 3(B)-(C) displayed more fibrous in topographical surface than the PVA10%. The AuNP-BS-GG2%PVA2%cys displayed in Figure 3(D) shows less fibrous than BS-GG2%PVA2%cys due to less crosslink, but due to thermal characteristics of AuNPs embebed into hydrogel, under the experimental conditions the release was faster (36%) in relation to BS-GG2%PVA2%cys alone.

3.4. FTIR Analysis of Hydrogel Composites

FTIR spectra was obtained with absorption in the region of 400 - 4000 cm^{-1} at room temperature and used to confirm the hydrogels structures. In Figure 4(A) is displayed the PVA 10% hydrogel FTIR spectra with a characteristic peak at 3343 cm^{-1} due typical OH stretching [16] . Also, there is a 2914 cm^{-1} the asymmetric stretching vibrations of methylene group [24] . At region of 1730 cm^{-1} it is possible to observe C = O stretching [10] . The peak in 1431 cm^{-1} and 1135 cm^{-1} indicate the presence of CH-OH [27] also in 1381 cm^{-1} peak is due to CH asymmetrical bending [26] , and in the region of 1095 cm^{-1} correspond to CO linkage [24] . In Figure 4(B) is displayed the GG2% hydrogel spectra showing the following peaks in the region 3432 cm^{-1} that correspond the OH group as shown before in the PVA hydrogel; 1620 cm^{-1} due to bending vibration of hydroxyl group, 1462 due to CH asymmetrical bending [28] . In the region of absorption of 1219 cm^{-1} is possible see the sulfate ion. At the region 1219 cm^{-1} has a peak that correspond ester linkages [27] and the peak in the 1043 cm^{-1} indicate the presence of C-O-C group. Both hydrogels of PVA10% and GG2% showed preservation of major groups. These characteristics indicate that have no news groups formed in the blend of this hydrogels. It is possible observe, in Figure 4(C) that the GG2% peaks were preserved as 1620 cm^{-1} shifted to absorption in 1607 cm^{-1}, ester linkages were also preserved, as show in the 1192 cm^{-1}. This phenomenon is shown in the same graphic with PVA10% hydrogel peaks. The C = O stretching in 1730 cm^{-1}, characteristic peak of this hydrogel, shifted to 1721 cm^{-1}. The infrared spectra did not show absorption bands of the typical bridges resulted from the reaction of the hydrogel and BS [10] [29] . It seem just characteristic bands from BS.

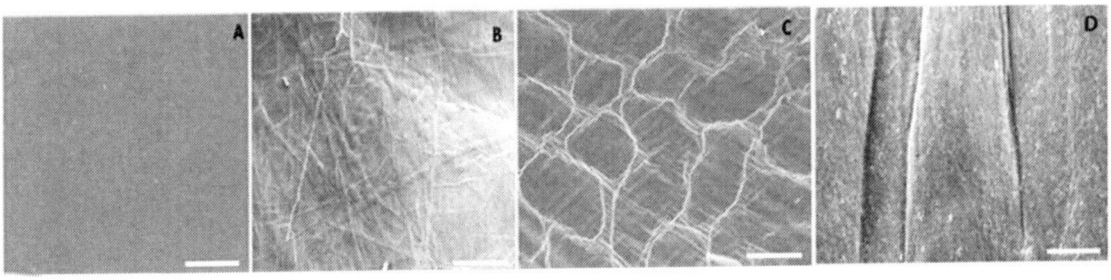

Figure 3. SEM images of hydrogel films. Surface of (a) BS-PVA10%, (b) BS-GG2%, (c) BS-GG2%PVA2%cys and (d) AuNP-BS-GG2%PVA2%cys hydrogel films (270× magnification).

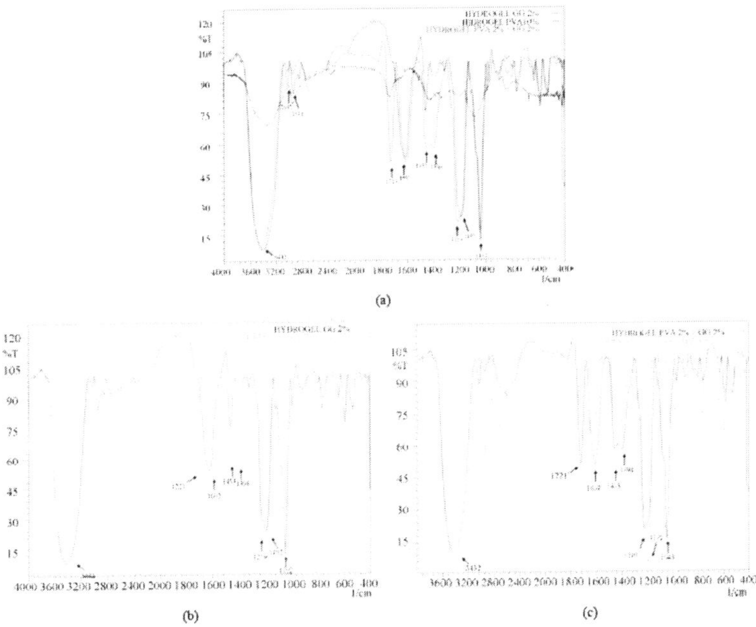

Figure 4. FTIR spectra of all hydrogel composite: (a) GG2%; PVA10%; GG2%PVA2%; (b) GG2% , GG2%PVA2%; and (c) BS; GG2%PVA2%; BS-GG2%PVA2%cys.

3.5. Thermal Analysis of Hydrogel Composites (DSC and TGA)

The DSC heating curves of all hydrogel samples displayed some endothermic peaks due to the melting of the various forms of water that freeze during the cooling stage (Figure 5). The endothermic peak around 40˚C - 420˚C displayed a peak, which have been ascribed previously to the freezing bound water (the sharp one) [30] -[34] . The thermogram is characterized by peaks crystallization (Tc), melting (Tm) and glass transition (Tg) of all hydrogel composite. The behavior observed for 10%PVA, GG2%, PVAGG2% were very similar showing its Tc in the range of 40˚C - 42˚C in the first peak and 190˚C - 260˚C in the

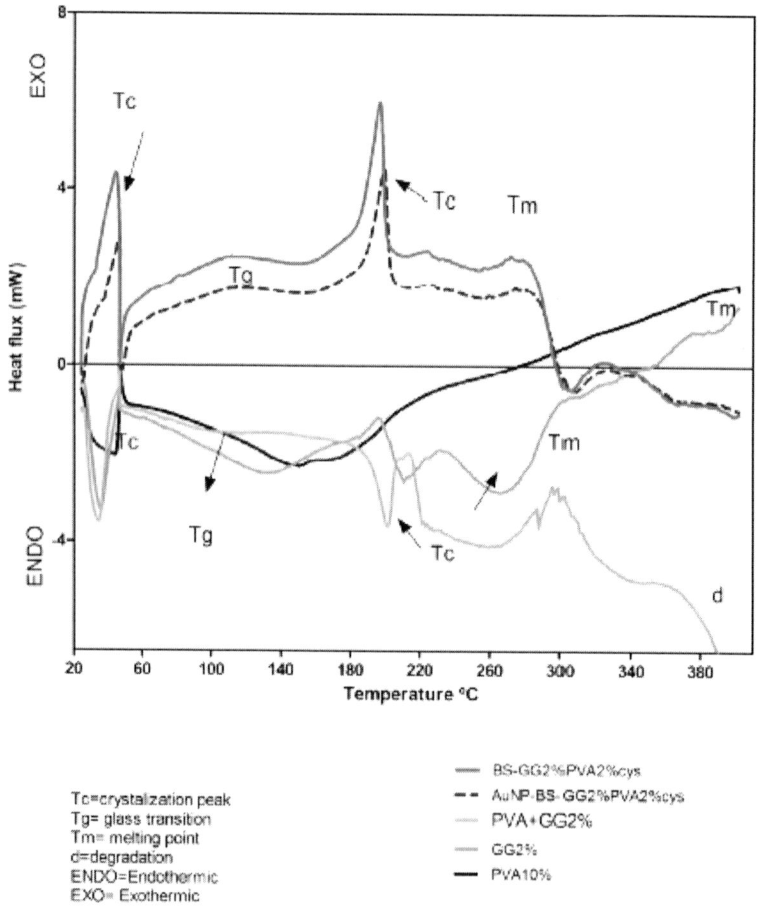

Figure 5. DSC spectra of hydrogel composite: PVA 10%; GG2 %; GG2%PVA2%cys; BS-GG2%PVA2%cys and AuNP-BS-GG2%PVA2%cys.

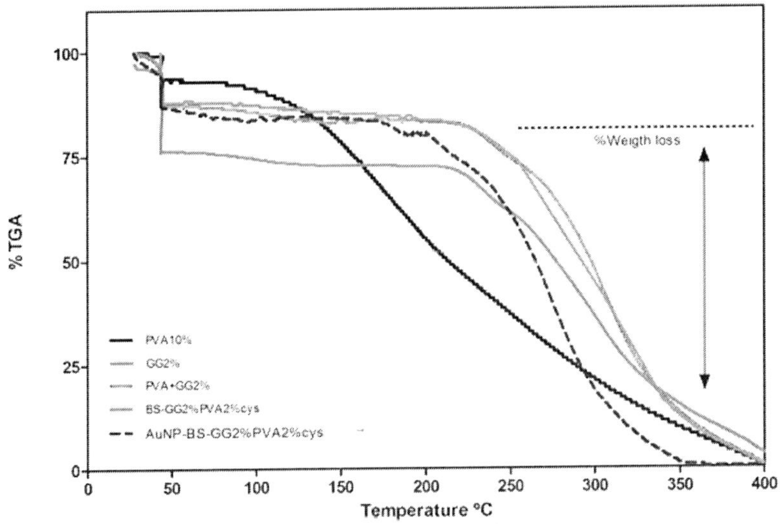

Figure 6. TGA spectra of hydrogel composite: PVA 10%; GG2 %; GG2% PVA2%cys; BS-GG2%PVA2%cys and AuNP-BS-GG2%PVA2%cys.

following transitions. The biodegradable hydrogel composite BS-GG2%PVA2%cys displayed a similar behavior, however most of the process occurs in exothermic profile. When association occurs, the formation of more structured complex so formed exhibits different characteristics in comparison to components-alone. AuNPs-BS-GG2%PVA2%cys showed simi- lar behavior

In Figure 6 is displayed the normalized TGA measurements of all components used in the synthesis biodegradable hydrogel composite. The evaporation process occurs more drastically in the GG2%-(23.0%) and the other component were respectively PVA10%-(5.02%); PVAGG2%-(12.1%); BS-GG2%PVA2%cys-(10.2%) and AuNP-BS-GG2%PVA2%cys-(12.1%). These results indicated that GG2% hydrogel lose more water than PVA10%, also when it is incorporated to PVA and the biodegradable hydrogel loaded with BS, this water lost is reduced indicating that the structure is modified entrapping the water inside the system. The percentage weight loss and the start temperature for all formulation were GG2% (71.5% at 214˚C); PVA10%-(90% at 100˚C);

PVAGG2%-(81.4% at 225°C); BS-GG2%PVA2%cys-(81.2% at 225°C) and AuNP-BS-GG2%PVA2%cys-(80% at 215°C) were observed for all system These results indicate that the GG2% has less mass to lose since its structure is less porous than the network achieved with PVAGG2% BS-GG2%PVA2%cys and AuNP-BS- GG2%PVA2%cys.

4. CONCLUSIONS

Polymeric drug delivery system allows the development of innovative concepts that could create more efficient systems to achieve a prolonged and controlled drug delivery. In this study, by the use of the crosslink method, we have prepared several hydrogel composite by varying amount of GG and PVA loaded with BS and its association to gold nanoparticles, and then characterized its water holding capacities, time course release profile; physical-chemical behavior (FTIR, DSC; TGA) and surface analysis (SEM).

The results have demonstrated distinct surface profile of the hydrogel composites and two different time course profiles, which could explain by the feature of hydrogel matrix.

Among all biodegradable hydrogel composites evaluated it was clear that the addition of GG associated to PVA and association to gold nanoparticle, produced the most suitable drug delivery system for BS, due to all characteristics (higher entrapment efficiency) of the matrix structure, making a promising drug delivery system for delivery hydrophilic drugs. Future application of gold nanoparticles (AuNPs) added into the transparent loaded hydrogel can be a promising efficient drug delivery system in skin, by enabling the cell activating capacity once its size is only 1/2000 as large as pores, very easy to penetrate into the dermis. It can carry the drug such as BS deep into the skin to activate skin cells, increases vasodilatation and can enhance the compactness of the fibrous tissue of collagen to turn the skin compact and elastic against aging and other process.

ACKNOWLEDGEMENTS

Camila Rufino Souza, Henrique R. Oliveira, Wagner M. Pinheiro, Lubhandwa S. Biswaro, Ricardo B. Azevedo, Anderson J. Gomes, Claure N. Lunardi* This material is based upon work supported by the CNPq, FAPDF, FINATEC, DPP-UnB, CAPES.

REFERENCES

1. Huang, Z.J., Zeng, Y., Lan, P., Sun, P.H. and Chen, W.M. (2011) Advances in Structural Modifications and Biological Activities of Berberine: An Active Compound in Traditional Chinese Medicine. Mini-Reviews in Medicinal Chemistry, 11, 1122-1129.

2. Tillhon, M., Guamán Ortiz, L.M., Lombardi, P. and Scovassi, A.I. (2012) Berberine: New Perspectives for Old Remedies. Biochemical Pharmacologyhem Pharmacol, 84, 1260-1267.

3. Xie, W. and Du, L. (2011) Diabetes Is an Inflammatory Disease: Evidence from Traditional Chinese Medicines. Diabetes, Obesity and Metabolism, 13, 289-301.

4. Wang, X.H., Jiang, S.M. and Sun, Q.W. (2011) Effects of Berberine on Human Rheumatoid Arthritis Fibroblast-Like Synoviocytes. Experimental Biology and Medicine (Maywood), 236, 859-866.

5. Chen, X.W., Di, Y.M., Zhang, J., Zhou, Z.W., Li, C.G. and Zhou, S.F. (2012) Interaction of Herbal Compounds with Biological Targets: A Case Study with Berberine. Scientific World Journal, 2012, Article ID: 708292.

6. Chen, Y., Wang, Y., Zhang, J., Sun, C. and Lopez, A. (2011) Berberine Improves Glucose Homeostasis in Streptozotocin-Induced Diabetic Rats in Association with Multiple Factors of Insulin Resistance. ISRN Endocrinology, 2011, Article ID: 519371.

7. Chidambara Murthy, K.N., Jayaprakasha, G.K. and Patil, B.S. (2012) The Natural Alkaloid Berberine Targets Multiple Pathways to Induce Cell Death in Cultured Human Colon Cancer Cells. European Journal of Pharmacology, 688, 14- 21.

8. Tan, W., Li, Y., Chen, M. and Wang, Y. (2011) Berberine Hydrochloride: Anticancer Activity and Nanoparticulate Delivery System. International Journal of Nanomedicine, 6, 1773-1777.

9. Trimarco, V., Cimmino, C.S., Santoro, M., Pagnano, G., Manzi, M.V., Piglia, A., et al. (2012) Nutraceuticals for Blood Pressure Control in Patients with High-Normal or Grade 1 Hypertension. High Blood Pressure & Cardiovascular Prevention, 19, 117-122. [Paper reference:1]

10. Wang, J., Liu, Q. and Yang, Q. (2012) Radiosensitization Effects of Berberine on Human Breast Cancer Cells. International Journal of Molecular Medicine, 30, 1166-1172. [Paper reference:2]

11. Wang, Y., Huang, Y., Lam, K.S., Li, Y., Wong, W.T., Ye, H., et al. (2009) Berberine Prevents Hyperglycemia-Induced Endothelial Injury and Enhances Vasodilatation via Adenosine Monophosphate-Activated Protein Kinase and Endothelial Nitric Oxide Synthase. Cardiovascular Research, 82, 484-492.

12. Zhou, L., Wang, X., Yang, Y., Wu, L., Li, F., Zhang, R., et al. (2011) Berberine Attenuates cAMP-Induced Lipolysis via Reducing the Inhibition of Phosphodiesterase in 3T3-L1 Adipocytes. Biochimica et Biophysica Acta (BBA)—Mole- cular Basis of Disease, 1812, 527-535.

13. Minhas, M.U., Ahmad, M., Ali, L. and Sohail, M. (2013) Synthesis of Chemically Cross-Linked Polyvinyl Alcohol-co- Poly (methacrylic acid) Hydrogels by Copolymerization; A Potential Graft-Polymeric Carrier for Oral Delivery of 5- Fluorouracil. DARU Journal of Pharmaceutical Sciences, 21.

14. Zhang, X.Z., Zhuo, R.X., Cui, J.Z. and Zhang, J.T. (2002) A Novel Thermo-Responsive Drug Delivery System with Positive Controlled Release. International Journal of Pharmaceutics, 235, 43-50.

15. Liu, L., Wang, B., Gao, Y. and Bai, T.C. (2013) Chitosan Fibers Enhanced Gellan Gum Hydrogels with Superior Mechanical Properties and Water-Holding Capacity. Carbohydrate Polymers, 97, 152-158.

16. Moura, M.J., Faneca, H., Lima, M.P., Gil, M.H. and Figueiredo, M.M. (2011) In Situ Forming Chitosan Hydrogels Prepared via Ionic/Covalent Co-Cross-Linking. Biomacromolecules, 12, 3275-3284.

17. Cencetti, C., Bellini, D., Pavesio, A., Senigaglia, D., Passariello, C., Virga, A., et al. (2012) Preparation and Characterization of Antimicrobial Wound Dressings Based on Silver, Gellan, PVA and Borax. Carbohydrate Polymers, 90, 1362-1370.

18. Cobley, C.M., Chen, J., Cho, E.C., Wang, L.V. and Xia, Y. (2011) Gold Nanostructures: A Class of Multifunctional Materials for Biomedical Applications. Chemical Society Reviews, 40, 44-56.

19. Bedford, E.E., Spadavecchia, J., Pradier, C.M. and Gu, F.X. (2012) Surface Plasmon Resonance Biosensors Incorporating Gold Nanoparticles. Macromolecular Bioscience, 12, 724-739.

20. Cristallini, C., Guerra, G.D., Barbani, N. and Bianchi, F. (2007) Biodegradable Bioartificial Materials Made with Chitosan and Poly(vinyl alcohol). Part I: Physicochemical Characterization. Journal of Applied Biomaterials & Biomechanics, 5, 184-191.

21. Cascone, M.G., Barbani, N., Cristallini, C., Giusti, P., Ciardelli, G. and Lazzeri, L. (2001) Bioartificial Polymeric Materials Based on Polysaccharides. Journal of Biomaterials Science, Polymer Edition, 12, 267-281.

22. Oliveira, J.T., Martins, L., Picciochi, R., Malafaya, P.B., Sousa, R.A., Neves, N.M., et al. (2010) Gellan Gum: A New Biomaterial for Cartilage Tissue Engineering Applications. Journal of Biomedical Materials Research Part A, 93, 852- 863.

23. Kimling, J., Maier, M., Okenve, B., Kotaidis, V., Ballot, H. and Plech, A. (2006) Turkevich Method for Gold Nanoparticle Synthesis Revisited. Journal of Physical Chemistry B, 110, 15700-15707.

24. Cai, X., Shao, W., Luan, Y., Pang, J., Li, F. and Li, Z. (2011) Metformin Hydrochloride-Loaded Poly(vinyl alcohol) Composites as Drug Delivery Systems. Journal of Nanoscience and Nanotechnology, 11, 8621-8627.

25. Chen, C.H., Wang, F.Y., Mao, C.F., Liao, W.T. and Hsieh, C.D. (2008) Studies of Chitosan: II. Preparation and Characterization of Chitosan/Poly(vinyl alcohol)/Gelatin Ternary Blend Films. International Journal of Biological Macromolecules, 43, 37-42

26. Lima, A.C., Sher, P. and Mano, J.F. (2012) Production Methodologies of Polymeric and Hydrogel Particles for Drug Delivery Applications. Expert Opinion on Drug Delivery, 9, 231-248.

27. Hu, Y., Wang, Q. and Tang, M. (2013) Preparation and Properties of Starch-g-PLA/Poly(vinyl alcohol) Composite Film. Carbohydrate Polymers, 96, 384-388.

28. Krauland, A.H., Leitner, V.M. and Bernkop-Schnürch, A. (2003) Improvement in the in Situ Gelling Properties of Deacetylated Gellan Gum by the Immobilization of Thiol Groups. Journal of Pharmaceutical Sciences, 92, 1234-1241.

29. Bashmakova, N., Kutovyy, S., Kornienko, M., Yashchuk, V., Hovorun, D. and Zhurakivsky, R. (2010) Experimental and Calculated by the DFT Method Vibration Spectra of Berberine.

Xxii International Conference on Raman Spectroscopy, 1267, 426-427.

30. Ahuja, M., Singh, S. and Kumar, A. (2013) Evaluation of Carboxymethyl Gellan Gum as a Mucoadhesive Polymer. International Journal of Biological Macromolecules, 53, 114-121.

31. Coutinho, D.F., Sant, S.V., Shin, H., Oliveira, J.T., Gomes, M.E., Neves, N.M., et al. (2010) Modified Gellan Gum Hydrogels with Tunable Physical and Mechanical Properties. Biomaterials, 31, 7494-7502.

32. Liu, Y., Geever, L.M., Kennedy, J.E., Higginbotham, C.L., Cahill, P.A. and McGuinness, G.B. (2010) Thermal Behavior and Mechanical Properties of Physically Crosslinked PVA/Gelatin Hydrogels. Journal of the Mechanical Behavior of Biomedical Materials, 3, 203-209.

33. Peng, Z., Kong, L.X., Li, S.D. and Spiridonov, P. (2006) Poly(vinyl alcohol)/Silica Nanocomposites: Morphology and Thermal Degradation Kinetics. Journal of Nanoscience and Nanotechnology, 6, 3934-3938.

34. Wang, H.Y., Lu, S.S. and Lun, Z.R. (2009) Glass Transition Behavior of the Vitrification Solutions Containing Propanediol, Dimethyl Sulfoxide and Polyvinyl Alcohol. Cryobiology, 58, 115-117.

Chapter 9

Coadjuvants in the Diabetic Complications: Nutraceuticals and Drugs with Pleiotropic Effects

Thiago Melo Costa Pereira [1,2], Fabio Silva Pimenta [1,3], Marcella Lima Porto [2], Marcelo Perim Baldo [4], Bianca Prandi Campagnaro [1], Agata Lages Gava [5,6], Silvana Santos Meyrelles [5] and Elisardo Corral Vasquez [1,5,*]

[1]*Pharmaceutical Sciences Graduate Program, Vila Velha University (UVV), Av. Comissario Jose Dantas Melo 21, Boa Vista, 29102-920 Vila Velha, Brazil*

[2]*Federal Institute of Education, Science and Technology (IFES), 29106-010 Vila Velha, Brazil*

[3]*Burn Treatment Center, Children State Hospital, 29056-030 Vitoria, Brazil*

[4]*Department of Pathophysiology, Montes Claros State University, 39401-089, Montes Claros, Brazil*

[5]*Laboratory of Translational Physiology, Federal University of Espirito Santo (Ufes), 29047-100 Vitoria, Brazil*

[6]*Division of Nephrology, McMaster University, Hamilton, ON L8N 4A6, Canada*

ABSTRACT

Because diabetes mellitus (DM) is a multifactorial metabolic disease, its prevention and treatment has been a constant challenge for basic and clinical investigators focused on translating their discoveries into clinical treatment of this complex disorder. In this review, we highlight recent experimental and clinical evidences of potential coadjuvants in the management of DM, such as polyphenols (quercetin, resveratrol and silymarin), cultured probiotic microorganisms and drugs acting through direct/indirect or pleiotropic effects on glycemic control in DM. Among several options, we highlight new promising therapeutic coadjuvants, including chemical scavengers, the probiotic kefir and the phosphodiesterase 5 inhibitors, which besides the reduction of hyperglycemia and ameliorate insulin resistance, they reduce oxidative stress and improve endothelial dysfunction in the systemic vascular circulation. In the near future, experimental studies are expected to clear the intracellular pathways involving coadjuvants. The design of clinical trials may also contribute to new strategies with coadjuvants against the harmful effects of diabetic complications.

Keywords: diabetes; quercetin; polyphenols; resveratrol; silymarin; kefir; probiotic; sildenafil; phosphodiesterase inhibitors; antioxidants

1. INTRODUCTION

Diabetes mellitus (DM) is an important public health issue because it is highly associated with increased morbidity and mortality [1]. In fact, the prevalence of diagnosed diabetes is increasing worldwide, as demonstrated by the rise from 6.5% (1999 to 2002) to 7.8% (2003 to 2006) of the population in just a few years [2]. Type 2 DM is the most common form of the disease and affects 90% to 95% of individuals with diabetes. The main issue of this pandemic is the increase in mortality associated with diabetes due to the risk of cardiovascular diseases (CVD), which are the leading cause of death in this population. This information became clear after an analysis of the First National Health and Nutrition Examination Survey (NHAHES), which covered the period of 1971–1993 and revealed that more than 65% of deaths of people with diabetes were due to CVD [3]. In addition, diabetes is a leading cause of morbidity and leads to microvascular and macrovascular complications [3,4,5].

Even with the already reported increase in the prevalence of diabetes over the years, only approximately 13% of individuals diagnosed as diabetic were in conformity with the control of the established levels of serum glucose, blood arterial pressure and total cholesterol at the same time [6]. Indeed, it is well known that most of the type 2 DM fail to control glycemia to normal levels when subjected only to diet and physical exercise and, consequently, it is necessary to treat them with anti-diabetic pharmacotherapy [1]. For instance, in a period of two years, among those patients who have been diagnosed as diabetics, the percentages of success in the control of glycated hemoglobin, blood pressure and total cholesterol are higher than 7%, 35% and 37%, respectively. As a result, good management of type 2 diabetes with pharmacological as well as non-pharmacological therapy (including reduction of caloric intake and intermittent fasting) is important [7,8]. Lately, with the mission of ameliorating this health problem, eight different classes of drugs for treatment of type 2 DM, with variations in their side effects and costs, have been approved by the US Food and Drug Administration (FDA) [9]. In this regard, investigators have been challenged to test potential therapies for DM based on functional foods, which are of low cost and very accessible (e.g., substances derived from marine algae [10]).

In the present review, we discuss some epidemiological aspects of diabetic complications resulting from hyperglycemia and the therapeutic advances with antioxidant substances based on experimental and clinical studies. Among different alternatives discussed in this review, we highlight the putative coadjuvants in the management of DM, such as functional foods rich in polyphenols and the probiotic kefir. In addition, we discuss drugs with pleiotropic effects, such as phosphodiesterase 5 (PDE5) inhibitors, which lately have been the main focus of investigation in our laboratory.

2. THE IMPACT OF CHRONIC HYPERGLYCEMIA ON DIABETIC COMPLICATION

2.1. Epidemiological Aspects of Diabetes

The high mortality and morbidity observed in DM patients characterized by chronic high levels of blood glucose and HbA1c, which compromises the function of the target organs heart and kidneys [11,12]. Therefore, the desired goal of treatment for diabetes is to maintain euglycemic levels as much as possible. Studies from early last century have also highlighted several effects of uncontrolled diabetes, such as dyslipidemia [13], reduced serum protein [14], skeletal muscle changes [15], and other complications. In the last decade, several epidemiological studies have been conducted to identify the risks associated to diabetes.

It is well known that diabetes doubles the risk for acute coronary syndrome with an additional risk once the event has occurred. This risk was evident in the Tehran Lipid and Glucose Study, a population-based cohort study that took place in Iran. The authors found that in type 2 diabetic patients, hypercholesterolemia and central adiposity were independent risk factors for death by cardiovascular causes, and poor glycemic control is an independent risk factor for both cardiovascular and all-cause mortality [16]. In the United Kingdom, a cohort study of myocardial infarction risk in men and women with and without diabetes was carried out using a large, nationwide primary care database. The overall adjusted relative risk of myocardial infarction was higher in individuals with diabetes versus no diabetes and was greater in women compared to men [17].

After a 23-year follow-up to determine the prevalence of diabetes and associated characteristics, the Da Qing IGT and Diabetes Study showed that CVD was the leading cause of death in individuals with diabetes (47.5% in men and 49.7% in women), and almost half of the deaths were due to stroke [18]. This excessive risk of stroke associated with diabetes was significantly higher in women than men, and there were no sex differences for other major cardiovascular risk factors [19]. It is noteworthy that high glucose levels alone did not account for the increased risk associated with diabetes. A meta-analysis of 15 prospective studies in approximately 760,000 patients showed that people with pre-diabetes, which was defined as impaired fasting glucose of 110 to 124 mg/dL (6.1 to 6.9 mmol/L) or both, exhibited a moderate higher risk of stroke events [20].

Another condition associated with diabetes is chronic kidney disease. In fact, diabetes is one of the leading causes of chronic kidney disease in the United States [21], where the prevalence of diabetic nephropathy in the population of patients with type 1 and 2 DM is 20% to 40% [22,23]. The Madrid Diabetes Study, which is a prospective cohort study of 3443 type-2 diabetic outpatients, showed that the unadjusted hazard ratio for all-cause mortality in diabetic patients with eGFR < 60 mL/min/1.73 m^2 was approximately 3 after five years of follow-up. Patients with chronic kidney disease at baseline had an increased risk of cardiovascular mortality [24].

2.2. Toxic Effects of Hyperglycemia

Chronic hyperglycemia can promote toxic effects in a myriad of tissues, especially in neurons, because they are more susceptible to glucose uptake [25].

Uncontrolled diabetes cam result in a pathological state characterized by severe hyperglycemia, elevation of plasma osmolarity and diabetic ketoacidosis [26]. Its classic manifestation consists of the biochemical triad of hyperglycemia, increased ketones in bloodstream, and metabolic acidosis, and it might be caused by several factors, including reduced secretion and action of insulin, and raised levels of anti-insulin hormones [27,28].

In general, patients with chronic hyperglycemia exhibit many other characteristics, such as altered expression of matrix degrading enzymes, increased synthesis and deposition of extracellular matrix

(ECM), generation of advanced glycation end products (AGE), upregulation of pro-inflammatory cytokines and growth factors, and augmented flux of hexosamines and polyols [29]. Moreover, in chronic hyperglycemia conditions, the augmented glycation of intracellular proteins appears to attack other proteins and worsen the exacerbate formation of AGEs [30,31]. Consequently, it leads to the inhibition of mitochondrial respiration, increased production of reactive oxygen species (ROS) and inflammatory cytokines, culminating with marked alterations in the systemic vascular function. Also, it is well known that the augmented production of ROS causes DNA damage and results in alteration in the expression of ECM glycoproteins, which corroborates the concept that augmented oxidative stress accounts for DM complications [32,33].

In chronic hyperglycemia, aldose reductase is activated and catalyzes the first reaction in the polyol pathway, resulting in exacerbated productions and accumulation of sorbitol [34,35,36] and causing cellular toxicity by osmotic effects. NADPH is consumed and NADH is produced with accumulation of sorbitol and fructose that can also affect cellular osmosis. While there is an oversupply of NADH in individuals with diabetes due to chronic hyperglycemia and enhanced fatty acid oxidation, NAD^+ could be depleted due to the activation of poly ADP ribose polymerase (PARP) by oxidative DNA damage during oxidative stress [37,38].

The activation of apoptosis in chronic hyperglycemia has received much attention in recent years. Several mechanisms regulate the complicated signaling pathways that mediate apoptosis by hyperglycemia. This process is initiated by interruption of mitochondrial electron transport, resulting in an incomplete reduction of molecular oxygen, generating superoxide anion (·O−2). This free radical can react with nitric oxide (NO), resulting in the production of peroxynitrite ($ONOO^-$), which is a highly toxic molecule [39,40] that causes endothelial cell death. Dysfunction of endothelial cells, which causes loss of multiple endothelium-derived substances, has been hypothesized to play a key role in the progression of vascular disease in diabetes [41,42].

2.3. Role of Oxidative Stress in Diabetic Complications

Oxidative stress is induced by elevations in glucose and free fatty acid levels and has a key role in the pathogenesis of both types of DM and on diabetic complications, as has been reviewed by Wei et al. [43]. Recent evidence suggests oxidative stress is a key participant in the development and progression of diabetes as well as its micro- and macrovascular complications [44,45,46]. Paradoxically, not much attention has been given to other possible therapeutic interventions besides glucose reduction.

ROS are a group of short-lived molecules derived from aerobic respiration and other oxygen reactions that include ·O−2, hydrogen peroxide (H_2O_2), hydroxyl radical (·OH), $ONOO^-$ and hydroxyl (OH^-) [47,48]. The major sources of ROS are the mitochondria, NADPH oxidases, xanthine oxidase, uncoupled NO synthase (NOS), lipoxygenase, cyclooxygenases and CYP450, but they vary in their pathological role and importance depending on the disease and the organ [40,49]. Mitochondria and NADPH oxidases (Nox) are the most important sites for ROS production and are responsible for cardiovascular complications in diabetes [50]. In 1999, Ide et al. [51] observed enhanced cardiomyocyte mitochondrial ·O−2 in the failing myocardium. Moreover, Selemidis et al. [52] suggested that NADPH is a primary ROS-producer not only in vascular smooth muscle cells but also in cardiomyocytes, vascular endothelial cells and adventitial fibroblasts. Furthermore, increased expression of Nox isoforms has been associated with myocardial hypertrophy and fibrosis in diabetes [52,53].

Hyperglycemia is characterized not only by a high-level production of ROS but also by an impairment of the intracellular antioxidant defense system, such as the nuclear factor (erythroid-derived 2)-like 2

(Nrf2), a master upregulator of several antioxidant enzymes [54,55]; consequently, the induction of genes encoding antioxidant molecules, including superoxide dismutase (SOD), glutathione peroxidase (GPx) and catalase is also affected [56]. Additionally, reduced SOD, catalase and GPx activity have been reported in both experimental and clinical diabetic conditions due to excessive glycation [57,58]. Batinic-Haberle et al. [59] found that diabetic blood vessels exhibited an improved endothelium-dependent relaxant response when treated with SOD. Interestingly, a recent study showed that the antioxidant curcumin may have a protective role against oxidative stress in diabetic mice (*db/db*) [60]. Therefore, it is important to emphasize that the nutraceutical compounds that require the activation of Nrf2 have been considered as relevant therapeutic strategy for prevention/treatment of diabetic complications [55,56].

Regardless of the imbalance between the generation of ROS and the activity/intracellular levels of the antioxidant defense mechanisms, excessive generation of ROS is a deleterious factor that leads to pathological consequences, including irreversible cellular damage by oxidation of proteins, lipids, carbohydrates and nucleic acids [61]. Recent evidence indicated that increased levels of urinary markers of oxidative DNA and RNA damage occur with diabetic complications [62]. Furthermore, Palem and Abraham [63] observed that diabetic patients taking both oral antidiabetic drugs and insulin still present high levels of oxidative stress, which emphasizes the need for adding antioxidants to reduce the impact of diabetic complications.

In addition to the direct damage to cells, increased ROS levels also cyclically activates pathways associated with diabetes complications, such as the polyol pathway, increased production of AGEs, activation of PKC isoforms and the hexosamine pathway [54,64]. ROS overproduction and increased oxidative stress can also cause vascular endothelial and smooth muscle dysfunction. On the other hand, it has been shown that neutralization of reactive molecules in patients with diabetes was capable of preventing cardiomyopathy, retinopathy, nephropathy and neuropathy [65]. To avoid diabetes disorders, hyperglycemia should be treated promptly through stimulation of insulin secretion (not the best choice) or increasing insulin sensitivity. However, adopting a causal antioxidant therapeutic approach might be a modern adjuvant strategy to prevent the overproduction of ROS and consequently complications from diabetes.

3. POTENTIAL OF NATURAL PRODUCTS WITH ANTIOXIDANT EFFECTS FOR TREATING DIABETES

Polyphenolic compounds are widely found in plants and provide several pharmacological properties, including antidiabetic effects [66,67,68]. Although not focused in the present discussion, it is important to recognize that the Chinese medicine has demonstrated the efficacy of several natural products that have been used in the treatment of DM as reviewed elsewhere [69]. In this subsection, the main polyphenols with potential antidiabetic activity investigated by us as well as others will be addressed.

3.1. Polyphenolic Compounds

3.1.1. Quercetin

Quercetin (2-(3,4-dihydroxyphenyl)-3,5,7-trihydroxychromen-4-one) is the major flavonoid involved in vegetables and fruits, and it exhibits metabolic, anti-oxidative, anti-apoptotic and renoprotective effects at adequate doses [45,46,68,70]. Although this molecule is widely consumed in the diet, it was surprisingly reported as mutagenic in the 1970s in a study with unusual methods and with no reproducible results [70]. Only in 1999 did the International Agency for Research on Cancer conclude that quercetin should not be classified as carcinogenic to humans [70]. However, in parallel, the investigations with quercetin related to diabetes began in 1975 with an initial interest in preventing cataracts through the inhibition of the aldose reductase that blocks polyol accumulation in intact lenses [71]. Only in the 1990s did quercetin studies extend to other targets in diabetes complications.

Many studies have demonstrated that this bioflavonoid may act through diverse pathways to decrease the tissue-damaging effects of chronic hyperglycemia, such as stimulation of glucose uptake via GLUT4 [72,73,74], inhibiting hepatic glycogenolysis and gluconeogenesis [72,75], and inhibiting α-glucosidase in the small intestine [76] or intestinal glucose transporter GLUT2 [77]. At the same time, another potential advantage is that quercetin exhibits all the characteristics of an adequate antioxidant for diabetes treatment: free radical scavenger ability [78,79], long half-life (~20 h in humans) [80,81], capacity to suppress pro-oxidant enzymes (NADPH oxidase, xanthine oxidase and CYP) [82,83,84] and the ability to stimulate antioxidant enzymes (SOD, catalase, glutathione peroxidase and glutathione reductase) [68,85,86] with high mitochondrial permeability [46,87], which are an important source of ROS in diabetes [88,89]. Given these multiple potential mechanisms, quercetin becomes an important protective molecule against the consequences of long-term diabetes (e.g., microvascular and macrovascular damage, nephropathy, neuropathy associated with the risks autonomic disturbance, amputations and foot ulcers) [67,90,91], as demonstrated in the experimental and clinical investigations as discussed below.

In streptozotocin (STZ)-induced type 1 diabetes models, varying doses of quercetin have shown several benefits. At 50 mg/kg/day (oral dose), quercetin prevented retinal degeneration [92] and vascular complications by inhibiting NF-κB signaling [93]. In rats, quercetin ameliorated erectile dysfunction by inhibiting oxidative stress and upregulating eNOS [94], and it protected against the progression of neuropathy even with a low dose of quercetin (10 mg/kg) as well as attenuating cold allodynia and hyperalgesia [95]. Recently, for the first time, we demonstrated that the same low dose of quercetin attenuates hyperglycemia and nephropathy in STZ-induced diabetes in apolipoprotein E-deficient mice [46] and in C57BL/6J mice [45] (or in rats in a study conducted by others [96,97]), and quercetin treatment exhibited antioxidant benefits. With different doses (25 to 100 mg/kg/day), quercetin was also capable of suppressing the kidney inflammatory response at least partly via anti-hyperuricemic and anti-dyslipidemic effects [98]. In *db/db* mice (the most popular mouse model for type 2 DM), quercetin also demonstrated satisfactory effects [76]. At doses ranging between 50 and 100 mg/kg/day, quercetin treatment improved postprandial blood glucose (similarly to acarbose) [76] in addition to avoiding hyperglycemia and hyperlipidemia and increasing the antioxidant status [99]. Although experimental studies clearly support the protective effects of quercetin in diabetes, clinical data with this isolated compound are still insufficient and inconclusive. Recently, 500 mg of daily quercetin (for four weeks) was capable of reducing hyperuricemia in healthy men [100], which is a relevant factor associated with insulin resistance and progression of diabetic complications [91]. On the other hand, quercetin administered at the same dosage in women with type 2 DM, has been shown to decrease systolic arterial pressure, without significant effects on other cardiovascular risk factors [101]. Similarly, recent data from Brüll et al. [102] revealed that quercetin (162 mg/day) decreased day- and nighttime systolic blood pressure in overweight-to-obese patients without changing any other metabolic risk factor. More recently, another study reported no effect on flow-mediated dilation or insulin resistance with an analogue of quercetin (quercetin-3-glucoside, at 160 mg/day) in healthy men and women aged 40–80 years [103]. Therefore, more studies about quercetin will be necessary to establish the ideal dosage and to identify the real efficacy in diabetic patients.

3.1.2. Resveratrol

This non-flavonoid polyphenolic compound (3,5,4′-trihydroxystilbene, notably present in peanuts, grapes, grape juice and red wine) might be the main molecule responsible for cardiovascular protective effects in the French population despite a high intake of saturated fats, which is known as “French Paradox” [66,104,105,106]. For that reason, this potent molecule (even with a short half-life) also would be highly beneficial as an adjuvant therapy for diabetes. Additionally, under in vitro [107,108] and in vivo [109,110,111] experimental conditions that mimic human diabetes, resveratrol has been shown to have a potential benefit in several multi-target mechanisms for diabetic complications, as presented below.

Recently, Yan et al. [112] showed that 40 mg/kg/day of oral resveratrol (a high dose—according to Zhou et al. [112]) reduced proteinuria and attenuated the progress of renal fibrosis in *db/db* mice [112,113]. At the other extreme, it was demonstrated that a low dose of oral resveratrol (0.5 mg/kg) ameliorated classical DM symptoms (e.g., polydipsia, polyphagia, and body weight loss) and delayed the onset of insulin resistance in an STZ model [66], which probably occurred through improved glucose homeostasis. This evidence was supported by Palsamy et al., who in 2009 [114] showed decreased activity of key enzymes for gluconeogenesis by treating rats with mild diabetes (STZ-nicotinamide model) with a low dose (5 mg/kg) of resveratrol. Moreover, several in vitro studies have shown that resveratrol can increase glucose uptake by targeting insulin-affected cells (skeletal muscle, adipocytes and hepatocytes) [115,116,117,118,119], thereby improving the insulin signaling probably through improvement of insulin sensitivity in a SIRT1-dependent manner [120,121,122] or by other distinct mechanisms [66]. This stimulation of SIRT1 (a pivotal mediator of the metabolic effects of resveratrol) also may promote an increase of antioxidant enzymes (SOD, catalase, GPx and glutathione-*S*-transferase) in pancreatic β-cells and decrease the function of pro-inflammatory mediators (IL-6, NF-kB and COX-2) in many diabetic target tissues [119,123,124,125], which explains the relevant protective effects against apoptosis, neurodegeneration and cardiovascular complications [106,126,127]. Interestingly, resveratrol also seems to contribute to endothelial repair (which is an important tissue affected by chronic diabetes) through free-radical scavenging and/or restoration of eNOS functionality that culminates with increased bioavailability of NO [106,109,127,128] and consequently reduces diabetic complications. Recently, Neves et al. [129] showed another possible pathway of cellular protection through the regulation of cell membrane structure and fluidity (similar to cholesterol). In addition, it was observed that resveratrol might reduce endoplasmic reticulum stress by avoiding misglycosylation, depletion of calcium stores and DNA damage [127]. Therefore, resveratrol not only acts by glycemic control per se but also provides antioxidant and other pleiotropic effects [125,129,130].

Even though the preclinical evidence includes experimental evidence that clearly demonstrated that resveratrol has a significant antidiabetic effect in a wide dose range (0.1 to 1.500 mg/kg body weight), recommending resveratrol as a therapeutic supplement or treatment for diabetes patients is still controversial, and there is a similar controversy for quercetin [119,127,131,132]. This is a problem because it has generated serious doubts about the potential usefulness of these substances, particularly for dietary prevention strategies [133,134,135,136]. For instance, Thazhath et al. [137] have recently demonstrated that 1000 mg/day resveratrol in diet-controlled type-2 DM patients for five weeks did not change body weight, glycemic control or GLP-1 secretion. Similar data were also obtained by Poulsen et al. [132], who gave 1500 mg/day of resveratrol for four weeks to obese patients and found no effects on metabolic biomarkers, blood pressure or resting energy expenditure. These apparent unsuccessful studies also may be explained by variability between volunteers (age, body weight, nutrition, severity of diabetes) and/or duration of treatments [119]. In agreement with this hypothesis, another study of patients with metabolic syndrome treated the patients with 1500 mg/day of resveratrol for 90 days (~13 weeks) and revealed a significant reduction in body weight and insulin secretion [137]. Additionally, Goh et al. [138] showed improvement of insulin sensitivity via SIRT1 through 3000 mg of resveratrol for 12 weeks in type-2 diabetic patients. The advantage of this regulation is the promotion of survival and longevity, associated with telomere length [7]. Even for a shorter period of time, it was shown that resveratrol (1000 mg daily in first week followed by 2000 mg daily in second week) was able to reduce hepatic and intestinal lipoprotein production [139]. It is important to consider that although there are several investigations on the tolerability of resveratrol in humans, we cannot ignore the fact that studies about long-term resveratrol toxicity (or analogues such as pterostilbene) are still needed.

3.1.3. Silymarin

Silymarin is a dry flavonoid mixture extracted after processing the seeds of *Silybum marium* with ethanol, methanol, and acetone [140], which contains seven major components: taxifolin (the most effective antioxidant), silychristin, silydianin, silybin A, silybin B, isosilybin A and isosilybin B [141,142]. Although silymarin has mainly been used to treat liver diseases [143], its antidiabetic activity was recently reported and is associated with an anti-glycation profile [144,145], inhibition of aldose reductase [143], partial agonist activity in peroxisome proliferator-activated receptor γ (PPARγ) [143], antioxidant capacity and radical scavenging [144,146]. All these characteristics make silymarin an interesting candidate for the prevention and treatment of diabetic complications, which has recently been demonstrated both in experimental models and in humans (the same as for quercetin and resveratrol).

In 2013, Sheela et al. [146] demonstrated more fully that silymarin (60 and 120 mg/kg/day, i.m., for eight weeks) was able of reduce the classical signs of DM and attenuate the progression of the disease in a STZ-nicotinamide-induced nephropathy model (although the possible pathways were not investigated). However, in parallel, an in vitro study revealed that podocytes exposed to high glucose restored the $\cdot O{-}2$production and NADPH oxidase activity to basal levels through 10 μM of isolated compound silybin. In the same paper, Khazim et al. [147] obtained similar results in an in vivo experiment using 100 mg/kg/day of same substance (i.p., six weeks) in an advanced new model of diabetic nephropathy (OVE26 mice) with an additional reduction in albuminuria. These data also corroborated the findings of Vessal et al. [148], who used silymarin (100 mg/kg/day, i.p., for four weeks) in an STZ-rat model to obtain a reduction in kidney lipid peroxidation and increase the activity of catalase and GPx under hyperglycemia conditions.

Further studies are necessary to explore the other cytoprotective effects of silymarin. For example, Tuorkey et al. [140] recently showed that this flavonoid mixture (120 mg/kg, i.p., for 10 days) could protect cardiomyocytes against apoptosis in diabetic (alloxan) rats via restoration of caspase-3 and Bcl-2 to control levels. For neuroprotection, silymarin (100 mg/kg/day for eight weeks) ameliorated hyperalgesia and sciatic motor nerve conduction velocity in STZ-diabetic neuropathic rat by reducing lipoperoxidation and increasing SOD activity [149]. Moreover, silibinin in *db/db* mice provided DNA protection and reduced oxidative stress in a brain-specific area in rodents [150]. Therefore, these preliminary studies also revealed the potential of silymarin as a valid tool to counteract oxidative stress in the central nervous system under diabetic conditions [151].

Although there are still only a few clinical studies with silymarin, the results have reflected the findings of the laboratory studies. Approximately two decades ago, a study with silymarin supplementation (600 mg/day for 12 months) was conducted in insulin-treated diabetics with alcoholic cirrhosis, and the study had encouraging results. Beyond the antioxidant effects, there was a reduction of insulin resistance, a decrease in endogenous insulin hypersecretion and a reduced need for exogenous insulin administration [152]. Corroborating this observation, 10 years later, 25 diabetic (but non-cirrhotic) patients treated with silymarin (600 mg/day, for 16 weeks) showed reductions in glycemia, glycated hemoglobin, and an improved lipid profile in liver biomarkers [153]. In addition, Hussain et al. [154] showed that silymarin (200 mg/day, for 12 weeks) could be an important adjuvant for improving the glycemic control target by increasing insulin sensitivity in peripheral tissues through sulfonylureas (glibenclamide). This finding was recently corroborated by a study in which type 2 DM patients aged 25–50 years old who were on stable medications were supplemented with silymarin (420 mg/day, for six weeks). These patients also showed improvements in some antioxidant indices (SOD, GPx and total antioxidant capacity) as well as decreased lipid peroxidation besides hs-CRP levels without reporting any adverse effects of silymarin treatment [155]. Based on these results, more studies are still needed for the evaluation of the possible synergistic effects of silymarin with other antidiabetic classes (e.g., biguanides/metformin, dipeptidyl peptidase-4 inhibitors/sitagliptin; glucagon-like peptide-1 analogues/liraglutide; sodium-glucose cotransporter 2 inhibitors/dapagliflozin). Interestingly, silymarin has also been demonstrated to be an alternative treatment for diabetic renal patients who are using the maximum doses of angiotensin-converting enzyme (ACE) inhibitors or AT1 antagonists; even after a short duration treatment with silymarin (420 mg/day, for 12 weeks), these patients showed a reduction of 50% in albuminuria, urinary TNFα levels besides serum and urinary lipid peroxidation [156,157], which reflects a potential nephroprotective activity.

Although clinical trials with these polyphenols are still insufficient to define the optimal doses for treatment, the dosing range of silymarin used for diabetic patients is the closest to the ideal (when compared to diverse doses of resveratrol and quercetin) because it has clinically been investigated in several studies since the 1970s [143,158] compared to quercetin in 1995 [159] and resveratrol in 2007 [160]. The literature still describes that the therapeutic dose for the benefits of silymarin ranges between 210–800 mg/day, and silymarin appears to be safe and well tolerated up to 2100 mg/day [161], which reflects a wide therapeutic index [162]. Another additional advantage offered by silymarin in DM compared to other isolated polyphenols might be related to the relevance of silymarin use in combination with other antioxidants, which prevents individual antioxidant vulnerability and promotes synergistic effects against the chronic oxidative stress induced by diabetes [15].

4. BENEFICIAL EFFECTS OF PROBIOTICS: HIGHLIGHTS OF TREATMENTS WITH KEFIR

In recent years, besides traditional drug treatments for DM, many efforts have been made in complementary or adjuvant therapy for the treatment of this complex disease [163]. Inadequate human dietary changes have been thought to be of major importance for the increased prevalence of DM. Overall, DM is estimated to afflict 350 million people globally and cost hundreds of billions of dollars annually [1,2]. Millions of cases could be prevented by including dietary modification to functional nutrition, which is a primary option for preventing metabolic disturbances and for reducing undesirable outcomes in DM [164,165]. Intestinal microbiota is a relevant therapeutic source for treatment of different diseases. Although there have been proposed different strategies including pre/probiotics and fecal microbiota transplantation interventions [166], in this section we review the main experimental and clinical studies that have focused on the beneficial effects of dairy cultured probiotics (live microorganisms) as coadjuvants in the prevention/treatment of this metabolic disorder.

Although many studies have been focused on the identification and use of innately occurring dairy components for the prevention and correction of metabolic dysfunctions accompanying DM [167], there is a growing and remarkable body of research showing the beneficial effects of non-innately cultured probiotics or bioactive end products [168]. These health benefits are achieved by stimulating beneficial gastrointestinal indigenous microflora proliferation [169]. Fermented milk kefir, which originated in the Northern Caucasus Mountains, is now commercially available in some countries, and in others it has been domestically produced and is spreading hand-to-hand [170]. The probiotic kefir has been associated with a range of health benefits, which have been reviewed by others [171], and its continuous intake has been shown to modulate complex cardiovascular and metabolic dysfunctions, including arterial hypertension [172] and DM [164].

In contrast with non-cultured dairy products, kefir grains are small clusters of microorganisms held together by an exopolysaccharide matrix named kefiran, which is the main functional component of the beverage [169,173,174,175]. Kefir grains are produced during the fermentation of milk by a complex symbiotic mixture of yeasts as well as lactic and acetic acid bacteria [170,173,174,176]. The dominating populations of bacterial genera in cultured kefir are *Lactobacillus*, *Lactococcus* and *Streptococcus* [169].

Rats administered with STZ (type 1 DM) or fed a hypercaloric diet (type 2 DM) are experimental models of DM [177]. In STZ-induced DM, it has been shown that daily administration of kefir caused an improvement in the increased levels of glycemia and glucose tolerance compared to conventional fermented milk [168,178,179]. Interestingly, kefiran, which is an exopolysaccharide isolated from kefir grains, has been shown to decrease blood pressure and blood glucose in animal models of hypertension [180] and an animal model of intolerance to glucose overload [181]. Kefiran-kefir also enhanced glucose uptake into insulin-responsive muscle cells, probably through activation of PI 3-kinases or another related signaling pathway [182]. Kefir also decreased polyuria, polydipsia and polyphagia [178]. In this model of DM, it has also been shown that administration of kefir results in a decrease in total cholesterol, triglycerides, LDL-cholesterol and an increase of HDL-cholesterol levels [179]. Moreover, kefir treatment of type 1 DM rats led to a decrease in the pro-inflammatory cytokines IL-1 and IL-6 as well as an increase of anti-inflammatory IL-10 compared to control groups [167]. These studies support the concept that kefir can be useful as a complementary or adjuvant therapy for better control of glycemia. However, the mechanisms by which probiotic kefir modulate hyperglycemia are not fully understood.

The beneficial effects of cultured probiotics have also been demonstrated in experimental type 2 DM. Administration of a strain of the probiotic microorganism *Lactococcus lactis* in rats with type 2 DM induced by a high-fructose diet resulted in significantly lower fasting blood glucose, HbA1c, insulin, free fatty acids and triglyceride levels than untreated DM rats [183]. By reducing the hyperglycemia, insulin resistance and hyperlipidemia, kefir actions were reflected in amelioration of the intracellular metabolic imbalance. In untreated DM animals, the excessive production of ROS overwhelmed the endogenous antioxidant defenses and resulted in oxidative stress, but this sequence of events can be attenuated through kefir treatment [183].

The use of antioxidant agents for therapeutic approaches in DM has been an attractive focus [184,185]. Accordingly, Friques et al. [172] observed through flow cytometry assays that kefir attenuated the endothelial dysfunction of spontaneously hypertensive rats by reducing the production of ·O−2, $ONOO^-$ and H_2O_2. Augmented oxidative stress has also been shown to play a role in DM [185,186,187,188] and arterial hypertension [172]. First, it was shown that kefir reduced the intracellular levels of ROS in insulin-responsive muscle cells [182]. Second, the antioxidative effects of kefir in STZ-induced DM led to an improvement in the ROS levels [178,179]. The antioxidative effect seems to be the main mechanism by which kefir reduced proteinuria and azotemia, which consequently improved the progression of renal injury in type 1 DM rats [178]. These results indicated that kefir treatment may exert beneficial effects on the oxidative stress that accompanies DM and suggests it could be used as a non-pharmacological adjuvant to delay the progression of this disease [178].

Recently, our laboratory has assessed the actions of kefir on cardiac dysautonomia and impaired baroreflex control of cardiovascular function in SHR [189]. The main action of kefir on cardiac autonomic imbalance and impaired baroreflex appears to be through attenuation of the cardiac and vascular sympathetic hyperactivity as well as augmenting cardiac parasympathetic hypoactivity [189]. Some of these effects are also expected to occur in animal models of diabetes because they present similar disturbances in the cardiovascular system [190]. For example, in the model of type 1 DM, an important imbalance of the cardiac autonomic nerves, located at both tissues and molecular pathways, has been observed. Recently, in the first 10 weeks of experimental DM, a marked cardiac dysfunction and an incomplete recovery of the cardioinhibitory vagal nerves, accompanied by a remodeling process in the stimulatory noradrenergic nerves [191], have been shown.

Most clinical studies, including trials, have been conducted with patients who have type 2 DM, and most were treated with probiotic fermented milk kefir containing one, two or multi-strains of bacteria, such as*Lactobacillus casei*, *L. acidophilus*, *L. bulgaricus*, *Streptococcus thermophiles* and *Bifidobacterium lactis* [169]. The kefir effects observed on primary outcomes included decreased fasting blood glucose and HbA1c levels as well as improved insulin resistance [166,192,193,194]. The latter effect could be a consequence of a kefir-induced reduction in the inflammatory response [192]. In agreement with these results, it has been shown that kefir reduced pro-inflammatory cytokines, including TNFα, in DM [168,195]. The secondary outcomes included an improved lipid profile, blood pressure and hs-CRP, but kefir administration did not significantly change these parameters [191]. In contrast with experimental studies, it is still not clear whether kefir has beneficial effects on the lipid profile. An important finding after comparing the quantity of*Lactobacillus* and *Bifidobacterium* before and after the intervention was that there was successful passage of the probiotic supplement through the gastrointestinal tract [166,196]. The above studies support the concept that kefir can be useful as a complementary or adjuvant therapy for a better control of glycemia, insulin resistance and kidney function in diabetic individuals.

An important characteristic of DM is endothelial dysfunction, which has been shown in experimental and clinical studies [197]. Our laboratory has demonstrated that kefir administered for at least 60 days in spontaneously hypertensive rats resulted in a significant attenuation of endothelial dysfunction [172]. Therefore, there is a need for more studies to test the hypothesis that kefir administration also exhibits benefits against this abnormality.

A limitation in the therapeutic use of the probiotic kefir in DM is that this is a heterogeneous and a multiple systems-derived disease that results in multiple complications. Therefore, it makes it hard to prevent or to treat DM with traditional medicine and functional nutrition, especially when treating different people with different needs. However, there is evidence that kefir has great potential to become an adjuvant alternative for control of glycemia and other diabetes-related outcomes. Further studies are needed not only to clarify the mechanisms behind the effects of kefir but also to determine which microorganisms in kefir are responsible for its benefits.

5. BENEFICIAL EFFECTS OF PHOSPHODIESTERASE INHIBITORS IN DIABETES MELLITUS: NEW INSIGHTS

Several investigations have demonstrated that increased cyclic GMP (cGMP) signaling might be an important strategy for reducing the progression of diabetes through multiple pathways [198]. Concerning glycemic control, even if an increase in intracellular calcium is the principal signal that activates insulin exocytosis, cGMP may also participate through distinct signals [199,200] and potentiating the stimulation of glucose [201,202,203]. In parallel, some in vitro studies have shown that cGMP may enhance insulin sensitivity in target organs (muscle and adipocytes) by stimulating GLUT4 recruitment into the plasma membrane [204,205,206]. In addition, because NO/cGMP signaling is fundamental to vascular protection [207,208,209], the increment of this pathway may be an attractive strategy to attenuate endothelial dysfunction development in diabetic complications, which is as major cause of disability and death in patients with DM [4,44].

Pharmacological strategies to increase cGMP signaling may be achieved through two main routes: (1) direct activation of guanylate cyclase directly by augmentation of NO; and/or (2) decreasing cGMP hydrolysis through PDE5 inhibitors (sildenafil/Viagra™, vardenafil/Levitra™, tadalafil/Cialis™, avanafil/Stendra™), which is currently considered an important tool to treat endothelial dysfunction in DM [209,210,211]. Because PDE5 is expressed in some tissues of the body (e.g., corpus cavernosum, platelets, systemic arteries and veins) [209,212], the diminished NO bioavailability in diabetic vasculature can be partially compensated through PDE5 inhibitors. Interestingly, although some recent studies demonstrated that association with antioxidants (e.g., polyphenols or vitamin E) potentiates vascular protection [213,214], sildenafil may also provide intrinsic antioxidant effects through NADPH oxidase activity inhibition [215]. This evidence was complemented by our research in various models of hypertension, nephropathy or atherosclerosis and demonstrated protective effects for endothelial, cardiac and kidney functions in physiological parameters, such as morphological analyses (Figure 1) [209,212,216,217,218,219]. Therefore, our studies and other experimental evidence support the clinical findings of improvement in endothelial function, reduction of markers of vascular inflammation, and beneficial effects for conditions beyond erectile dysfunction [220,221,222,223,224].

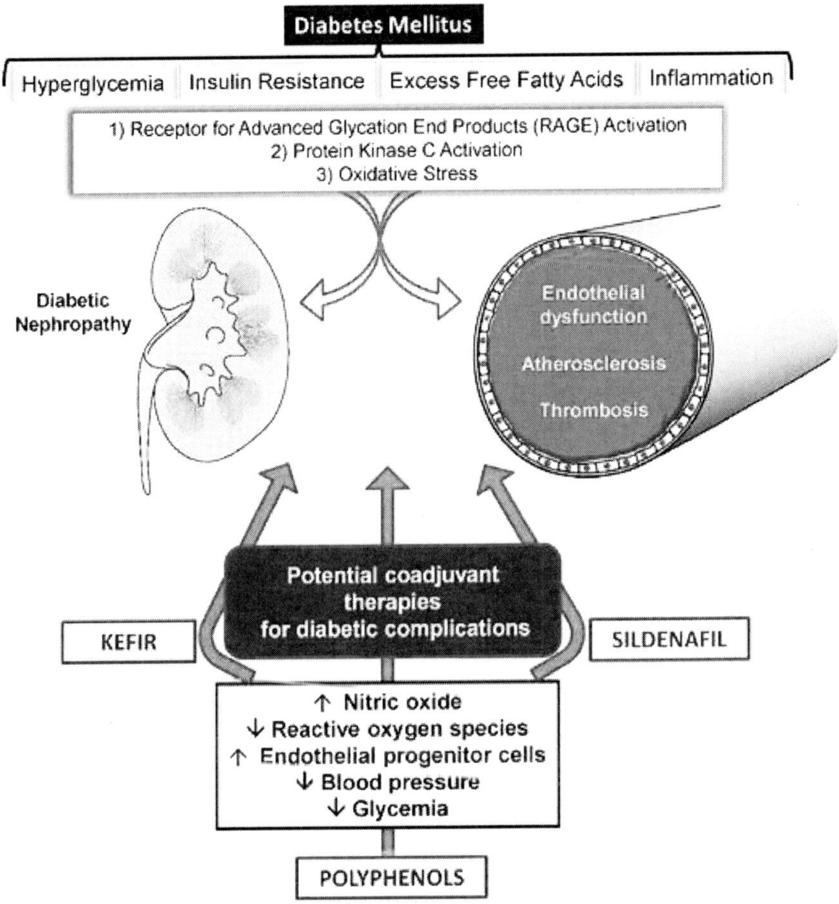

Figure 1. Schematic representation of metabolic complications of diabetes mellitus in two important target organs, and the main effects exhibited by three important coadjuvants currently under investigation with the aim of preventing and treating this complex disease. Arrows up (↑): increase; arrows down (↓): decrease.

In relation to glycemic control, PDE5 inhibitors may have improved insulin sensitivity both in isolated human endothelial cells [225] and in high fat-fed mice [226], which corroborates the results related to cGMP that were previously discussed. Moreover, recent findings showed that chronic treatment with tadalafil reduced inflammatory cytokines, infarct size and oxidative stress in the hearts of diabetic mice by reducing NADPH oxidase activity, oxidized glutathione and lipid peroxidation [227,228]. These results show a potential role for PDE5 inhibitors in treating diabetes-related cardiac and inflammatory complications. Interestingly, clinical investigations confirmed that sildenafil could improve insulin sensitivity in addition to fibrinolytic balance and albuminuria in hyperglycemic patients [198,229]. These studies suggest that PDE inhibitors can be effective (and safely used) in patients with multiple comorbidities and therapies, except for patients treated with continuous nitrates [209,223,230].

6. CONCLUSIONS

In the present review, besides showing the importance of lifestyle modification, diet and weight control to prevent DM and its aggravation, we highlight recent experimental and clinical evidences of potential coadjuvants in the management of DM without compromising the function of β-cells via hyperinsulinism. Here, we have discussed the substances that exhibit direct/indirect or pleiotropic effects on glycemic control in DM and on oxidative stress that is one of the most contributors to the complications of this disease by affecting the different target organs. Among several options, we have highlighted new promising therapeutic coadjuvants, including the cultured probiotic microorganisms (such as kefir grains) and the PDE5 inhibitors (such as sildenafil), which besides the reduction of hyperglycemia and ameliorate insulin resistance, they have been shown to reduce the oxidative stress and improved the endothelial dysfunction in the systemic vascular circulation. In the near future, there are expected experimental studies designed to clear the intracellular pathways involving those coadjuvants discussed in this review as well as promoting clinical trials that may contribute to new strategies against the harmful effects of diabetic complications.

ACKNOWLEDGMENTS

Elisardo Corral Vasquez is supported by National Council for the Development of Science and Technology (CNPq) (Grant 303001/2015-1) and State Foundation for Science and Technology (Fapes) (Grant Universal 2014 Proc 67597483). Silvana S. Meyrelles is supported by CNPq (307584/2015-1). Bianca P. Campagnaro is supported by CNPq (445736/2014-3). Thiago Melo C. Pereira is supported by CNPq (445080/2014-0).

AUTHOR CONTRIBUTIONS

Elisardo Corral Vasquez supervised the analysis of publication data, and edited and approved the final version of this review. The contribution of the collaborators for each section is as follows. Section 1: Marcelo Perim Baldo and Silvana Santos Meyrelles; Section 2: Marcella Lima Porto and Agata Lages Gava; Section 3: Thiago Melo Costa Pereira and Bianca Prandi Campagnaro; Section 4: Fabio Silva Pimenta and Silvana Santos Meyrelles; Section 5: Thiago Melo Costa Pereira and Elisardo Corral Vasquez and creation of Figure 1: Thiago Melo Costa Pereira and Elisardo Corral Vasquez.

CONFLICTS OF INTEREST

The authors declare no conflict of interest.

REFERENCES

1. Garcia-Perez, L.E.; Alvarez, M.; Dilla, T.; Gil-Guillen, V.; Orozco-Beltran, D. Adherence to therapies in patients with type 2 diabetes. Diabetes Ther. 2013, 4, 175–194.

2. Cheung, B.M.; Ong, K.L.; Cherny, S.S.; Sham, P.C.; Tso, A.W.; Lam, K.S. Diabetes prevalence and therapeutic target achievement in the United States, 1999 to 2006. Am. J. Med. 2009, 122, 443–453.

3. Gu, K.; Cowie, C.C.; Harris, M.I. Mortality in adults with and without diabetes in a national cohort of the U.S. population, 1971–1993. Diabetes Care 1998, 21, 1138–1145.

4. Potenza, M.A.; Gagliardi, S.; Nacci, C.; Carratu, M.R.; Montagnani, M. Endothelial dysfunction in diabetes: From mechanisms to therapeutic targets. Curr. Med. Chem. 2009, 16, 94–112.

5. Santi, D.; Giannetta, E.; Isidori, A.M.; Vitale, C.; Aversa, A.; Simoni, M. Therapy of endocrine disease. Effects of chronic use of phosphodiesterase inhibitors on endothelial markers in type 2 diabetes mellitus: A meta-analysis. Eur. J. Endocrinol. 2015, 172, R103–R114.

6. Ong, K.L.; Cheung, B.M.; Wong, L.Y.; Wat, N.M.; Tan, K.C.; Lam, K.S. Prevalence, treatment, and control of diagnosed diabetes in the U.S. National Health and Nutrition Examination Survey 1999–2004. Ann. Epidemiol. 2008, 18, 222–229.

7. Wegman, M.P.; Guo, M.H.; Bennion, D.M.; Shankar, M.N.; Chrzanowski, S.M.; Goldberg, L.A.; Xu, J.; Williams, T.A.; Lu, X.; Hsu, S.I.; et al. Practicality of intermittent fasting in humans and its effect on oxidative stress and genes related to aging and metabolism. Rejuvenation Res. 2015, 18, 162–172.

8. Wang, Y. Molecular Links between Caloric Restriction and Sir2/SIRT1 Activation. Diabetes Metab. J.2014, 38, 321–329.

9. Kuecker, C.M.; Vivian, E.M. Patient considerations in type 2 diabetes—Role of combination dapagliflozin-metformin XR. Diabetes Metab. Syndr. Obes. 2016, 9, 25–35.

10. Sharma, B.R.; Kim, H.J.; Rhyu, D.Y. Caulerpa lentillifera extract ameliorates insulin resistance and regulates glucose metabolism in C57BL/KsJ-db/db mice via PI3K/AKT signaling pathway in myocytes.J. Transl. Med. 2015, 13, 62.

11. Shera, A.S.; Jawad, F.; Maqsood, A.; Jamal, S.; Azfar, M.; Ahmed, U. Prevalence of chronic complications and associated factors in type 2 diabetes. J. Pak. Med. Assoc. 2004, 54, 54–59.

12. Siddiqui, F.J.; Avan, B.I.; Mahmud, S.; Nanan, D.J.; Jabbar, A.; Assam, P.N. Uncontrolled diabetes mellitus: Prevalence and risk factors among people with type 2 diabetes mellitus in an Urban District of Karachi, Pakistan. Diabetes Res. Clin. Pract. 2015, 107, 148–156.

13. Hamwi, G.J.; Garcia, O.; Kruger, F.A.; Gwinup, G.; Cornwell, D.G. Hyperlipidemia in uncontrolled diabetes. Metabolism 1962, 11, 850–862.

14. Moinat, P.; Nichols, N.; Tuller, E.F. Changes in serum proteins and polysaccharides in rats with uncontrolled diabetes. Diabetes 1956, 5, 468–474.

15. Litchfield, J.A. Biochemical changes in skeletal muscle in patients with uncontrolled diabetes mellitus.Diabetes 1959, 8, 257–260.

16. Afsharian, S.; Akbarpour, S.; Abdi, H.; Sheikholeslami, F.; Moeini, A.S.; Khalili, D.; Momenan, A.A.; Azizi, F.; Hadaegh, F. Risk factors for cardiovascular disease and mortality events in adults with type 2 diabetes: A 10 year follow-up: Tehran lipid and glucose study. Diabetes Metab. Res. Rev. 2016.

17. Mulnier, H.E.; Seaman, H.E.; Raleigh, V.S.; Soedamah-Muthu, S.S.; Colhoun, H.M.; Lawrenson, R.A.; de Vries, C.S. Risk of myocardial infarction in men and women with type 2 diabetes in the UK: A cohort study using the General Practice Research Database. Diabetologia 2008, 51, 1639–1645.

18. An, Y.; Zhang, P.; Wang, J.; Gong, Q.; Gregg, E.W.; Yang, W.; Li, H.; Zhang, B.; Shuai, Y.; Chen, Y.; et al. Cardiovascular and all-cause mortality over a 23-year period among chinese with newly diagnosed diabetes in the Da Qing IGT and Diabetes Study. Diabetes Care 2015, 38, 1365–1371.

19. Peters, S.A.; Huxley, R.R.; Woodward, M. Diabetes as a risk factor for stroke in women compared with men: A systematic review and meta-analysis of 64 cohorts, including 775,385 individuals and 12,539 strokes. Lancet 2014, 383, 1973–1980.

20. Lee, M.; Saver, J.L.; Hong, K.S.; Song, S.; Chang, K.H.; Ovbiagele, B. Effect of pre-diabetes on future risk of stroke: Meta-analysis. BMJ 2012, 344.

21. Collins, A.J.; Foley, R.N.; Herzog, C.; Chavers, B.; Gilbertson, D.; Ishani, A.; Kasiske, B.; Liu, J.; Mau, L.W.; McBean, M.; et al. US renal data system 2010 annual data report. Am. J. Kidney Dis. 2011, 57, e1–e526.

22. Radbill, B.; Murphy, B.; LeRoith, D. Rationale and strategies for early detection and management of diabetic kidney disease. Mayo Clin. Proc. 2008, 83, 1373–1381.

23. de Boer, I.H.; Rue, T.C.; Hall, Y.N.; Heagerty, P.J.; Weiss, N.S.; Himmelfarb, J. Temporal trends in the prevalence of diabetic kidney disease in the United States. JAMA 2011, 305, 2532–2539.

24. Salinero-Fort, M.Á.; San Andrés-Rebollo, F.J.; de Burgos-Lunar, C.; Abánades-Herranz, J.C.; Carrillo-de-Santa-Pau, E.; Chico-Moraleja, R.M.; Jiménez-García, R.; López-de-Andrés, A.; Gómez-Campelo, P. Cardiovascular and all-cause mortality in patients with type 2 diabetes mellitus in the MADIABETES Cohort Study: Association with chronic kidney disease. J. Diabetes Complic. 2016, 30, 227–236.

25. Brownlee, M. The pathobiology of diabetic complications: A unifying mechanism. Diabetes 2005, 54, 1615–1625.

26. Kitabchi, A.E.; Umpierrez, G.E.; Miles, J.M.; Fisher, J.N. Hyperglycemic crises in adult patients with diabetes. Diabetes Care 2009, 32, 1335–1343.

27. Kitabchi, A.E.; Nyenwe, E.A. Hyperglycemic crises in diabetes mellitus: Diabetic ketoacidosis and hyperglycemic hyperosmolar state. Endocrinol. Metab. Clin. N. Am. 2006, 35, 725–751.

28. Davis, S.N.; Umpierrez, G.E. Diabetic ketoacidosis in type 2 diabetes mellitus-pathophysiology and clinical presentation. Nat. Clin. Pract. Endocrinol. Metab. 2007, 3, 730–731.

29. Lewko, B.; Stepinski, J. Hyperglycemia and mechanical stress: Targeting the renal podocyte. J. Cell. Physiol. 2009, 221, 288–295.

30. Di Mario, U.; Pugliese, G. 15th Golgi lecture: From hyperglycaemia to the dysregulation of vascular remodelling in diabetes. Diabetologia 2001, 44, 674–692.

31. Beisswenger, P.J.; Howell, S.K.; Nelson, R.G.; Mauer, M.; Szwergold, B.S. α-Oxoaldehyde metabolism and diabetic complications. Biochem. Soc. Trans. 2003, 31, 1358–1363.

32. Nishikawa, T.; Edelstein, D.; Du, X.L.; Yamagishi, S.; Matsumura, T.; Kaneda, Y.; Yorek, M.A.; Beebe, D.; Oates, P.J.; Hammes, H.P.; et al. Normalizing mitochondrial superoxide production blocks three pathways of hyperglycaemic damage. Nature 2000, 404, 787–790.

33. Lee, H.B.; Yu, M.R.; Yang, Y.; Jiang, Z.; Ha, H. Reactive oxygen species-regulated signaling pathways in diabetic nephropathy. J. Am. Soc. Nephrol. 2003, 14, S241–S245.

34. Dunlop, M. Aldose reductase and the role of the polyol pathway in diabetic nephropathy. Kidney Int. Suppl. 2000, 77, S3–S12.

35. Tomlinson, D.R.; Gardiner, N.J. Glucose neurotoxicity. Nat. Rev. Neurosci. 2008, 9, 36–45.

36. Luo, X.; Wu, J.; Jing, S.; Yan, L.J. Hyperglycemic stress and carbon stress in diabetic glucotoxicity.Aging Dis. 2016, 7, 90–110.

37. Ying, W. NAD+/NADH and NADP+/NADPH in cellular functions and cell death: Regulation and biological consequences. Antioxid. Redox Signal. 2008, 10, 179–206.

38. Dolle, C.; Rack, J.G.; Ziegler, M. NAD and ADP-ribose metabolism in mitochondria. FEBS J. 2013, 280, 3530–3541.

39. Du, X.L.; Edelstein, D.; Rossetti, L.; Fantus, I.G.; Goldberg, H.; Ziyadeh, F.; Wu, J.; Brownlee, M. Hyperglycemia-induced mitochondrial superoxide overproduction activates the hexosamine pathway and induces plasminogen activator inhibitor-1 expression by increasing Sp1 glycosylation. Proc. Natl. Acad. Sci. USA 2000, 97, 12222–12226.

40. Porto, M.L.; Rodrigues, B.P.; Menezes, T.N.; Ceschim, S.L.; Casarini, D.E.; Gava, A.L.; Pereira, T.M.; Vasquez, E.C.; Campagnaro, B.P.; Meyrelles, S.S. Reactive oxygen species contribute to dysfunction of bone marrow hematopoietic stem cells in aged C57BL/6 J mice. J. Biomed. Sci. 2015, 22, 97.

41. Nakagami, H.; Morishita, R.; Yamamoto, K.; Yoshimura, S.I.; Taniyama, Y.; Aoki, M.; Matsubara, H.; Kim, S.; Kaneda, Y.; Ogihara, T. Phosphorylation of p38 mitogen-activated protein kinase downstream of bax-caspase-3 pathway leads to cell death induced by high D-glucose in human endothelial cells.Diabetes 2001, 50, 1472–1481.

42. Nakagami, H.; Kaneda, Y.; Ogihara, T.; Morishita, R. Endothelial dysfunction in hyperglycemia as a trigger of atherosclerosis. Curr. Diabetes Rev. 2005, 1, 59–63.

43. Wei, W.; Liu, Q.; Tan, Y.; Liu, L.; Li, X.; Cai, L. Oxidative stress, diabetes, and diabetic complications.Hemoglobin 2009, 33, 370–377.

44. Domingueti, C.P.; Dusse, L.M.; Carvalho, M.D.; de Sousa, L.P.; Gomes, K.B.; Fernandes, A.P. Diabetes mellitus: The linkage between oxidative stress, inflammation, hypercoagulability and vascular complications. J. Diabetes Complic. 2016, 30, 738–745.

45. Gomes, I.B.; Porto, M.L.; Santos, M.C.; Campagnaro, B.P.; Pereira, T.M.; Meyrelles, S.S.; Vasquez, E.C. Renoprotective, anti-oxidative and anti-apoptotic effects of oral low-dose quercetin in the C57BL/6J model of diabetic nephropathy. Lipids Health Dis. 2014, 6, 184.

46. Gomes, I.B.; Porto, M.L.; Santos, M.C.; Campagnaro, B.P.; Gava, A.L.; Meyrelles, S.S.; Pereira, T.M.; Vasquez, E.C. The protective effects of oral low-dose quercetin on diabetic nephropathy in hypercholesterolemic mice. Front. Physiol. 2015, 6, 247.

47. Holmström, K.M.; Finkel, T. Cellular mechanisms and physiological consequences of redox-dependent signaling. Nat. Rev. Mol. Cell Biol. 2014, 15, 411–421.

48. Kayama, Y.; Raaz, U.; Jagger, A.; Adam, M.; Schellinger, I.N.; Sakamoto, M.; Suzuki, H.; Toyama, K.; Spin, J.M.; Tsao, P.S. Diabetic cardiovascular disease induced by oxidative stress. Int. J. Mol. Sci. 2015,16, 25234–25263.

49. Münzel, T.; Gori, T.; Bruno, R.M.; Taddei, S. Is oxidative stress a therapeutic target in cardiovascular disease? Eur. Heart J. 2010, 31, 2741–2748.

50. Ceriello, A.; Testa, R.; Genovese, S. Clinical implications of oxidative stress and potential role of natural antioxidants in diabetic vascular complications. Nutr. Metab. Cardiovasc. Dis. 2016, 26, 285–292.

51. Ide, T.; Tsutsui, H.; Kinugawa, S.; Utsumi, H.; Kang, D.; Hattori, N.; Uchida, K.; Arimura, K.; Egashira, K.; Takeshita, A. Mitochondrial electron transport complex I is a potential source of oxygen free radicals in the failing myocardium. Circ. Res 1999, 85, 357–363.

52. Selemidis, S.; Sobey, C.G.; Wingler, K.; Schmidt, H.H.; Drummond, G.R. NADPH oxidases in the vasculature: Molecular features, roles in disease and pharmacological inhibition. Pharmacol. Ther.2008, 120, 254–291.

53. Zhou, G.; Li, X.; Hein, D.W.; Xiang, X.; Marshall, J.P.; Prabhu, S.D.; Cai, L. Metallothionein suppresses angiotensin II-induced nicotinamide adenine dinucleotide phosphate oxidase activation, nitrosative stress, apoptosis, and pathological remodeling in the diabetic heart. J. Am. Coll. Cardiol. 2008, 52, 655–666.

54. Brownlee, M. Biochemistry and molecular cell biology of diabetic complications. Nature 2001, 414, 813–820.

55. Tan, S.M.; de Haan, J.B. Combating oxidative stress in diabetic complications with Nrf2 activators: How much is too much? Redox Rep. 2014, 19, 107–117.

56. Xu, X.; Luo, P.; Wang, Y.; Cui, Y.; Miao, L. Nuclear factor (erythroid-derived 2)-like 2 (NFE2L2) is a novel therapeutic target for diabetic complications. J. Int. Med. Res. 2013, 41, 13–19.

57. Murali, R.; Karthikeyan, A.; Saravanan, R. Protective effects of D-limonene on lipid peroxidation and antioxidant enzymes in streptozotocin-induced diabetic rats. Basic Clin. Pharmacol. Toxicol. 2013, 112, 175–181.

58. Ghattas, M.H.; Abo-Elmatty, D.M. Association of polymorphic markers of the catalase and superoxide dismutase genes with type 2 diabetes mellitus. DNA Cell Biol. 2012, 31, 1598–1603.

59. Batinic-Haberle, I.; Reboucas, J.S.; Spasojevic, I. Superoxide dismutase mimics: Chemistry, pharmacology, and therapeutic potential. Antioxid. Redox Signal. 2010, 13, 877–918.

60. Soto-Urquieta, M.G.; López-Briones, S.; Pérez-Vázquez, V.; Saavedra-Molina, A.; González-Hernández, G.A.; Ramírez-Emiliano, J. Curcumin restores mitochondrial functions and decreases lipid peroxidation in liver and kidneys of diabetic db/db mice. Biol. Res. 2014, 47, 74.

61. Pitocco, D.; Tesauro, M.; Alessandro, R.; Ghirlanda, G.; Cardillo, C. Oxidative stress in diabetes: Implications for vascular and other complications. Int. J. Mol. Sci. 2013.

62. Liu, X.; Gan, W.; Zou, Y.; Yang, B.; Su, Z.; Deng, J.; Wang, L.; Cai, J. Elevated levels of urinary markers of oxidative DNA and RNA damage in type 2 diabetes with complications. Oxid. Med. Cell. Longev.2016, 2016, 4323198.

63. Palem, S.P.; Abraham, P. A study on the level of oxidative stress and inflammatory markers in type 2 diabetes mellitus patients with different treatment modalities. J. Clin. Diagn. Res. 2015.

64. Araki, E.; Nishikawa, T. Oxidative stress: A cause and therapeutic target of diabetic complications. J. Diabetes Investig. 2010, 1, 90–96.

65. Zatalia, S.R.; Sanusi, H. The role of antioxidants in the pathophysiology, complications, and management of diabetes mellitus. Acta Med. Indones 2013, 45, 141–147.

66. Su, H.C.; Hung, L.M.; Chen, J.K. Resveratrol, a red wine antioxidant, possesses an insulin-like effect in streptozotocin-induced diabetic rats. Am. J. Physiol. Endocrinol. Metab. 2006, 290, E1339–E1346.

67. Zhang, Z.; Li, Y.; Li, Y. Grape seed proanthocyanidin extracts prevent hyperglycemia-induced monocyte adhesion to aortic

endothelial cells and ameliorates vascular inflammation in high-carbohydrate/high-fat diet and streptozotocin-induced diabetic rats. Int. J. Food Sci. Nutr. 2015, 67, 524–534.

68. D'Andrea, G. Quercetin: A flavonol with multifaceted therapeutic applications? Fitoterapia 2015, 106, 256–271.

69. Liu, J.Y.; Chen, X.X.; Tang, S.C.; Sze, S.C.; Feng, Y.; Lee, K.F.; Zhang, K.Y. Chinese medicines in the treatment of experimental diabetic nephropathy. Chin. Med. 2016, 11, 6.

70. Okamoto, T. Safety of quercetin for clinical application (Review). Int. J. Mol. Med. 2005, 16, 275–278.

71. Varma, S.D.; Mikuni, I.; Kinoshita, J.H. Flavonoids as inhibitors of lens aldose reductase. Science 1975,188, 1215–1216.

72. Alam, M.M.; Meerza, D.; Naseem, I. Protective effect of quercetin on hyperglycemia, oxidative stress and DNA damage in alloxan induced type 2 diabetic mice. Life Sci. 2014, 109, 8–14.

73. Xu, M.; Hu, J.; Zhao, W.; Gao, X.; Jiang, C.; Liu, K.; Liu, B.; Huang, F. Quercetin differently regulates insulin-mediated glucose transporter 4 translocation under basal and inflammatory conditions in adipocytes. Mol. Nutr. Food Res. 2014, 58, 931–941.

74. Henagan, T.M.; Lenard, N.R.; Gettys, T.W.; Stewart, L.K. Dietary quercetin supplementation in mice increases skeletal muscle PGC1α expression, improves mitochondrial function and attenuates insulin resistance in a time-specific manner. PLoS ONE 2014, 9, e89365.

75. Eid, H.M.; Nachar, A.; Thong, F.; Sweeney, G.; Haddad, P.S. The molecular basis of the antidiabetic action of quercetin in cultured skeletal muscle cells and hepatocytes. Pharmacogn. Mag. 2015, 11, 74–81.

76. Kim, J.H.; Kang, M.J.; Choi, H.N.; Jeong, S.M.; Lee, Y.M.; Kim, J.I. Quercetin attenuates fasting and postprandial hyperglycemia in animal models of diabetes mellitus. Nutr. Res. Pract. 2011, 5, 107–111.

77. Kwon, O.; Eck, P.; Chen, S.; Corpe, C.P.; Lee, J.H.; Kruhlak, M.; Levine, M. Inhibition of the intestinal glucose transporter GLUT2 by flavonoids. FASEB J. 2007, 21, 366–377.

78. Mahesh, T.; Menon, V.P. Quercetin allievates oxidative stress in streptozotocin-induced diabetic rats.Phytother. Res. 2004, 18, 123–127.

79. Oršolić, N.; Gajski, G.; Garaj-Vrhovac, V.; Dikić, D.; Prskalo, Z.Š.; Sirovina, D. DNA-protective effects of quercetin or naringenin in alloxan-induced diabetic mice. Eur. J. Pharmacol. 2011, 656, 110–118.

80. Hollman, P.C.; van Trijp, J.M.; Buysman, M.N.; van der Gaag, M.S.; Mengelers, M.J.; de Vries, J.H.; Katan, M.B. Relative bioavailability of the antioxidant flavonoid quercetin from various foods in man.FEBS Lett. 1997, 418, 152–156.

81. De Boer, V.C.; Dihal, A.A.; van der Woude, H.; Arts, I.C.; Wolffram, S.; Alink, G.M.; Rietjens, I.M.; Keijer, J.; Hollman, P.C. Tissue distribution of quercetin in rats and pigs. J. Nutr. 2005, 135, 1718–1725.

82. Bakhshaeshi, M.; Khaki, A.; Fathiazad, F.; Khaki, A.A.; Ghadamkheir, E. Anti-oxidative role of quercetin derived from Allium cepa on aldehyde oxidase (OX-LDL) and hepatocytes apoptosis in streptozotocin-induced diabetic rat. Asian Pac. J. Trop. Biomed. 2012, 2, 528–531.

83. Dodda, D.; Ciddi, V. Plants used in the management of diabetic complications. Indian J. Pharm. Sci.2014, 76, 97–106.

84. Umathe, S.N.; Dixit, P.V.; Kumar, V.; Bansod, K.U.; Wanjari, M.M. Quercetin pretreatment increases the bioavailability of pioglitazone in rats: Involvement of CYP3A inhibition. Biochem. Pharmacol. 2008,75, 1670–1676.

85. Sanders, R.A.; Rauscher, F.M.; Watkins, J.B. Effects of quercetin on antioxidant defense in streptozotocin-induced diabetic rats. J. Biochem. Mol. Toxicol. 2001, 15, 143–149.

86. Elbe, H.; Esrefoglu, M.; Vardi, N.; Taslidere, E.; Ozerol, E.; Tanbek, K. Melatonin, quercetin and resveratrol attenuates oxidative hepatocellular injury in streptozotocin-induced diabetic rats. Hum. Exp. Toxicol. 2015, 34, 859–868.

87. Ortega, R.; García, N. The flavonoid quercetin induces changes in mitochondrial permeability by inhibiting adenine nucleotide translocase. J. Bioenerg. Biomembr. 2009, 41, 41–47.

88. Sivitz, W.I.; Yorek, M.A. Mitochondrial dysfunction in diabetes: From molecular mechanisms to functional significance and therapeutic opportunities. Antioxid. Redox Signal. 2010, 12, 537–577.

89. Kowluru, R.A.; Mishra, M. Oxidative stress, mitochondrial damage and diabetic retinopathy. Biochim. Biophys. Acta 2015, 1852, 2474–2483.

90. Gonzalez Suarez, M.L.; Thomas, D.B.; Barisoni, L.; Fornoni, A. Diabetic nephropathy: Is it time yet for routine kidney biopsy? World J. Diabetes 2013, 4, 245–255.

91. Kushiyama, A.; Tanaka, K.; Hara, S.; Kawazu, S. Linking uric acid metabolism to diabetic complications. World J. Diabetes 2014, 5, 787–795.

92. Kumar, B.; Gupta, S.K.; Nag, T.C.; Srivastava, S.; Saxena, R.; Jha, K.A.; Srinivasan, B.P. Retinal neuroprotective effects of

quercetin in streptozotocin-induced diabetic rats. Exp. Eye Res. 2014, 125, 193–202.

93. Mahmoud, M.F.; Hassan, N.A.; El Bassossy, H.M.; Fahmy, A. Quercetin protects against diabetes-induced exaggerated vasoconstriction in rats: Effect on low grade inflammation. PLoS ONE 2013, 8, e63784.

94. Zhang, W.; Wang, Y.; Yang, Z.; Qiu, J.; Ma, J.; Zhao, Z.; Bao, T. Antioxidant treatment with quercetin ameliorates erectile dysfunction in streptozotocin-induced diabetic rats. J. Biosci. Bioeng. 2011, 112, 215–218.

95. Anjaneyulu, M.; Chopra, K. Quercetin attenuates thermal hyperalgesia and cold allodynia in STZ-induced diabetic rats. Indian J. Exp. Biol. 2004, 42, 766–769.

96. Anjaneyulu, M.; Chopra, K. Quercetin, an anti-oxidant bioflavonoid, attenuates diabetic nephropathy in rats. Clin. Exp. Pharmacol. Physiol. 2004, 31, 244–248.

97. Chen, P.; Chen, J.; Zheng, Q.; Chen, W.; Wang, Y.; Xu, X. Pioglitazone, extract of compound Danshen dripping pill, and quercetin ameliorate diabetic nephropathy in diabetic rats. J. Endocrinol. Investig.2013, 36, 422–427.

98. Wang, C.; Pan, Y.; Zhang, Q.Y.; Wang, F.M.; Kong, L.D. Quercetin and allopurinol ameliorate kidney injury in STZ-treated rats with regulation of renal NLRP3 inflammasome activation and lipid accumulation. PLoS ONE 2012, 7, e38285.

99. Jeong, S.M.; Kang, M.J.; Choi, H.N.; Kim, J.H.; Kim, J.I. Quercetin ameliorates hyperglycemia and dyslipidemia and improves antioxidant status in type 2 diabetic db/db mice. Nutr. Res Pract. 2012, 6, 201–207.

100. Shi, Y.; Williamson, G. Quercetin lowers plasma uric acid in pre-hyperuricaemic males: A randomised, double-blinded, placebo-controlled, cross-over trial. Br. J. Nutr. 2016, 115, 800–806.

101. Zahedi, M.; Ghiasvand, R.; Feizi, A.; Asgari, G.; Darvish, L. Does quercetin improve cardiovascular risk factors and inflammatory biomarkers in women with type 2 diabetes: A double-blind randomized controlled clinical trial. Int. J. Prev. Med. 2013, 4, 777–785.

102. Brüll, V.; Burak, C.; Stoffel-Wagner, B.; Wolffram, S.; Nickenig, G.; Müller, C.; Langguth, P.; Alteheld, B.; Fimmers, R.; Naaf, S.; et al. Effects of a quercetin-rich onion skin extract on 24 h ambulatory blood pressure and endothelial function in overweight-to-obese patients with (pre-)hypertension: A randomised double-blinded placebo-controlled cross-over trial. Br. J. Nutr. 2015, 114, 1263–1277.

103. Dower, J.I.; Geleijnse, J.M.; Gijsbers, L.; Zock, P.L.; Kromhout, D.; Hollman, P.C. Effects of the pure flavonoids epicatechin and quercetin on vascular function and cardiometabolic health: A randomized, double-blind, placebo-controlled, crossover trial. Am. J. Clin. Nutr. 2015, 101, 914–921.

104. Renaud, S.; de Lorgeril, M. Wine, alcohol, platelets, and the French paradox for coronary heart disease. Lancet 1992, 339, 1523–1526.

105. Nishizuka, T.; Fujita, Y.; Sato, Y.; Nakano, A.; Kakino, A.; Ohshima, S.; Kanda, T.; Yoshimoto, R.; Sawamura, T. Procyanidins are potent inhibitors of LOX-1: A new player in the French Paradox. Proc. Jpn. Acad. Ser. B Phys. Biol. Sci. 2011, 87, 104–113.

106. Bonnefont-Rousselot, D. Resveratrol and cardiovascular diseases. Nutrients 2016, 8, E250.

107. Lin, Y.L.; Chang, H.C.; Chen, T.L.; Chang, J.H.; Chiu, W.T.; Lin, J.W.; Chen, R.M. Resveratrol protects against oxidized LDL-induced breakage of the blood-brain barrier by lessening disruption of tight junctions and apoptotic insults to mouse cerebrovascular endothelial cells. J. Nutr. 2010, 140, 2187–2192.

108. Posadino, A.M.; Cossu, A.; Giordo, R.; Zinellu, A.; Sotgia, S.; Vardeu, A.; Hoa, P.T.; Nguyen le, H.V.; Carru, C.; Pintus, G. Resveratrol alters human endothelial cells redox state and causes mitochondrial-dependent cell death. Food Chem. Toxicol. 2015, 78, 10–16.

109. Zhang, H.; Zhang, J.; Ungvari, Z.; Zhang, C. Resveratrol improves endothelial function: Role of TNFα and vascular oxidative stress. Arterioscler. Thromb. Vasc. Biol. 2009, 29, 1164–1171.

110. Petit, M.; Guihot, A.L.; Grimaud, L.; Vessieres, E.; Toutain, B.; Menet, M.C.; Nivet-Antolne, V.; Arnal, J.F.; Loufrani, L.; Procaccio, V.; et al. Resveratrol improved flow-mediated outward arterial remodellng in ovaricctomized rats with hypertrophic effect at high dose. PLoS ONE 2016, 11, e0146148.

111. Hu, M.; Liu, B. Resveratrol via activation of LKB1-AMPK signaling suppresses oxidative stress to prevent endothelial dysfunction in diabetic mice. Clin. Exp. Hypertens. 2016, 5, 1–7.

112. Yan, C.; Xu, W.; Huang, Y.; Li, M.; Shen, Y.; You, H.; Liang, X. HRD1-mediated IGF-1R ubiquitination contributes to renal protection of resveratrol in db/db mice. Mol. Endocrinol. 2016.

113. Zhou, Y.; Chen, K.; He, L.; Xia, Y.; Dai, W.; Wang, F.; Li, J.; Li, S.; Liu, T.; Zheng, Y.; et al. The Protective effect of resveratrol on concanavalin-A-induced acute hepatic injury in mice. Gastroenterol. Res. Pract. 2015, 2015, 506390.

114. Palsamy, P.; Subramanian, S. Ameliorative potential of resveratrol on proinflammatory cytokines, hyperglycemia

mediated oxidative stress, and pancreatic β-cell dysfunction in streptozotocin-nicotinamide-induced diabetic rats. J. Cell. Physiol. 2010, 224, 423–432.

115. Breen, D.M.; Sanli, T.; Giacca, A.; Tsiani, E. Stimulation of muscle cell glucose uptake by resveratrol through sirtuins and AMPK. Biochem. Biophys. Res. Commun. 2008, 374, 117–122.

116. Borriello, A.; Cucciolla, V.; della Ragione, F.; Galletti, P. Dietary polyphenols: Focus on resveratrol, a promising agent in the prevention of cardiovascular diseases and control of glucose homeostasis.Nutr. Metab. Cardiovasc. Dis. 2010, 20, 618–625.

117. Patel, M.I.; Gupta, A.; Dey, C.S. Potentiation of neuronal insulin signaling and glucose uptake by resveratrol: The involvement of AMPK. Pharmacol. Rep. 2011, 63, 1162–1168.

118. Gomez-Zorita, S.; Tréguer, K.; Mercader, J.; Carpéné, C. Resveratrol directly affects in vitro lipolysis and glucose transport in human fat cells. J. Physiol. Biochem. 2013, 69, 585–593.

119. Szkudelski, T.; Szkudelska, K. Resveratrol and diabetes: From animal to human studies. Biochim. Biophys. Acta 2015, 1852, 1145–1154.

120. Sun, C.; Zhang, F.; Ge, X.; Yan, T.; Chen, X.; Shi, X.; Zhai, Q. SIRT1 improves insulin sensitivity under insulin-resistant conditions by repressing PTP1B. Cell Metab. 2007, 6, 307–319.

121. Deng, J.Y.; Hsieh, P.S.; Huang, J.P.; Lu, L.S.; Hung, L.M. Activation of estrogen receptor is crucial for resveratrol-stimulating muscular glucose uptake via both insulin-dependent and -independent pathways. Diabetes 2008, 57, 1814–1823.

122. Wang, Q.; Sun, X.; Li, X.; Dong, X.; Li, P.; Zhao, L. Resveratrol attenuates intermittent hypoxia-induced insulin resistance in rats: Involvement of Sirtuin 1 and the phosphatidylinositol-4,5-

bisphosphate 3-kinase/AKT pathway. Mol. Med. Rep. 2015, 11, 151–158.

123. Bagul, P.K.; Deepthi, N.; Sultana, R.; Banerjee, S.K. Resveratrol ameliorates cardiac oxidative stress in diabetes through deacetylation of NFκB-p65 and histone 3. J. Nutr. Biochem. 2015, 26, 1298–1307.

124. Diaz-Gerevini, G.T.; Repossi, G.; Dain, A.; Tarres, M.C.; Das, U.N.; Eynard, A.R. Beneficial action of resveratrol: How and why? Nutrition 2016, 32, 174–178.

125. Granados-Soto, V. Pleiotropic effects of resveratrol. Drug News Perspect. 2003, 16, 299–307.

126. Rodrigo, R.; Miranda, A.; Vergara, L. Modulation of endogenous antioxidant system by wine polyphenols in human disease. Clin. Chim. Acta 2011, 412, 410–424.

127. Kakoti, B.B.; Hernandez-Ontiveros, D.G.; Kataki, M.S.; Shah, K.; Pathak, Y.; Panguluri, S.K. Resveratrol and Omega-3 Fatty Acid: Its Implications in Cardiovascular Diseases. Front. Cardiovasc. Med. 2015, 11, 38.

128. Xia, N.; Förstermann, U.; Li, H. Resveratrol and endothelial nitric oxide. Molecules 2014, 19, 16102–16121.

129. Neves, A.R.; Nunes, C.; Amenitsch, H.; Reis, S. Effects of resveratrol on the structure and fluidity of lipid bilayers: A membrane biophysical study. Soft Matter 2016, 12, 2118–2126.

130. Marques, F.Z.; Markus, M.A.; Morris, B.J. Resveratrol: Cellular actions of a potent natural chemical that confers a diversity of health benefits. Int. J. Biochem. Cell Biol. 2009, 41, 2125–2128.

131. Cho, S.J.; Jung, U.J.; Choi, M.S. Differential effects of low-dose resveratrol on adiposity and hepatic steatosis in diet-induced obese mice. Br. J. Nutr. 2012, 108, 2166–2175.

132. Poulsen, M.M.; Vestergaard, P.F.; Clasen, B.F.; Radko, Y.; Christensen, L.P.; Stødkilde-Jørgensen, H.; Møller, N.; Jessen, N.; Pedersen, S.B.; Jørgensen, J.O. High-dose resveratrol supplementation in obese men: An investigator-initiated, randomized, placebo-controlled clinical trial of substrate metabolism, insulin sensitivity, and body composition. Diabetes 2013, 62, 1186–1195.

133. Walle, T.; Hsieh, F.; DeLegge, M.H.; Oatis, J.E., Jr.; Walle, U.K. High absorption but very low bioavailability of oral resveratrol in humans. Drug Metab. Dispos. 2004, 32, 1377–1382.

134. la Porte, C.; Voduc, N.; Zhang, G.; Seguin, I.; Tardiff, D.; Singhal, N.; Cameron, D.W. Steady-State pharmacokinetics and tolerability of trans-resveratrol 2000 mg twice daily with food, quercetin and alcohol (ethanol) in healthy human subjects. Clin. Pharmacokinet. 2010, 49, 449–454.

135. Kapetanovic, I.M.; Muzzio, M.; Huang, Z.; Thompson, T.N.; McCormick, D.L. Pharmacokinetics, oral bioavailability, and metabolic profile of resveratrol and its dimethylether analog, pterostilbene, in rats. Cancer Chemother. Pharmacol. 2011, 68, 593–601.

136. Malhotra, A.; Bath, S.; Elbarbry, F. An organ system approach to explore the antioxidative, anti-inflammatory, and cytoprotective actions of resveratrol. Oxid. Med. Cell. Longev. 2015, 2015, 803971.

137. Thazhath, S.S.; Wu, T.; Bound, M.J.; Checklin, H.L.; Standfield, S.; Jones, K.L.; Horowitz, M.; Rayner, C.K. Administration of resveratrol for 5 wk has no effect on glucagon-like peptide 1 secretion, gastric emptying, or glycemic control in type 2 diabetes: A randomized controlled trial. Am. J. Clin. Nutr.2016, 103, 66–70.

138. Goh, K.P.; Lee, H.Y.; Lau, D.P.; Supaat, W.; Chan, Y.H.; Koh, A.F. Effects of resveratrol in patients with type 2 diabetes mellitus on skeletal muscle SIRT1 expression and energy expenditure. Int. J. Sport Nutr. Exerc. Metab. 2014, 24, 2–13.

139. Dash, S.; Xiao, C.; Morgantini, C.; Szeto, L.; Lewis, G.F. High-dose resveratrol treatment for 2 weeks inhibits intestinal and hepatic lipoprotein production in overweight/obese men. Arterioscler. Thromb. Vasc. Biol. 2013, 33, 2895–2901.

140. Tuorkey, M.J.; El-Desouki, N.I.; Kamel, R.A. Cytoprotective effect of silymarin against diabetes-induced cardiomyocyte apoptosis in diabetic rats. Biomed. Environ. Sci. 2015, 28, 36–43.

141. Lee, D.Y.; Liu, Y. Molecular structure and stereochemistry of silybin A, silybin B, isosilybin A, and isosilybin B, Isolated from Silybum marianum (milk thistle). J. Nat. Prod. 2003, 66, 1171–1174.

142. Anthony, K.P.; Saleh, M.A. Free radical scavenging and antioxidant activities of silymarin components. Antioxidants 2013, 2, 398–407.

143. Kazazis, C.E.; Evangelopoulos, A.A.; Kollas, A.; Vallianou, N.G. The therapeutic potential of milk thistle in diabetes. Rev. Diabet. Stud. 2014, 11, 167–174.

144. Wu, C.H.; Huang, S.M.; Yen, G.C. Silymarin: A novel antioxidant with antiglycation and antiinflammatory properties in vitro and in vivo. Antioxid. Redox Signal. 2011, 14, 353–366.

145. Shin, S.; Lee, J.A.; Kim, M.; Kum, H.; Jung, E.; Park, D. Anti-glycation activities of phenolic constituents from Silybum marianum (Milk Thistle) flower in vitro and on human explants. Molecules2015, 20, 3549–3564.

146. Sheela, N.; Jose, M.A.; Sathyamurthy, D.; Kumar, B.N. Effect of silymarin on streptozotocin-nicotinamide-induced type 2

diabetic nephropathy in rats. Iran J. Kidney Dis. 2013, 7, 117–123.

147. Khazim, K.; Gorin, Y.; Cavaglieri, R.C.; Abboud, H.E.; Fanti, P. The antioxidant silybin prevents high glucose-induced oxidative stress and podocyte injury in vitro and in vivo. Am. J. Physiol. Ren. Physiol.2013, 305, F691–F700.

148. Vessal, G.; Akmali, M.; Najafi, P.; Moein, M.R.; Sagheb, M.M. Silymarin and milk thistle extract may prevent the progression of diabetic nephropathy in streptozotocin-induced diabetic rats. Ren. Fail.2010, 32, 733–739.

149. Baluchnejadmojarad, T.; Roghani, M.; Khastehkhodaie, Z. Chronic treatment of silymarin improves hyperalgesia and motor nerve conduction velocity in diabetic neuropathic rat. Phytother. Res. 2010, 24, 1120–1125.

150. Marrazzo, G.; Bosco, P.; la Delia, F.; Scapagnini, G.; di Giacomo, C.; Malaguarnera, M.; Galvano, F.; Nicolosi, A.; Li Volti, G. Neuroprotective effect of silibinin in diabetic mice. Neurosci. Lett. 2011, 504, 252–256.

151. Borah, A.; Paul, R.; Choudhury, S.; Choudhury, A.; Bhuyan, B.; Das Talukdar, A.; Dutta Choudhury, M.; Mohanakumar, K.P. Neuroprotective potential of silymarin against CNS disorders: Insight into the pathways and molecular mechanisms of action. CNS Neurosci. Ther. 2013, 19, 847–853.

152. Velussi, M.; Cernigoi, A.M.; De Monte, A.; Dapas, F.; Caffau, C.; Zilli, M. Long-term (12 months) treatment with an anti-oxidant drug (silymarin) is effective on hyperinsulinemia, exogenous insulin need and malondialdehyde levels in cirrhotic diabetic patients. J. Hepatol. 1997, 26, 871–879.

153. Huseini, H.F.; Larijani, B.; Heshmat, R.; Fakhrzadeh, H.; Radjabipour, B.; Toliat, T.; Raza, M. The efficacy of Silybum marianum (L.) Gaertn. (silymarin) in the treatment of type II

diabetes: A randomized, double-blind, placebo-controlled, clinical trial. Phytother. Res. 2006, 20, 1036–1039.

154. Hussain, S.A. Silymarin as an adjunct to glibenclamide therapy improves long-term and postprandial glycemic control and body mass index in type 2 diabetes. J. Med. Food 2007, 10, 543–547.

155. Ebrahimpour Koujan, S.; Gargari, B.P.; Mobasseri, M.; Valizadeh, H.; Asghari-Jafarabadi, M. Effects ofSilybum marianum (L.) Gaertn. (silymarin) extract supplementation on antioxidant status and hs-CRP in patients with type 2 diabetes mellitus: A randomized, triple-blind, placebo-controlled clinical trial.Phytomedicine 2015, 22, 290–296.

156. Fallahzadeh, M.K.; Dormanesh, B.; Sagheb, M.M.; Roozbeh, J.; Vessal, G.; Pakfetrat, M.; Daneshbod, Y.; Kamali-Sarvestani, E.; Lankarani, K.B. Effect of addition of silymarin to renin-angiotensin system inhibitors on proteinuria in type 2 diabetic patients with overt nephropathy: A randomized, double-blind, placebo-controlled trial. Am. J. Kidney Dis. 2012, 60, 896–903.

157. Gueutin, V.; Gauthier, M.; Cazenave, M.; Izzedine, H. Diabetic nephropathy: Emerging treatments.Nephrol. Ther. 2014, 10, 210–215.

158. Magliulo, E.; Gagliardi, B.; Fiori, G.P. Results of a double blind study on the effect of silymarin in the treatment of acute viral hepatitis, carried out at two medical centres. Med. Klin. 1978, 73, 1060–1065.

159. Hollman, P.C.; de Vries, J.H.; van Leeuwen, S.D.; Mengelers, M.J.; Katan, M.B. Absorption of dietary quercetin glycosides and quercetin in healthy ileostomy volunteers. Am. J. Clin. Nutr. 1995, 62, 1276–1282.

160. Boocock, D.J.; Faust, G.E.; Patel, K.R.; Schinas, A.M.; Brown, V.A.; Ducharme, M.P.; Booth, T.D.; Crowell, J.A.; Perloff, M.; Gescher, A.J.; et al. Phase I dose escalation pharmacokinetic

study in healthy volunteers of resveratrol, a potential cancer chemopreventive agent. Cancer Epidemiol. Biomark. Prev.2007, 16, 1246–1252.

161. Hawke, R.L.; Schrieber, S.J.; Soule, T.A.; Wen, Z.; Smith, P.C.; Reddy, K.R.; Wahed, A.S.; Belle, S.H.; Afdhal, N.H.; Navarro, V.J.; et al. Silymarin ascending multiple oral dosing phase I study in noncirrhotic patients with chronic hepatitis C. J. Clin. Pharmacol. 2010, 50, 434–449.

162. Lecomte, J. Pharmacologic properties of silybin and silymarin. Rev. Med. Liege 1975, 30, 110–114.

163. O'Connor, L.M.; Lentjes, M.A.; Luben, R.N.; Khaw, K.T.; Wareham, N.J.; Forouhi, N.G. Dietary dairy product intake and incident type 2 diabetes: A prospective study using dietary data from a 7-day food diary. Diabetologia 2014, 57, 909–917.

164. Pasin, G.; Comerford, K.B. Dairy foods and dairy proteins in the management of type 2 diabetes: A systematic review of the clinical evidence. Adv. Nutr. 2015, 6, 245–259.

165. Astrup, A. Yogurt and dairy product consumption to prevent cardiometabolic diseases: Epidemiologic and experimental studies. Am. J. Clin. Nutr. 2014, 99, 1235S–1242S.

166. Ejtahed, H.S.; Soroush, A.R.; Angoorani, P.; Larijani, B.; Hasani-Ranjbar, S. Gut microbiota as a target in the pathogenesis of metabolic disorders: A new approach to novel therapeutic agents. Horm. Metab. Res. 2016, 48, 349–358.

167. Aune, D.; Norat, T.; Romundstad, P.; Vatten, L.J. Dairy products and the risk of type 2 diabetes: A systematic review and dose-response meta-analysis of cohort studies. Am. J. Clin. Nutr. 2013, 98, 1066–1083.

168. Hadisaputro, S.; Djokomoeljanto, R.R.; Judiono Soesatyo, M.H. The effects of oral plain kefir supplementation on

proinflammatory cytokine properties of the hyperglycemia Wistar rats induced by streptozotocin. Acta Med. Indones. 2012, 44, 100–104.

169. Bourrie, B.C.; Willing, B.P.; Cotter, P.D. The microbiota and health promoting characteristics of the fermented beverage kefir. Front. Microbiol. 2016, 7, 647.

170. Magalhães, K.T.; de Melo Pereira, G.V.; Campos, C.R.; Dragone, G.; Schwan, R.F. Brazilian kefir: Structure, microbial communities and chemical composition. Braz. J. Microbiol. 2011, 42, 693–702.

171. De Oliveira Leite, A.M.; Miguel, M.A.; Peixoto, R.S.; Rosado, A.S.; Silva, J.T.; Paschoalin, V.M. Microbiological, technological and therapeutic properties of kefir: A natural probiotic beverage. Braz. J. Microbiol. 2013, 44, 341–349.

172. Friques, A.G.; Arpini, C.M.; Kalil, I.C.; Gava, A.L.; Leal, M.A.; Porto, M.L.; Nogueira, B.V.; Dias, A.T.; Andrade, T.U.; Pereira, T.M.; et al. Chronic administration of the probiotic kefir improves the endothelial function in spontaneously hypertensive rats. J. Transl. Med. 2015, 13, 390.

173. Zhou, J.; Liu, X.; Jiang, H.; Dong, M. Analysis of the microflora in Tibetan kefir grains using denaturing gradient gel electrophoresis. Food Microbiol. 2009, 26, 770–775.

174. Leite, A.M.; Mayo, B.; Rachid, C.T.; Peixoto, R.S.; Silva, J.T.; Paschoalin, V.M.; Delgado, S. Assessment of the microbial diversity of Brazilian kefir grains by PCR-DGGE and pyrosequencing analysis. Food Microbiol. 2012, 31, 215–221.

175. Hamet, M.F.; Londero, A.; Medrano, M.; Vercammen, E.; van Hoorde, K.; Garrote, G.L.; Huys, G.; Vandamme, P.; Abraham, A.G. Application of culture-dependent and culture-independent methods for the identification of Lactobacillus kefiranofaciens in

microbial consortia present in kefir grains.Food Microbiol. 2013, 36, 327–334.

176. Marsh, A.J.; O'Sullivan, O.; Hill, C.; Ross, R.P.; Cotter, P.D. Sequencing-based analysis of the bacterial and fungal composition of kefir grains and milks from multiple sources. PLoS ONE 2013, 8, e69371.

177. Gonçalves, N.; Gomes-Ferreira, C.; Moura, C.; Roncon-Albuquerque, R., Jr.; Leite-Moreira, A.F.; Falcão-Pires, I. Worse cardiac remodeling in response to pressure overload in type 2 diabetes mellitus.Int. J. Cardiol. 2016, 217, 195–204.

178. Punaro, G.R.; Maciel, F.R.; Rodrigues, A.M.; Rogero, M.M.; Bogsan, C.S.; Oliveira, M.N.; Ihara, S.S.; Araujo, S.R.; Sanches, T.R.; Andrade, L.C.; et al. Kefir administration reduced progression of renal injury in STZ-diabetic rats by lowering oxidative stress. Nitric Oxide 2014, 37, 53–60.

179. Yadav, H.; Jain, S.; Sinha, P.R. Oral administration of dahi containing probiotic Lactobacillus acidophilus and Lactobacillus casei delayed the progression of streptozotocin-induced diabetes in rats. J. Dairy Res. 2008, 75, 189–195.

180. Maeda, H.; Zhu, X.; Omura, K.; Suzuki, S.; Kitamura, S. Effects of an exopolysaccharide (kefiran) on lipids, blood pressure, blood glucose, and constipation. Biofactors 2004, 22, 197–200.

181. Maeda, H.; Zhu, X.; Suzuki, S.; Suzuki, K.; Kitamura, S. Structural characterization and biological activities of an exopolysaccharide kefiran produced by Lactobacillus kefiranofaciens WT-2B(T). J. Agric. Food Chem. 2004, 52, 5533–5338.

182. Teruya, K.; Yamashita, M.; Tominaga, R.; Nagira, T.; Shim, S.Y.; Katakura, Y.; Tokumaru, S.; Tokumaru, K.; Barnes, D.; Shirahata, S. Fermented milk, Kefram-Kefir enhances glucose uptake into

insulin-responsive muscle cells. Cytotechnology 2002, 40, 107–116.

183. Yadav, H.; Jain, S.; Sinha, P.R. Effect of Dahi containing Lactococcus lactis on the progression of diabetes induced by a high-fructose diet in rats. Biosci. Biotechnol. Biochem. 2006, 70, 1255–1258.

184. Asemi, Z.; Zare, Z.; Shakeri, H.; Sabihi, S.S.; Esmaillzadeh, A. Effect of multispecies probiotic supplements on metabolic profiles, hs-CRP, and oxidative stress in patients with type 2 diabetes. Ann. Nutr. Metab. 2013.

185. Rudich, A.; Kozlovsky, N.; Potashnik, R.; Bashan, N. Oxidant stress reduces insulin responsiveness in 3T3-L1 adipocytes. Am. J. Physiol. 1997, 272, E935–E940.

186. Rudich, A.; Tirosh, A.; Potashnik, R.; Hemi, R.; Kanety, H.; Bashan, N. Prolonged oxidative stress impairs insulin-induced GLUT4 translocation in 3T3-L1 adipocytes. Diabetes 1998, 47, 1562–1569.

187. Baynes, J.W. Role of oxidative stress in development of complications in diabetes. Diabetes 1991, 40, 405–412.

188. Wolff, S.P.; Jiang, Z.Y.; Hunt, J.V. Protein glycation and oxidative stress in diabetes mellitus and ageing. Free Radic. Biol. Med. 1991, 10, 339–352.

189. Klippel, B.F.; Duemke, L.B.; Leal, M.A.; Friques, A.G.F.; Dantas, E.M.; Dalvi, R.F.; Gava, A.L.; Pereira, T.M.C.; Andrade, T.U.; Meyrelles, S.S.; et al. Effects of kefir on the cardiac autonomic tones and baroreflex sensitivity in spontaneously hypertensive rats. Front. Physiol. 2016, 7, 211.

190. Liu, Y.; Liu, S.X.; Zheng, F.; Cai, Y.; Xie, K.L.; Zhang, W.L. Cardiovascular autonomic neuropathy in patients with type 2 diabetes. J. Diabetes Investig. 2015.

191. Li, X.; Jiang, Y.H.; Jiang, P.; Lin, H.Q.; Yang, J.L.; Ma, D.F.; Wang, X.; Yang, C.H. Analysis of heart rate variability and cardiac autonomic nerve remodeling in streptozotocin-induced diabetic rats. Exp. Clin. Endocrinol. Diabetes 2015, 123, 272–281.

192. Firouzi, S.; Majid, H.A.; Ismail, A.; Kamaruddin, N.A.; Barakatun-Nisak, M.Y. Effect of multi-strain probiotics (multi-strain microbial cell preparation) on glycemic control and other diabetes-related outcomes in people with type 2 diabetes: A randomized controlled trial. Eur. J. Nutr. 2016.

193. Ostadrahimi, A.; Taghizadeh, A.; Mobasseri, M.; Farrin, N.; Payahoo, L.; Beyramalipoor Gheshlaghi, Z.; Vahedjabbari, M. Effect of probiotic fermented milk (kefir) on glycemic control and lipid profile in type 2 diabetic patients: A randomized double-blind placebo-controlled clinical trial. Iran J. Public Health 2015, 44, 228–237.

194. Hulston, C.J.; Churnside, A.A.; Venables, M.C. Probiotic supplementation prevents high-fat, overfeeding-induced insulin resistance in human subjects. Br. J. Nutr. 2015, 113, 596–602.

195. Tonucci, L.B.; Olbrich Dos Santos, K.M.; Licursi de Oliveira, L.; Rocha Ribeiro, S.M.; Duarte Martino, H.S. Clinical application of probiotics in type 2 diabetes mellitus: A randomized, double-blind, placebo-controlled study. Clin. Nutr. 2015.

196. Manaer, T.; Yu, L.; Zhang, Y.; Xiao, X.J.; Nabi, X.H. Anti-diabetic effects of shubat in type 2 diabetic rats induced by combination of high-glucose-fat diet and low-dose streptozotocin. J. Ethnopharmacol.2015, 169, 269–274.

197. Kuschnerus, K.; Landmesser, U.; Kränkel, N. Vascular repair strategies in type 2 diabetes: Novel insights. Cardiovasc. Diagn. Ther. 2015, 5, 374–386.

198. Ramirez, C.E.; Nian, H.; Yu, C.; Gamboa, J.L.; Luther, J.M.; Brown, N.J.; Shibao, C.A. Treatment with sildenafil improves insulin

sensitivity in prediabetes: A randomized, controlled trial. J. Clin. Endocrinol. Metab. 2015, 100, 4533–4540.

199. Gromada, J.; Høy, M.; Renström, E.; Bokvist, K.; Eliasson, L.; Göpel, S.; Rorsman, P. CaM kinase II-dependent mobilization of secretory granules underlies acetylcholine-induced stimulation of exocytosis in mouse pancreatic B-cells. J. Physiol. 1999, 518, 745–759.

200. Fu, Z.; Gilbert, E.R.; Liu, D. Regulation of insulin synthesis and secretion and pancreatic β-cell dysfunction in diabetes. Curr. Diabetes Rev. 2013, 9, 25–53.

201. Nyström, T.; Ortsäter, H.; Huang, Z.; Zhang, F.; Larsen, F.J.; Weitzberg, E.; Lundberg, J.O.; Sjöholm, Å. Inorganic nitrite stimulates pancreatic islet blood flow and insulin secretion. Free Radic. Biol. Med.2012, 53, 1017–1023.

202. Méndez-del Villar, M.; González-Ortiz, M.; Martínez-Abundis, E.; Pérez-Rubio, K.G.; Lizárraga-Valdez, R. Effect of resveratrol administration on metabolic syndrome, insulin sensitivity, and insulin secretion. Metab. Syndr. Relat. Disord. 2014, 12, 497–501.

203. Otunola, G.A.; Oloyede, O.B.; Oladiji, A.T.; Afolayan, A.J. Selected spices and their combination modulate hypercholesterolemia-induced oxidative stress in experimental rats. Biol. Res. 2014, 47, 5.

204. Bergandi, L.; Silvagno, F.; Russo, I.; Riganti, C.; Anfossi, G.; Aldieri, E.; Ghigo, D.; Trovati, M.; Bosia, A. Insulin stimulates glucose transport via nitric oxide/cyclic GMP pathway in human vascular smooth muscle cells. Arterioscler. Thromb. Vasc. Biol. 2003, 23, 2215–2221.

205. Tanaka, T.; Nakatani, K.; Morioka, K.; Urakawa, H.; Maruyama, N.; Kitagawa, N.; Katsuki, A.; Araki-Sasaki, R.; Hori, Y.; Gabazza, E.C.; et al. Nitric oxide stimulates glucose transport through

insulin-independent GLUT4 translocation in 3T3-L1 adipocytes. Eur. J. Endocrinol. 2003, 149, 61–67.

206. Lira, V.A.; Soltow, Q.A.; Long, J.H.; Betters, J.L.; Sellman, J.E.; Criswell, D.S. Nitric oxide increases GLUT4 expression and regulates AMPK signaling in skeletal muscle. Am. J. Physiol. Endocrinol. Metab.2007, 293, E1062–E1068.

207. Furchgott, R.F.; Zawadzki, J.V. The obligatory role of endothelial cells in the relaxation of arterial smooth muscle by acetylcholine. Nature 1980, 288, 373–376.

208. Ignarro, L.J. Nitric oxide: A unique endogenous signaling molecule in vascular biology. Biosci. Rep.1999, 19, 51–71.

209. Vasquez, E.C.; Gava, A.L.; Graceli, J.B.; Balarini, C.M.; Campagnaro, B.P.; Pereira, T.M.; Meyrelles, S.S. Novel therapeutic targets for phosphodiesterase 5 inhibitors: Current state-of-the-art on systemic arterial hypertension and atherosclerosis. Curr. Pharm. Biotechnol. 2016, 17, 347–364.

210. Behr-Roussel, D.; Oudot, A.; Caisey, S.; Coz, O.L.; Gorny, D.; Bernabé, J.; Wayman, C.; Alexandre, L.; Giuliano, F.A. Daily treatment with sildenafil reverses endothelial dysfunction and oxidative stress in an animal model of insulin resistance. Eur. Urol. 2008, 53, 1272–1280.

211. Maiorino, M.I.; Bellastella, G.; Esposito, K. Diabetes and sexual dysfunction: Current perspectives.Diabetes Metab. Syndr. Obes. 2014, 7, 95–105.

212. Leal, M.A.; Balarini, C.M.; Dias, A.T.; Porto, M.L.; Gava, A.L.; Pereira, T.M.; Meyrelles, S.S.; Vasquez, E.C. Mechanisms of enhanced vasoconstriction in the mouse model of atherosclerosis: The beneficial effects of sildenafil. Curr. Pharm. Biotechnol. 2015, 16, 517–530.

213. Bai, Y.; An, R. Resveratrol and sildenafil synergistically improve diabetes-associated erectile dysfunction in streptozotocin-induced diabetic rats. Life Sci. 2015, 135, 43–48.

214. Dalaklioglu, S.; Bayram, Z.; Tasatargil, A.; Ozdem, S. Resveratrol reverses diabetes-related decrement in sildenafil-induced relaxation of corpus cavernosum in aged rats. Aging Clin. Exp. Res. 2016.

215. Bivalacqua, T.J.; Sussan, T.E.; Gebska, M.A.; Strong, T.D.; Berkowitz, D.E.; Biswal, S.; Burnett, A.L.; Champion, H.C. Sildenafil inhibits superoxide formation and prevents endothelial dysfunction in a mouse model of secondhand smoke induced erectile dysfunction. J. Urol. 2009, 181, 899–906.

216. Balarini, C.M.; Leal, M.A.; Gomes, I.B.; Pereira, T.M.; Gava, A.L.; Meyrelles, S.S.; Vasquez, E.C. Sildenafil restores endothelial function in the apolipoprotein E knockout mouse. J. Transl. Med. 2013,11, 3.

217. Dias, A.T.; Cintra, A.S.; Frossard, J.C.; Palomino, Z.; Casarini, D.E.; Gomes, I.B.; Balarini, C.M.; Gava, A.L.; Campagnaro, B.P.; Pereira, T.M.; et al. Inhibition of phosphodiesterase 5 restores endothelial function in renovascular hypertension. J. Transl. Med. 2014, 12, 250.

218. Fahning, B.M.; Dias, A.T.; Oliveira, J.P.; Gava, A.L.; Porto, M.L.; Gomes, I.B.; Nogueira, B.V.; Campagnaro, B.P.; Pereira, T.M.; Vasquez, E.C.; et al. Sildenafil improves vascular endothelial structure and function in renovascular hypertension. Curr. Pharm. Biotechnol. 2015, 16, 823–831.

219. de Almeida, L.S.; Barboza, J.R.; Freitas, F.P.; Porto, M.L.; Vasquez, E.C.; Meyrelles, S.S.; Gava, A.L.; Pereira, T.M. Sildenafil prevents renal dysfunction in contrast media-induced nephropathy in Wistar rats. Hum. Exp. Toxicol. 2016.

220. Aversa, A.; Vitale, C.; Volterrani, M.; Fabbri, A.; Spera, G.; Fini, M.; Rosano, G.M. Chronic administration of Sildenafil improves markers of endothelial function in men with Type 2 diabetes.Diabet Med. 2008, 25, 37–44.

221. Kondoh, N.; Higuchi, Y.; Maruyama, T.; Nojima, M.; Yamamoto, S.; Shima, H. Salvage therapy trial for erectile dysfunction using phosphodiesterase type 5 inhibitors and vitamin E: Preliminary report.Aging Male 2008, 11, 167–170.

222. Mandosi, E.; Giannetta, E.; Filardi, T.; Lococo, M.; Bertolini, C.; Fallarino, M.; Gianfrilli, D.; Venneri, M.A.; Lenti, L.; Lenzi, A.; et al. Endothelial dysfunction markers as a therapeutic target for Sildenafil treatment and effects on metabolic control in type 2 diabetes. Expert Opin. Ther. Targets 2015, 19, 1617–1622.

223. Balhara, Y.P.; Sarkar, S.; Gupta, R. Phosphodiesterase-5 inhibitors for erectile dysfunction in patients with diabetes mellitus: A systematic review and meta-analysis of randomized controlled trials. Indian J. Endocrinol. Metab. 2015, 19, 451–461.

224. Das, A.; Durrant, D.; Salloum, F.N.; Xi, L.; Kukreja, R.C. PDE5 inhibitors as therapeutics for heart disease, diabetes and cancer. Pharmacol. Ther. 2015, 147, 12–21.

225. Mammi, C.; Pastore, D.; Lombardo, M.F.; Ferrelli, F.; Caprio, M.; Consoli, C.; Tesauro, M.; Gatta, L.; Fini, M.; Federici, M.; et al. Sildenafil reduces insulin-resistance in human endothelial cells. PLoS ONE2011, 6, e14542.

226. Ayala, J.E.; Bracy, D.P.; Julien, B.M.; Rottman, J.N.; Fueger, P.T.; Wasserman, D.H. Chronic treatment with sildenafil improves energy balance and insulin action in high fat-fed conscious mice. Diabetes2007, 56, 1025–1033.

227. Varma, A.; Das, A.; Hoke, N.N.; Durrant, D.E.; Salloum, F.N.; Kukreja, R.C. Anti-inflammatory and cardioprotective effects of tadalafil in diabetic mice. PLoS ONE 2012, 7, e45243.

228. Koka, S.; Das, A.; Salloum, F.N.; Kukreja, R.C. Phosphodiesterase-5 inhibitor tadalafil attenuates oxidative stress and protects against myocardial ischemia/reperfusion injury in type 2 diabetic mice.Free Radic. Biol. Med. 2013, 60, 80–88.

229. Grover-Páez, F.; Villegas Rivera, G.; Guillén Ortíz, R. Sildenafil citrate diminishes microalbuminuria and the percentage of A1c in male patients with type 2 diabetes. Diabetes Res. Clin. Pract. 2007, 78, 136–140.

230. Chrysant, S.G.; Chrysant, G.S. The pleiotropic effects of phosphodiesterase 5 inhibitors on function and safety in patients with cardiovascular disease and hypertension. J. Clin. Hypertens. 2012, 14, 644–649.

Chapter 10

The Clinical Characteristics of Older People with Chronic Multiple-Site Joint Pains and Their Utilisation of Therapeutic Interventions: Data from a Prospective Cohort Study

Rafi Raja, Bright Dube, Elizabeth M. A. Hensor, Sarah F. Hogg, Philip G. Conaghan* and Sarah R. Kingsbury

Leeds Institute of Rheumatic and Musculoskeletal Medicine, Chapel Allerton Hospital, University of Leeds and NIHR Leeds Musculoskeletal Biomedical Research Unit, Chapeltown Rd, Leeds LS7 4SA, UK

ABSTRACT

Background

Chronic multiple-site joint pain (MSJP) is common in older people and associated with poor outcomes, yet under-researched. Our aim was to detail the clinical characteristics of people with MSJP and their utilisation of therapies.

Methods

MSJP was defined as pain in at least one large joint and one other joint for >6 weeks in the last three months. A mixed community, primary and secondary care cohort of people >50 years old underwent detailed history and examination by a single clinician. Treatment utilisation was recorded comprehensively.

Results

201 adults were recruited, 82 % women, mean age 63, BMI 31 kg/m^2. Median number of painful joints per patient was 6 (IQR 4–9; range 2–17); most common painful sites were knee (84 %), lower back (62 %) and shoulder (47 %). 194/201 (96 %) had an osteoarthritis (OA) diagnosis, 155/194 (80 %) also had soft tissue pathology and 72 % had back problems. 85 % had OA at multiple sites. Upper and lower limb weakness was common (90 and 77 % respectively). Lower limb weakness was significantly associated with obesity. Only 26 % had received written information about their joints. Though 79 % had attended physiotherapy, the majority (93 %) had muscle weakness. Only 36 % of overweight participants had accessed weight-loss support. Half of those with foot pain had seen a podiatrist or used appliances. Multiple concurrent pharmacological therapies were used by 47 %.

Conclusion

MSJP represents a combination of OA, back pain and soft tissue disorders; muscle weakness is extremely common. Therapies appear underutilised in people with MJSP. Identifying the reasons for this should guide effective intervention research.

Keywords: Joint pain Multiple site Osteoarthritis Back pain Soft tissue disorders Therapeutics

BACKGROUND

Musculoskeletal (MSK) problems are now the second most significant cause of disability worldwide, with low back pain remaining the leading specific cause of years lived with disability, and osteoarthritis (OA)

significantly rising in importance [1]. Large epidemiological studies have reported that chronic multiple-site joint pain (MSJP) is more common than single joint problems in older adults and is associated with poor outcomes [2, 3]. Increased numbers of painful joints is related to poor physical function [3, 4] and increased work disability [5].

Despite the frequent prevalence of MSJP and the associated poor outcomes, the characteristics of MSJP have not been well described or researched. Of note, there have been extremely few therapeutic trials in this area. The majority of MSK pain trials have involved selecting a single predominantly painful joint, whilst guidelines have focused on individual disease areas such as OA or back pain [6, 7]. The effectiveness of currently available therapies in people with MSJP is therefore not known. A recent survey of the approach of UK general practitioners (GPs) on pharmacological management of MSJP found that most did aim to treat multiple-site pains concurrently, using the same therapies for all sites irrespective of diagnosis [8].

Although clinicians have long recognised MSJP, the lack of characterisation and understanding of this condition, and the lack of management strategies, in the context of a rapidly ageing and increasingly obese society, makes this an increasingly important area for further research. The aim of this study was therefore to examine the detailed clinical characteristics of people with MSJP and their utilisation of therapeutic interventions.

METHODS

Study population and eligibility criteria

Prospective participants were identified through the following sources: referral by general practitioners from primary care services; referral by physiotherapists from musculoskeletal services; identification by clinicians within secondary and tertiary care rheumatology, musculoskeletal and orthopaedic clinics; patient public involvement organisations in West Yorkshire. Patients were screened via a telephone interview and those meeting the inclusion criteria were recruited.

The inclusion criteria were patients aged 50 years and above, having pain in at least one large joint and one other joint for more than six weeks within the last three months, and capable of understanding and signing an informed consent form. The definition of a large joint area in this study included the spine, shoulders, elbows, hips, knees and ankles. Exclusion criteria included i) previous diagnosis of a primary inflammatory arthritis including rheumatoid arthritis, gout, polymyalgia rheumatica or connective tissue disease, ii) previous clinician-diagnosed fibromyalgia, iii) a chronic medical condition requiring long term use of oral corticosteroids or immunosuppressants and iv) unable or unwilling to give informed consent.

Ethics, consent and permissions

Ethical approval was received from the Yorkshire and the Humber (Leeds Central) Ethics Committee (Ref: 12/YH/0345) and all participants gave written informed consent.

Design

The Leeds MSJP study involves observational, longitudinal evaluation of this under-researched group; here we present the baseline cross-sectional data. Participants completed a series of questionnaires and underwent a detailed history and clinical examination of painful joints by a single rheumatologist to document medical history and musculoskeletal diagnoses. A patient and public involvement group representative was involved in the development of the study and design of the participant case report form.

Information on age, gender, ethnicity, smoking status, alcohol consumption, employment history and medical co-morbidities, including joint related co-morbidities (duration of joint pain, previous joint surgery and family history), and comprehensive therapy use (current and previous pharmacological therapies, including over-the-counter (OTC), and local therapies) were recorded (see Additional file 1). Clinical diagnoses for the painful joints were based on established diagnostic criteria (Additional file 1). Where diagnostic criteria were not available, the clinician's judgement was used. Where previous radiographic information was available, this was used to support the clinical diagnosis. Upper limb strength was measured using a Jamar hand dynamometer (Sammons Preston Rolyan, Bolingbrook, IL, USA). Three attempts were recorded (measured in pounds) for each hand, and the three trials then averaged to create scores for analysis. For lower limb muscle strength, the Medical Research Council (MRC) scale was used. The MRC scale is an established test for muscle grading on a 0 to 5 scale which has been previously shown to be reliable for assessing lower limb weakness [9] (Additional file 1).

Participants completed a set of questionnaires that asked about their joint pain and function over the past week. Joint pain was also assessed using a manikin that included the neck, upper back, lower back, shoulders, elbows, wrists, hands or fingers, thumbs, hips, groin, knees, ankles, feet and ball of feet or toes. 11-point numerical rating scales were used to assess overall pain severity from all joints and pain from the most painful joint.

Statistical analysis

Statistical analysis was carried out with Stata 13.1 software (StataCorp LP, College Station, TX, USA) [10] and R version 3.1.1 [11].

Descriptive statistics were used to describe the main characteristics of the study population and are presented as arithmetic mean (S.D) or medians where appropriate for continuous variables and frequency and percentages for categorical variables. The prevalence of pain at each site was evaluated and correlations between reported pain at each site compared with other sites using phi correlation coefficients for binary data. These associations between pain at pairs of sites were also explored using logistic models and findings summarised using odds ratios (ORs) and 95 % confidence intervals having adjusted for age and sex. Muscle weakness was split into upper limb (based on hand grip measurements) and lower limb (using quadriceps strength measurements). For upper limb strength, the average of 3 attempts from the dynamometer readings was used, these were then converted to kilograms and the determination of whether an individual's upper limb was weak was adjusted based on their gender and BMI. For males the cut offs were: (obese men < 40 kg; overweight men <39 kg and normal men 37 kg) while in female the cut off was uniformly 21 kg for one to be considered to have weakness in that limb [12]. For lower limb weakness any score less than 5 on the MRC scale was considered as weakness for that limb. The MRC scale grades weakness from 0 to 5 with zero being no movement observed and five representing the muscle fully contracting under resistance (Additional file 1). Associations between site of muscle weakness (upper limb weakness vs lower limb weakness) and associations between limb pain and muscle weakness (upper limb pain vs upper limb weakness and lower limb weakness vs lower limb pain), and also associations between muscle weakness and specific joint pain (for example lower limb weakness vs shoulder pain) were evaluated using chi-square (X^2) tests or Fisher's exact test where appropriate. Differences were considered significant at $P < 0.05$.

RESULTS

Among 424 people who were approached to participate in the study, 210 people were screened. Three failed screening (fibromyalgia $n = 2$, chronic illness on long term corticosteroid therapy $n = 1$). Six participants with pain limited to one large joint at the time of the baseline assessment were not included in this analysis, leaving 201 participants. The mean ± SD age of the cohort was 63 ± 8.77 years (range 50–88) with 82 % of the cohort being female. The mean BMI ± SD was 31 ± 6.42 kg/m^2. The mean duration of symptoms was 13.7 years (range 1–50). Table 1 shows the demographics and baseline characteristics of the participants.

Table 1. Demographics and baseline characteristics

Characteristic	N (%)
Age, years, mean ± SD (range)	63 ± 8.77 (50–88)
Female	164 (82)
BMI, kg/m^2, mean ± SD	31.0 ± 6.42
Ethnicity	
Caucasian	193 (96)
African/Caribbean	5 (3)
Asian	3 (1)
Smoking status	
Current smoker	16 (8)
Previous smoker	81 (40)
Pack years, mean (range)	20 (1–75)
Alcohol consumption	
Units per week, mean (range)	4 (0–38)
Employment history	
Employed	49 (24)
Self-employed	14 (7)
Retired	110 (55)
Unemployed	28 (14)
Job activity (current or previous)	
Heavy manual	94/192 (49)
Repetitive use of hands	21/192 (11)
Prolonged key boarding or typing	46/192 (24)
Prolonged standing	26/192 (14)
Median number of painful joints (IQR)	

Overall in all participants	6 (4–9)
Current/previous smokers	7 (5–9)
Never smoked	6 (4–8)
Heavy manual job	7 (4–9)
Repetitive use of hands	7 (6–10)
Prolonged keyboarding/typing	6 (5–8)
Prolonged standing	6 (5–8)
Comorbidities	
Cardiovascular disease (including hypertension, ischaemic heart disease)	94 (47)
Pulmonary condition (including asthma, emphysema, chronic bronchitis)	44 (22)
Gastro-intestinal disease (including gastro-oesophageal reflux, peptic ulcer)	108 (54)
Diabetes	20 (10)
Depression	63 (31)
Medical history	
Joint replacement or fusion	57 (28)
Joint related soft tissue repair	53 (26)
Non-orthopaedic surgery	160 (80)
Family history of OA	135 (67)

BMI body mass index, *IQR* interquartile range

Examination findings

A total of 1342 painful joints were reported by participants with the median number of painful joints per person being six (inter-quartile range 4–9, range 2–17). Peripheral joint pain was more common (82 %, 1107/1342) than axial joint pain (18 %, 235/1342). The most commonly involved painful joints by participant were the knee (84 %, 168/201), lower back (62 %, 125/201) and shoulder (47 %, 95/201), while the least commonly painful was the foot excluding the toes (12 %, 25/201). The joint with the highest proportion of bilateral pain for that particular joint was the hand/finger with 90 % of all the participants with involvement in that joint having the condition affecting both sides. This was followed by the thumb (71 %) and knee (67 %).

Of the painful joints, 51 % (688/1342) were diagnosed with OA, 30 % (408/1342) as having soft tissue pathology, 18 % with axial pain and 1 % non-specific joint pain. Most participants (96 %, 194/201) had at least one joint with an OA diagnosis, 81 % (162/201) had soft tissue pathology and 77 % (155/194) had both OA and soft tissue pathology. The prevalence of soft tissue pathology was as common as OA in the upper limbs whereas OA was more common in the lower limbs (Table 2).

Table 2. Symptomatic joint and diagnosis

	N (%) by region	(%) of total number of joints
Upper limb		
Osteoarthritis	277/520 (53)	20
Soft tissue pathology	242/520 (47)	18
Lower limb		
Osteoarthritis	411/588 (70)	31
Soft tissue pathology	166/588 (28)	12
Other (including referred pain)	11/588 (2)	1
Axial		
Mechanical	219/235 (93)	16
Mechanical with radiculopathy	16/235 (7)	2

The most common joint-specific diagnosis was knee OA (20.8 %, 279/1342) followed by hand OA (11.2 %, 150/1342), trochanteric bursitis (9.6 %, 129/1342), subacromial impingement syndrome (9.5 %, 128/1342), thumb OA (9.2 %, 124/1342) and mechanical low back pain (8.3 %, 112/1342). OA accounted for 99 % of knee pain, 92 % of hand pain, 86 % of foot/ball-of-foot/toe pain and 74 % of groin pain. 99 % of "hip" pain was due to trochanteric bursitis and 96 % of shoulder pain was due to subacromial impingement syndrome.

Figure 1 shows the correlations of pain at each of the 25 anatomical sites. Pain was reported most frequently in the right knee (73.6 %), left knee (66.2 %) and lower back (62.1 %), and least often in the left ankle (8.0 %) and right foot (8.5 %). Higher correlations were observed for pain at bilateral joints (correlation for right hand and left hand 0.91; left and right thumbs 0.75) and also anatomically adjacent joints (shoulder with ipsilateral elbow 0.22 and groin and ipsilateral hip 0.21). Exploratory analyses using adjusted logistic regression models revealed similar results but with wide confidence intervals. The strongest associations were for pain at corresponding sites bilaterally (ORs 706 for right and left hand, 95.2 for right and left wrists, 56.2 for right and left thumb). Higher ORs were also observed for pain at adjacent anatomical sites in the upper limb (shoulder with ipsilateral elbow, 4.7), and lower limb (right groin with ipsilateral hip, 4.3) (Additional file 2: Table S1).

Muscle weakness

Four participants were unable to perform the handgrip strength test due to hand pain, whilst 21 participants were unable to complete the quadriceps strength test due to lower limb pain. Muscle weakness was very common, affecting the upper limb in 90 % (178/197), lower limb in 77 % (139/180), and both locations in 74 % (131/178). There was a statistically significant association between lower limb weakness and

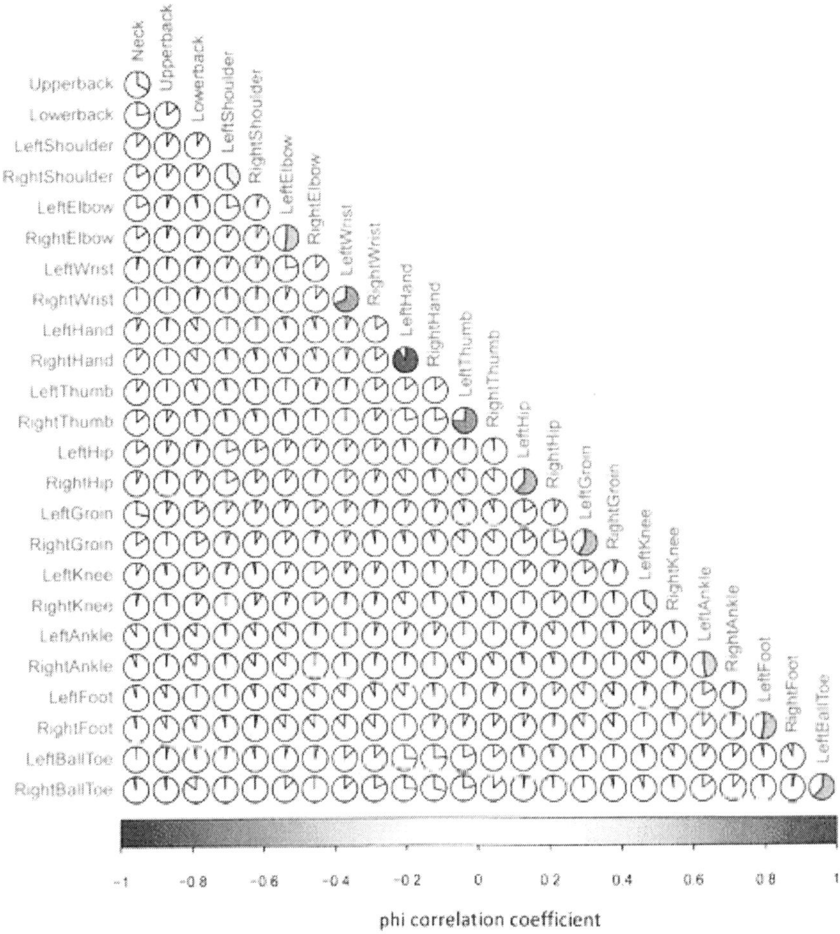

Figure 1. Association between painful joints. Clockwise shading represents positive correlation and anti-clockwise shading represents negative correlation

upper limb weakness ($X^2 = 20.21$, $p < 0.001$). 90 % of participants with upper limb pain had upper limb muscle weakness (149/165) and 78 % with lower limb pain had lower limb weakness (134/172). A statistically significant association was also demonstrated between having lower limb weakness and having shoulder pain ($X^2 = 8.39$, $p = 0.004$), with 87 % of participants with shoulder pain having lower limb weakness compared to 69 % of participants that had no reported shoulder pain. In participants classified as obese (BMI > 30), 86 % of these reported lower limb weakness compared to 69 % of those not classified as obese ($X^2 = 7.11$, $p = 0.008$).

Therapy

Information

Provision of written information about the participant's joint problem was infrequent, with only 26 % (53/201) recalling receiving such information or being referred to other resources (e.g. internet website) following a GP or specialist consultation.

Non-pharmacological treatment use

Non-pharmacological therapy use was infrequent. 173 participants were classed as being overweight, of which 36 % (62/173) recalled receiving weight loss treatment (advice, written information, weight loss programme or dietician input). The majority (79 %, 159/201) had attended physiotherapy, 62 % (99/159) of these reported continuing their exercises. Only half (51 %, 32/63) of those with foot pain had used a podiatry service or a shoe appliance. The most common reason for using specific non-pharmacological therapies were: physiotherapy for knee OA (40 %, 81/201) and mechanical neck/back pain (39 %, 79/201), exercise for knee OA (33 %, 67/201), transcutaneous electrical nerve stimulation (TENS) for back pain (16 %, 33/201), acupuncture for back pain (21 %, 43/201), occupational therapy for hand/thumb OA (10 %, 20/201), appliances for hand/thumb OA (17 %, 34/201) and surgery for knee OA (20 %, 40/201).

Current pharmacological treatment use

Analgesia use was self-reported by 95 % of participants. Of these, 71 % were using one or more prescription medications, 74 % were using over-the-counter (OTC) medication and 44 % were using both prescription and OTC medications. Paracetamol (62 %) was the most commonly used medication, with 62 % of paracetamol users reporting this as OTC use. Opioids were the second most common medication (51 %) and were mainly reported as prescription medication (81 % for co-codamol and 100 % other opioids) (Table 3). Oral co-codamol (a fixed combination agent including paracetamol and codeine) was the most commonly used opioid medication, although other oral opioid (codeine phosphate, tramadol, oral morphine) use was also reported. Transdermal opioid use was low (buprenorphine patch and fentanyl patch). Most participants on opioid therapy used a single opioid (77 %, 79/103) rather than combination oral opioid therapies (8 %, 8/103). NSAIDs were used in 38 % (77/201), with the majority using a non-selective NSAID (*n* = 71). Almost half of NSAID users reported them as an OTC medication (44 %) Gastro-protective agent (GPA) use among all non-selective NSAID or COX-2 inhibitor users was 48 % (34/71) and 67 % (4/6) respectively. In participants taking OTC NSAIDs, only 35 % of these used a GPA compared to 58 % of those taking prescription NSAIDs. Nutraceutical use was limited with only 6 % reporting use of glucosamine/chondroitin (Table 3).

Combination oral analgesia use was common (59 %, 113/191) and is outlined in Table 4. The most common local pharmacological therapies were topical NSAID for knee OA (43 %, 87/201) and intra-articular corticosteroid injection for subacromial impingement syndrome (24 %, 49/201) and knee OA (24 %, 49/201).

Table 3. Overall pattern of current and previous medication use

	Paracetamol	NSAID	Cox2 inhibitor	Oral co-codamol	Other oral opioid[a]	Transdermal opioid	Glucosamine/ Chondroitin	Hydroxychloroquine
Current drug use	124 (62)	71 (35)	6 (3)	58 (29)	47 (23)	14 (7)	12 (6)	4 (2)
Prescription drug	47 (38)	40 (56)	6 (100)	47 (81)	47 (100)	14 (100)	0 (0)	4 (100)
Reason for use								
For most painful joint	68 (55)	46 (65)	3 (50)	36 (62)	22 (47)	2 (14)	1 (12)	2 (50)
For overall pain	56 (45)	25 (35)	3 (50)	22 (38)	25 (53)	12 (86)	11 (88)	2 (50)
Drug experience								
Effective	50 (40)	49 (69)	3 (50)	32 (55)	29 (62)	6 (43)	7 (58)	3 (75)
Not effective	74 (60)	22 (31)	3 (50)	26 (45)	18 (38)	8 (57)	5 (42)	1 (25)
Side effects	3 (2)	12 (17)	6 (100)	24 (41)	24 (51)	3 (21)	0 (0)	0 (0)
Frequency of use								
Regular use	28 (23)	18 (25)	5 (83)	19 (33)	22 (47)	12 (86)	11 (88)	4 (100)
Only when in pain	96 (77)	53 (75)	1 (17)	39 (67)	25 (53)	2 (14)	1 (12)	0 (0)
Previous drug use	52 (26)	119 (60)	4 (2)	87 (43)	53 (26)	9 (4)	70 (35)	5 (3)
Reason stopped[b]								
Side effects	1 (2)	78 (66)	4 (100)	52 (60)	43 (81)	4 (44)	4 (5)	4 (80)
Inefficacy	42 (81)	32 (26)	0 (0)	20 (23)	6 (11)	3 (33)	58 (83)	1 (20)
Loss of efficacy	9 (17)	7 (5)	0 (0)	7 (7)	1 (2)	0 (0)	3 (4)	0 (0)
Doesn't like taking pills	0 (0)	1 (1)	0 (0)	5 (5)	1 (2)	2 (22)	4 (5)	0 (0)
Pain not severe enough	0 (0)	4 (3)	0 (0)	5 (5)	2 (0)	1 (11)	2 (3)	0 (0)

Values shown are number of participants (%)
[a]Other oral opioid includes codeine phosphate, tramadol and oral morphine
[b]Some participants had more than one reason for stopping medication

Participants using non-selective NSAIDs or oral co-codamol tended to use the analgesia for the most painful joint rather than for overall pain. Most participants did not use oral analgesia regularly, instead reporting to use it only when in pain. In general efficacy was lowest among participants that reported use of paracetamol (40 %, 50/124) and highest for NSAID (69 %, 49/71) and other oral opioid users (62 %, 29/47). NSAID and co-codamol users who found their medication to be effective were significantly more likely to be using it for their most painful joint (36/49, 73 % and 25/32, 78 % respectively) than for all of their joints (13/49, 27 %, $X^2 = 5.22$, $p = 0.022$; 7/32, 22 %, $X^2 = 7.82$, $p = 0.005$). For paracetamol users and opioid users effectiveness was equally as likely in participants reporting use for their most painful joint or for overall pain. Side effects were least common among paracetamol users and most common in those using oral opioid therapy. The overall pattern of current pharmacological therapy use is described in Table 3. The most common reason for stopping NSAID and all opioid (oral and transdermal) medication was side effects whereas inefficacy was the most common reason for stopping paracetamol and glucosamine/chondroitin (Table 4).

Table 4. Analgesic combinations in 191 participants [a]

Type of treatment	Number of patients (%)
Monotherapy	78 (41)
Paracetamol	36 (19)
NSAID	12 (6)
Opioids	38 (20)
Nutraceuticals	0 (0)
Combination therapy	113 (59)
Paracetamol	
with NSAID	31 (16)
with opioids	30 (16)
with nutraceuticals	4 (2)
with NSAID and opioids	15 (8)
with NSAID and nutraceuticals	3 (2)
with opioids and nutraceuticals	3 (2)
NSAID	
with opioids	12 (6)
with nutraceuticals	1 (1)
with opioids and nutraceuticals	1 (1)
Opioids	
with nutraceuticals	2 (1)
Nutraceuticals	
with NSAID and opioids	1 (1)
with all drugs	2 (1)

NSAID nonsteroidal anti-inflammatory drugs

[a] 10 participants did not take any medication

DISCUSSION

This is the first comprehensive study to examine the detailed clinical characteristics of whole-body MSJP and peoples' utilisation of therapeutic interventions. This study confirms that MSJP is a heterogeneous condition comprised of a range of musculoskeletal pathologies. It can be conceptualised as different combinations of peripheral joint OA, soft tissue disorders and mechanical back pain.

In this study we included participants on the basis of at least one large joint with pain. Previous studies have specified knee OA as the index joint whilst others have reported patients with multiple painful joints only if they meet the ACR criteria for fibromyalgia; such studies therefore do not necessarily reflect a true representation of mechanical MSJP patients [13, 14, 15]. Many previous MSJP studies, whether postal questionnaire or interview based, have reported the number of painful joints without characterisation of the involved joints [16]. Our study included detailed clinical diagnosis of all involved joints, both upper and lower limbs as well as the axial joints. We found that nearly all participants had at least one joint with an OA diagnosis, with most also having soft tissue pathology in at least one joint. A previous study which characterised upper limb joint pain reported that specific soft-tissue disorders were common in the upper limb [17]. In line with this, we found that soft-tissue disorders were common in the setting of MSJP especially in the upper limb compared to the lower limbs. This study highlights the heterogeneity of MSJP and demonstrates that a combination of OA, back pain and soft tissue disorders is common in this phenotypic setting.

Association between reported painful sites was strongest for contralateral and adjacent sites, which may be attributed to shared risk factors. Our findings are similar to those from a 12,400 patient questionnaire study which found similar associations (ORs) for self-reported pain at 10 anatomical sites [18].

Muscle weakness captured as a component of MSJP in previous studies has been limited to the upper limbs. Andersson et al. observed that individuals with generalised pain were more likely to have reduced hand muscle strength compared to regional pain [19]. We recorded both upper and lower limb muscle strength and found that both were common in the setting of MSJP. Obesity and shoulder pain showed a statistically significant association with lower limb muscle weakness, whilst the majority (87 %) of participants with shoulder pain had lower limb weakness. These results suggest that obesity and/or lower limb muscle weakness may contribute to upper limb symptoms, perhaps through changes to the use of the upper limbs, as has recently been reported [20]. The longitudinal data from this study may shed more light on this putative biomechanical chain of events.

Previous studies have mainly recorded non-pharmacological management in the setting of knee OA [21, 22]. The majority (79 %) of participants in our study had attended a physiotherapy appointment, with two-thirds of these reportedly continuing with exercises. This is considerably higher than a recent OA study which reported physiotherapy attendance of 46 % [23], but should be interpreted with some caution since we did not capture exact numbers and details of sessions attended or details of adherence. With regards to education, only a quarter of participants recalled ever receiving written information on their joint problem. Although this finding may be influenced by recall bias, nonetheless it suggests that there may be a lack of readily available information (particularly about specific soft tissue disorders) at health practices. This highlights an important area of management that needs further consideration. The majority of participants in this study were overweight/obese (86 %), with only low numbers (36 %) reporting to have ever received any type of weight management therapy. With obesity rates increasing in Western societies, this remains an important issue [24], particularly in light of a recent randomised clinical trial which found that even a modest weight reduction leads to improvement in function in people with knee OA [25].

A recent GP survey revealed a belief that different classes of analgesia have equal efficacy when used across the range of different musculoskeletal pathologies that comprise MSJP [8]. However, research is lacking to examine efficacy across classes of oral analgesia for different musculoskeletal pathologies, especially for opioids, providing limited evidence-base for how to best approach and treat MSJP. Compared to previous studies, this study provides a more detailed description of analgesic use in the setting of MSJP by separately reporting paracetamol, co-codamol, non-selective NSAIDs, cox-2 inhibitors and the different types of opioid (oral and transdermal), as well as examining whether participants used agents for their most painful joint or for overall pain. Although paracetamol was the most commonly used medication in our study, opioid use was frequent with 48 % of participants using at least one opioid. Co-codamol was the most commonly used opioid-containing analgesia, with the large majority prescribed by the GP despite its availability over the counter in the UK. The high use of opioids in our cohort is in line with Grimby et al. who suggested that in their older (>75 years) cohort, 'light' opioids were more likely to be used in MSJP than NSAIDs [26]. In contrast our recent study of medication use in people across Europe with OA, found that NSAIDs were the most commonly used medication in this population [27]. The higher use of opioids in the MSJP setting may reflect increased incidence of co-morbidities in this population, which preclude the use of NSAIDs or may reflect physician preference of opioids. In this study, 80 % of participants reported at least one comorbidity related to cardiac, pulmonary or gastrointestinal disease, demonstrating the high prevalence of comorbidities in this population.

Medication efficacy was reportedly higher among those using NSAID or opioid therapy and lowest with paracetamol use. Paracetamol was most commonly stopped due to inefficacy. The lack of efficacy for paracetamol reported by our population is in line with for the very low effect size for paracetamol reported in recent systematic reviews of OA therapies [28, 29]. Notably, for both NSAIDs and co-codamol users, effectiveness was more likely to be reported by participants using the therapy to reduce pain in their most painful joint, compared to those reporting to use the therapy to reduce their overall pain. Most participants did not use oral analgesia on a regular basis, perhaps offering opportunity for optimisation of therapy. Although there is no standard definition for 'under-utilisation' in this context, the level of utilisation of therapy which translates into efficacy in such a population is unknown. Further work to establish appropriate levels of therapeutic utilisation and to understand why therapies are currently under-utilised in MSJP is required.

There are limitations to this study. Intra-rater reliability for the different joint diagnoses, which were performed by the single study clinician, was not examined; however the clinician was a fully qualified Consultant Rheumatologist. Although recruitment was from a variety of sources including primary, secondary and tertiary centres, most participants were from the hospital rheumatology clinics. This may have introduced some selection bias, as patients seen in these clinics may have a more complex presentation compared to those managed in primary care. When compared to another Yorkshire community-based postal survey of 16,222 people [2], the median number of painful joints in the present cohort was higher (6 vs. 4). Inclusion of patients with at least one large joint pain may also have introduced some selection bias leading to a cohort mainly with large joint OA, whilst the lack of radiological assessment may have precluded accurate diagnosis of OA in joints not included in ACR criteria e.g. shoulder, elbow and ankle. Whilst we endeavored to capture as many therapies as possible in this study the list was not exhaustive. As such we did not collect information on non-pharmacological therapies such as yoga and Tai Chi, and their current uptake in this group is therefore unknown. There are limitations in using the MRC scale to measure lower limb weakness due to the subjective nature of the test and lack of specificity, which may have resulted in an under-estimation of the true prevalence of lower limb weakness. As with other questionnaire-based studies, findings may also be limited by recall bias.

CONCLUSIONS

In conclusion, MSJP reflects a combination of OA, soft tissue disorders and mechanical back pain. Muscle weakness and obesity are very common within this population. Both systemic and local therapies appear to be underutilised in people with MSJP. Identifying the reasons for this should guide effective intervention research.

ACKNOWLEDGEMENT

We would like to thank the LMBRU PPI group for their help in designing study documents; Christine Thomas, Jill Halstead, Jackie Nam, David Pickles, Hazel Rowling, Angela Nauth and Sharon Ferdinandus for their help with participant recruitment; and Helen Skinner and Emily Norman for their help with data entry.

Funding

RR is funded by the Rose Hellaby Scholarship (Guardian Trust) New Zealand, The Royal Australasian College of Physicians (RACP)/Australian Rheumatology Association & Starr Fellowship (Australia), New Zealand Rheumatology Association and Health Workforce New Zealand. SRK and PGC are funded in part by the Arthritis Research UK Experimental Osteoarthritis Treatment Centre (grant number 20083) and the NIHR Leeds Musculoskeletal Biomedical Research Unit. This study has been part funded by the National Institute for Health Research (NIHR) through the Leeds Musculoskeletal Biomedical Research Unit. This article presents independent research funded by the NIHR. This research was supported by the National Institute for Health Research Leeds Clinical Research Facility. The views expressed are those of the authors and not necessarily those of the NHS, the NIHR or the Department of Health.

COMPETING INTERESTS

The authors declare that they have no competing interests.

AUTHORS' CONTRIBUTIONS

PC, SK, RR designed the study. RR, SH conducted the study. RR, BD, SK, EH conducted the statistical analysis. RR, BD, SK drafted the manuscript. All authors read and approved the final manuscript.

REFERENCES

1. Vos T, Flaxman AD, Naghavi M, Lozano R, Michaud C, Ezzati M, et al. Years lived with disability (YLDs) for 1160 sequelae of 289 diseases and injuries 1990-2010: a systematic analysis for the Global Burden of Disease Study 2010. Lancet. 2012;380(9859):2163–96.

2. Keenan AM, Tennant A, Fear J, Emery P, Conaghan PG. Impact of multiple joint problems on daily living tasks in people in the community over age fifty-five. Arthritis Rheum. 2006;55(5):757–64.

3. Peat G, Thomas E, Wilkie R, Croft P. Multiple joint pain and lower extremity disability in middle and old age. Disabil Rehabil. 2006;28(24):1543–9.

4. Croft P, Jordan K, Jinks C. "Pain elsewhere" and the impact of knee pain in older people. Arthritis Rheum. 2005;52(8):2350–4.

5. Miranda H, Kaila-Kangas L, Heliovaara M, Leino-Arjas P, Haukka E, Liira J, et al. Musculoskeletal pain at multiple sites and its effects on work ability in a general working population. Occup Environ Med. 2010;67(7):449–55.

6. Osteoarthritis. Care and management in adults. NICE Clinical Guideline 177. February 2014. Available from: http://www.nice.org.uk/guidance/CG177. 2014. http://www.nice.org.uk/Guidance/CG177. Accessed 4 August 2014.

7. National Institute for Health and Care Excellence. Low back pain: Early management of persistent non-specific low back pain. May 2009. Available from: http://www.nice.org.uk/guidance/CG88. 2009.

8. Raja R, Kingsbury SR, Wise E, Conaghan PG. Primary care approaches to musculoskeletal multiple-site joint pain pharmacological therapy: a survey of general practitioners. Prim Health Care Res Dev. 2014;15(4):476–81.

9. Florence JM, Pandya S, King WM, Robison JD, Baty J, Miller JP, et al. Intrarater reliability of manual muscle test (Medical Research Council scale) grades in Duchenne's muscular dystrophy. Phys Ther. 1992;72(2):115–22. discussion 22-6.

10. StataCorp. Stata Statistical Software: Release 13. College Station: StataCorp LP; 2013.

11. R Core Team. R: A language and environment for statistical computing. Vienna: R Foundation for Statistical Computing; 2014. http://www.R-project.org/.

12. Sallinen J, Stenholm S, Rantanen T, Heliovaara M, Sainio P, Koskinen S. Hand-grip strength cut points to screen older persons at risk for mobility limitation. J Am Geriatr Soc. 2010;58(9):1721–6.

13. Suri P, Morgenroth DC, Kwoh CK, Bean JF, Kalichman L, Hunter DJ. Low back pain and other musculoskeletal pain comorbidities in individuals with symptomatic osteoarthritis of the knee: data from the osteoarthritis initiative. Arthritis Care Res (Hoboken). 2010;62(12):1715–23.

14. Carnes D, Parsons S, Ashby D, Breen A, Foster NE, Pincus T, et al. Chronic musculoskeletal pain rarely presents in a single body site: results from a UK population study. Rheumatology (Oxford). 2007;46(7):1168–70.

15. Harkness EF, Macfarlane GJ, Silman AJ, McBeth J. Is musculoskeletal pain more common now than 40 years ago?: Two population-based cross-sectional studies. Rheumatology (Oxford). 2005;44(7):890–5.

16. Cuperus N, Vliet Vlieland TP, Mahler EA, Kersten CC, Hoogeboom TJ, van den Ende CH. The clinical burden of generalized osteoarthritis represented by self-reported health-related quality of life and activity limitations: a cross-sectional study. Rheumatol Int. 2015;35(5):871–7.

17. Walker-Bone K, Palmer KT, Reading I, Coggon D, Cooper C. Prevalence and impact of musculoskeletal disorders of the upper limb in the general population. Arthritis Rheum. 2004;51(4):642–51.

18. Coggon D, Ntani G, Palmer KT, Felli VE, Hararl R, Barrero LH, et al. Patterns of multisite pain and associations with risk factors. Pain. 2013;154(9):1769–77.

19. Andersson HI, Ejlertsson G, Leden I, Rosenberg C. Characteristics of subjects with chronic pain, in relation to local and widespread pain report. A prospective study of symptoms, clinical findings and blood tests in subgroups of a geographically defined population. Scand J Rheumatol. 1996;25(3):146–54.

20. Laslett LL, Otahal P, Hensor EM, Kingsbury SR, Conaghan PG. Why does joint pain 'spread'? Knee pain predicts later shoulder pain, due to muscle weakness. Data from the Osteoarthritis Initiative. Intern Med J. 2015;45:10.

21. Jordan KM, Sawyer S, Coakley P, Smith HE, Cooper C, Arden NK. The use of conventional and complementary treatments for knee osteoarthritis in the community. Rheumatology (Oxford). 2004;43(3):381–4.

22. Porcheret M, Jordan K, Jinks C, Croft P. Primary care treatment of knee pain--a survey in older adults. Rheumatology (Oxford). 2007;46(11):1694–700.

23. Conaghan PG, Porcheret M, Kingsbury SR, Gammon A, Soni A, Hurley M, et al. Impact and therapy of osteoarthritis: the Arthritis Care OA Nation 2012 survey. Clin Rheumatol. 2014.

24. [Health and Social Care Information Centre (UK) [Internet]. Statistics in obesity, physical activity and diet; publication date 20th February 2013; [cited 2014]. Available from:http://www.hscic.gov.uk/catalogue/PUB10364].

25. Christensen R, Astrup A, Bliddal H. Weight loss: the treatment of choice for knee osteoarthritis? A randomized trial. Osteoarthritis Cartilage. 2005;13(1):20–7.

26. Grimby C, Fastbom J, Forsell Y, Thorslund M, Claesson CB, Winblad B. Musculoskeletal pain and analgesic therapy in a very old population. Arch Gerontol Geriatr. 1999;29(1):29–43.

27. Kingsbury SR, Gross HJ, Isherwood G, Conaghan PG. Osteoarthritis in Europe: impact on health status, work productivity and use of pharmacotherapies in five European countries. Rheumatology (Oxford). 2014.

28. Zhang W, Nuki G, Moskowitz RW, Abramson S, Altman RD, Arden NK, et al. OARSI recommendations for the management of hip and knee osteoarthritis: part III: Changes in evidence following systematic cumulative update of research published through January 2009. Osteoarthritis Cartilage. 2010;18(4):476–99.

29. Machado GC, Maher CG, Ferreira PH, Pinheiro MB, Lin CW, Day RO, et al. Efficacy and safety of paracetamol for spinal pain and osteoarthritis: systematic review and meta-analysis of randomised placebo controlled trials. BMJ. 2015;350:h1225.

Chapter 11

Development and Testing of Gold Nanoparticles for Drug Delivery and Treatment of Heart Failure: A Theranostic Potential for PPP Cardiology

Mykola Ya Spivak[1,2], Rostyslav V Bubnov[1,3]*, Ilya M Yemets[4] , Liudmyla M Lazarenko[1], Natalia O Tymoshok[1] and Zoia R Ulberg[5]

[1]Zabolotny Institute of Microbiology and Virology, National Academy of Sciences of Ukraine, Zabolotny str., 154, Kyiv 03680, Ukraine.

[2]LCL "DIAPROF", Svitlycky str., 35, Kyiv 04123, Ukraine

[3]Centre of Ultrasound Diagnostics and Interventional Sonography, Clinical Hospital "Pheophania" of State Affairs Department, Zabolotny str., 21, Kyiv 03680, Ukraine.

[4]Scientific-Practical Centre of Pediatric Cardiology and Cardiac Health of Ukraine, Chornovil str., 28/1, Kyiv 01135, Ukraine.

[5]Ovcharenko Institute of Biocolloidal Chemistry, National Academy of Sciences of Ukraine, Acad. Vernadsky blvd, 42, Kyiv 03142, Ukraine

ABSTRACT

Introduction

Nanoscale gold particles (AuNPs) have wide perspectives for biomedical applications because of their unique biological properties, as antioxidative activity and potentials for drug delivery.

Aims and objectives

The aim was to test effects of AuNPs using suggested heart failure rat model to compare with proved medication Simdax, to test gold nanoparticle for drug delivery, and to test sonoporation effect to increase nanoparticles delivery into myocardial cells.

Material and methods

We performed biosafety and biocompatibility tests for AuNPs and conjugate with Simdax. For *in vivo* tests, we included Wistar rats weighing 180–200 g (n = 54), received doxorubicin in cumulative dose of 12.0 mg/kg to model advance heart failure, registered by ultrasonography. We formed six groups: the first three groups of animals received, respectively, 0.06 ml Simdax, AuNPs, and conjugate (AuNPs-Simdax), intrapleurally, and the second three received them intravenously. The seventh group was control (saline). We performed dynamic assessment of heart failure regression *in vivo* measuring hydrothorax. Sonoporation of gold nanoparticles to cardiomyocytes was tested.

Results

We designed and constructed colloidal, spherical gold nanoparticles, AuNPs-Simdax conjugate, both founded biosafety (in cytotoxicity, genotoxicity, and immunoreactivity). In all animals of the six groups after the third day post-medication injection, no ascites and liver enlargement were registered ($P < 0.001$ vs controls). Conjugate injection showed significantly higher hydrothorax reduction than Simdax injection only ($P < 0.01$); gold nanoparticle injection showed significantly higher results than Simdax injection ($P < 0.05$). AuNPs and conjugate showed no significant difference for rat recovery. Difference in rat life continuity was significant between Simdax vs AuNPs ($P < 0.05$) and Simdax vs conjugate ($P < 0.05$). Sonoporation enhances AuNP transfer into the cell and mitochondria that were highly localized, superior to controls ($P < 0.01$ for both).

Conclusions

Gold nanoparticles of 30 nm and its AuNPs-Simdax conjugate gave positive results in biosafety and biocompatibility *in vitro* and *in vivo*. AuNPs-Simdax and AuNPs have similar significant cardioprotective effects in rats with doxorubicin-induced heart failure, higher than that of Simdax. Intrapleural (local) delivery is preferred over intravenous (systemic) delivery according to all tested parameters. Sonoporation is able to enhance gold nanoparticle delivery to myocardial cells *in vivo*.

Keywords: Predictive Preventive Personalized medicine Nanomedicine Gold nanoparticles Heart failure Drug delivery Sonoporation Theranostics Animal model

OVERVIEW

Predictive, preventive, and personalized cardiovascular nanomedicine

In the developing paradigm of predictive, preventive, and personalized nanomedicine (PPPM), a crucial point is highly specific and sensitive, i.e., drug targeting, to make patients receive the right drug for their disease at the right dose and the right time [1]. One of the goals of PPPM is to diagnose, observe the process of treatment in tissue transformation, and analyze early parameters (biomarkers) to assess/predict the outcome, driven by a decision-making process.

Heart diseases are one of the main causes of death worldwide; heart failure is associated with a significantly reduced physical and mental health, resulting in a decreased quality of life [2, 3]. Although many patients with cardiovascular diseases survive for many years, the progressive disease is associated with an overall annual mortality rate of

10% [4]; heart failure is the leading cause of hospitalization in people older than 65 years [4].

Some of the outstanding achievements at the end of the last century are the studies on properties of biological and synthetic materials in nanometer size. The rapid development of nanoscience has caused the formation of fundamentally new directions for biotechnology research on nano-objects, which are characterized by peculiar, often unexpected properties that are different from the properties of both macro- and microscale particles.

Development of fundamentally new methods of diagnosis and treatment goes towards the use of nanomaterials (NPs) and nanotechnology, which has a very broad definition based on scale, and nanomedicines are likewise based not only on the type of medicine or their function but also on a nanosized range. While most nanotechnology is expected to have an upper size limit of 100 nm, in the drug delivery field, this is more generally accepted as medicines in the size range from a few nanometres to 1,000 nm in diameter. Advances in nanotechnology have led to the development of new materials and devices for various scientific and therapeutic purposes.

Modeling of heart failure

Mouse and rat models are widely used in biological and medical sciences, but these studies are still limited by the inability of noninvasive collection of anatomical and physiological data during the time of the study. The use of rats as animal models is rational from the economic viewpoint, and many techniques have been developed to measure relevant functional parameters. Animals have been used by humans to understand their own biology since many human diseases are studied on experimental animals. The appropriateness of animal models in the future is determined by the fact that even the most powerful computers using appropriate mathematical models are unable to reproduce the interaction between molecules of cells, organs, organisms, and environment [5].

In cardiovascular research, animal models have allowed the study of cardiovascular disease in the early stages, as well as the investigation on the mechanisms of the pathogenesis of cardiovascular disease and the effects of drug intervention. Doggrell et al. [6] suggest that an ideal animal model for any cardiovascular disease in humans should follow five characteristics: (1) mimic the human disease, (2) allow studies in chronic, stable disease, (3) produce symptoms which are predictable and controllable, (4) satisfy economical, technical, and animal welfare considerations, and (5) allow measurement of relevant cardiac, biochemical, and hemodynamic parameters. Cardiovascular disease is uncommon in young humans but markedly increases with age [7].

The numeral rat models of hypertension, cardiac hypertrophy, and heart failure were suggested for the following conditions [8]: hypertension, systemic spontaneously hypertensive rats (SHRs), stroke-prone SHR (SHR-SP), mineralocorticoids (DOCA salt), NO synthase inhibition (L-NAME administration), transgenics (TGR(mREN2) 27 rats), diabetic hypertensive rats (STZ-SHR, Zucker), renal renal artery occlusion (1K1C, 2K1C), pulmonary monocrotaline, hypoxia (normobaric, hypobaric), hypertrophy, spontaneously hypertensive rats (SHRs), renal artery occlusion; pressure loading (aortic banding), catecholamines (noradrenaline, isoprenaline), Transgenics, heart failure, systemic hypertension spontaneously hypertensive rats (SHRs-F), hypertensive HF prone rats, Dahl/Rapp salt-sensitive rats, ischemic heart failure non-occlusive coronary ligation, myocardial infarction coronary ligation, microembolization of coronary vessels, cardiomyopathy toxins (adriamycin, ethanol), myocarditis autoimmune, Chagas' disease, pulmonary hypertension, monocrotaline, hypoxia, and miscellaneous aortacaval fistula (shunts).

Imaging for heart failure assessment in rats

In the biological sciences, many studies using mouse models are limited by the inability to gather anatomical and physiological information noninvasively in a longitudinal manner. To investigate the changes, the experimental animal had to be killed and dissected. Therefore, reducing the losses and increasing the number of small animals as an experiment by intravital evaluation of changes in animal tissue is a very relevant task. Clinical ultrasound (US) diagnostics besides the human could be successfully used to study the structure of animal tissues, including small ones. The US method is used for research purposes. Ultrasound biomicroscopy (UBM) may overcome this obstacle as it confers near-microscopic resolution through the use of high-frequency ultrasound waves, which can be applied for echocardiography for a fetal study of the cardiovascular system in mouse embryos [9].

Still, preclinical imaging techniques in small animals, especially with the use of ultrasound technology, are used only in few research centers using special equipment around the world [10]. Recently, we performed a study describing the use of US equipment of general use for *in vivo* study of novel medicine testing in mice [11, 12] and patented the method of experiment on animals using US [8, 13], which consider registration of dynamic changes in the tissues of animals carried ultrasound small laboratory animals (rats, mice) using high-frequency probes using Doppler, sonoelastography, contrast media, motion detection of tissue, interventions under US guidance for administration of drugs, and obtaining material for study and create vector three-dimensional scenes using the received ultrasonic data.

The application of ultrasonic methods using special equipment for *in vivo* examination of cardiac function was also described in rats with echocardiography [14, 15, 16, 17, 18, 19, 20, 21,22, 23, 24]. Bjornerheim et al. [14], while evaluating echocardiography data, considered that Doppler data are more representative than the M-mode. The regional heart function is reported to be exactly evaluated using tissue Doppler and two-dimensional (2D) strain echocardiography [15]. Color Doppler-guided evaluation of aortic flow and aortic root measurement was reported for assessment of stroke volume and cardiac output in mice [16]. Recently, reports have emerged regarding the use of intravascular probes adapted for transesophageal study of the rat heart [15].

Few researches focus on the study of echocardiographic changes in post-infarction of rats with congestive heart failure (CHF) and spontaneous hypertension [18, 19, 25]. Sjaastad et al. [21] evaluated the post-infarction myocardial function of rats and determined echocardiographic criteria for heart failure CHF using high-performance echocardiography. Extensive myocardial infarction (MI) was induced in rats by left coronary occlusion. Sham-operated animals served as controls. Authors conclude that by high-frame-rate echocardiography, it is possible to obtain high-quality recordings in rats. It is feasible to distinguish MI rats from CHF rats due to the myocardial dysfunction from those without failure and since longitudinal studies are performed on myocardial function. Kokubo et al. [19] presented a study on hypertension, designed to provide a noninvasive evaluation of the time-dependent alteration of cardiac function in male spontaneously hypertensive rat at 4 to 24 weeks of age and age-matched Wistar-Kyoto rats. Echocardiographic studies were performed after blood pressure and heart rate were measured by a tail-cuff method. Rats are commonly used to study left ventricular (LV) hypertrophy and measure the LV mass and dimensions. De Simone et al. [22] determined the accuracy of echocardiography in rats. Blinded cross-sectional area and LV mass measurements using either the cube function or an elliptical model from high-resolution M-mode echocardiograms were compared to the necropsy LV weight (0.28 to 1.5 g) in 41 normotensive (body weight 116 to 762 g) and 17 hypertensive rats (350 to 560 g), comparing postmortem chamber volumes in 28 normal rats (0.02 to 0.19 ml) to echocardiographic volumes derived from the elliptical model. Echocardiography can be used to evaluate LV structure and function in rats and to detect *in vivo*LV anatomic differences induced by hypertension.

In studies of CHF treatment, it is essential to select animals with a similar degree of cardiac dysfunction. However, this is difficult to establish without hemodynamic evaluation in rat post-infarction-induced congestive heart failure. Martinez et al. [23] studied the diagnostics of congestive heart failure in long-term follow-up in post-infarction rats using only echocardiographic criteria through a J-tree cluster analysis and Fisher's linear discriminant function in two sets of sham and infarcted rats. Echocardiographic analysis has shown to be useful in accurately predicting congestive heart failure in postinfarction rats with 100% specificity and 80% sensitivity. However, ultrasound can cause complication in rats, such as pulmonary hemorrhage [24].

Doxorubicin for heart failure modeling

Doxorubicin, one of the most effective anticancer drugs, is characterized by severe cardiotoxic effects, which induce cardiac remodeling and congestive heart failure. The method of simulation of heart failure uses doxorubicin [26] by means of 10 intraperitoneal drug injection in dose of 1 mg/kg, followed by transesophageal echocardiography adapted intravascular probe. Kharin et al. [27] described chronic doxorubicin cardiotoxicity in rats in a cumulative dose of doxorubicin (15 mg/kg) by six equal intraperitoneal injections in a 2-week period. Authors registered remodeling of ventricular repolarization heterogeneity. The major findings were as follows: (1) activation-recovery intervals (ARIs) on the ventricular epicardium of both ventricles were significantly prolonged in the doxorubicin group and (2) this inhomogeneous prolongation of ARIs on the ventricular epicardium resulted in the increase in the dispersion of repolarization across the ventricular epicardium and the inhomogeneous alterations of the regional ARI gradients on the ventricular epicardium. These changes in repolarization could explain the electrocardiographic alterations, that is, the prolongation of the QT interval and flattening of the T wave.

In clinical practice, despite its cardiotoxic effects, doxorubicin remains in use because of its efficacy in the treatment of several types of tumors

[28]. According to Steinherz et al. [29], echocardiography in humans should be performed before every additional course of doxorubicin up to a total dose of 300 mg per square meter, given with or without concurrent radiation therapy. A change in the left ventricular ejection fraction, as determined by echocardiography, is a very good indicator of developing cardiomyopathy; monitoring for such a change should be frequent during treatment and regular thereafter throughout the patient's lifetime. Adjunctive therapy with an antioxidant such as probucol merits serious consideration. Endomyocardial biopsy remains the most sensitive method for early diagnosis of ensuing cardiomyopathy.

Dimitrakis et al. [30] tested the hypothesis of the dose-dependent cardiotoxicity of doxorubicin, affecting protein degradation pathways in adult cardiomyocytes connected to the effects of apoptosis, autophagy, and the proteasome/ubiquitin system in long-term-cultured adult rat cardiomyocytes. Thus, doxorubicin causes a down regulation of the protein degradation machinery of cardiomyocytes with a resulting accumulation of poly-ubiquitinated proteins and autophagosomes. Although autophagy is initially stimulated as a compensatory response to cytotoxic stress, it is followed by apoptosis and necrosis at higher doses and longer exposure times. This mechanism might contribute to the late cardiotoxicity of anthracyclines by accelerated aging of the postmitotic adult cardiomyocytes and to the susceptibility of the aging heart to anthracycline cancer therapy.

Al-Shabanah et al. [31] studied interaction of doxorubicin with iron and the consequent generation of reactive oxygen species as a major player in doxorubicin-induced cardiomyopathy.

It was supposed that the pericardial pores may function in an allied self-defense mechanism between the pleural and pericardial cavities in mice [32]. Numerous circular fenestrations or pores that indirectly connect the right and left pleural cavities were present in the pericardium of the golden hamster and rat [33]. This phenomena could be relevant in choosing the place of injection (the effect should be expected as similar).

However, in described models, focus mostly on local heart function assessed by echocardiography, the dynamic *in vivo* examination of systemic circulation of the animals was not sufficiently evaluated. All cited papers using ultrasound imaging, considered application of special US equipment.

We did not find any data regarding the use of precise injection under US guidance for heart failure modeling in rats. Without visual navigation, injection methods are still limited by introduction of agents orally, into the tail vein, intraperitoneally, and subtentorially. Finally, developing a comprehensive methodology for the cardiovascular system using Doppler, M-mode parameters, conduction systematic assessment of hemocirculation, injection drugs under US guidance in pericardial and pleural cavities remains to be an important task; optimal cardiotoxic dose of doxorubicin for extended and longitudinal observation of rats has not been determined.

Recently, we described and patented the method of doxorubicin-induced heart failure on the rat model using the US equipment, which focuses on peripheral circulation. The assessment suggested that optimal cardiotoxic dose of doxorubicin for extended and longitudinal observation of rats has not been determined [10, 34]. The modeling process for heart failure, which includes an experiment on laboratory animals (rats) introduced with a cardiotoxic drug (doxorubicin) and assessed *in vivo* using a dynamic ultrasound, can be used for research purposes, i.e., for basic preclinical studies of new drugs, and can be recommended for implementation purposes to research institutes, centers, departments of cardiology, ultrasound, and interventional ultrasonography. US is an effective modality for *in vivo*monitoring of the condition of rat organs targeted for experiment in the study of cardiovascular function. In this study, the optimal dose of doxorubicin was established. Thus, the dose higher than 23.1 mg/kg leads to the death of animals from the 20-day experiment, while the dose lower than 12.45 mg/kg did not induce significant clinical symptoms. US criteria to gain reproducible model and cardiovascular symptoms are compensated to the level of normal parameters in a short period. Four- and five-time administrations of doxorubicin showed similar results for modeling heart failure.

The experimental rat organs were investigated by authorities in similar criteria and patterns as ultrasound diagnostics are performed in humans. We obtained average ultrasonic linear parameters of the rat organs: (before receiving doxorubicin) the longitudinal liver size 15 ± 1.5 mm, longitudinal kidney size 16 ± 1.3 mm, longitudinal size of spleen 14 ± 1.7 mm, inferior vena cava diameter was 3.0 ± 2,3 mm, diameter of portal vein 1.5 ± 0.3 mm, ejection fraction 78% ± 6%, maximum systolic velocity in aortic root was 11 ± 1.3 cm/s, resistive index (RI) in the renal segmental arteries 0.68 ± 0.04. Sizes were compared with necropsies. These average linear parameters of the main organs of normal rats and rats with heart failure, which received a cumulative dose of doxorubicin (15 mg/kg; Sigma-Aldrich, St. Louis, MO, USA) had significant changes in mentioned organs (Table 1).

We concluded that US is an effective modality for *in vivo* monitoring of rat organs targeted in experiments for the study of cardiovascular function. Interventional ultrasonography is effective for expanding of the utility of modeling and drug testing. However, the method is operator related and requires US specialized training, particularly in small animals. A suggested model (The optimal dose of doxorubicin for simulation of CHF of 2.5 mg/animal is a cumulative dose of 12.45 mg/kg in four injections every 3 days) can be used for research purposes and basic or preclinical studies of new drugs and can be recommended for implementation purposes in research institutes.

Interventional experiments on rats showed [34] that the technique is feasible for an expanding experiment: injection into the pericardial and the pleural rat cavities showed a non-specified difference between the two approaches.

Table 1. Sonometry data of rats [34]

Parameter	Control group	Model of heart failure	*P*
Longitudinal liver size (mm)	15.0 ± 1.5	18.0 ± 1.7	<0.05
Longitudinal kidney size (mm)	16.0 ± 1.3	17.0 ± 1.4	>0.05
longitudinal spleen size (mm)	14.0 ± 1.7	17.0 ± 1.8	<0.05
Inferior vena cava, diameter (mm)	3.0 ± 2.3	3.7 ± 2.6	>0.05
Portal vein, diameter (mm)	1.5 ± 0.3	1.78 ± 0.2	<0.05
Ejection fraction (%)	78.0 ± 6.0	46.0 ± 8.0	<0.01
Maximum systolic velocity aortic root (cm/sec)	11.0 ± 1.3	6.5 ± 1.6	<0.01
Resistive index (RI) in the renal segmental arteries	0.68 ± 0.04	0.7 ± 0.04	>0.05

Simdax (levosimendan)

For comparison, we chose the calcium sensitizer *levosimendan* (Simdax) as the most effective inotropic agent that improves myocardial contractility in patients with heart failure; although, its effects on inflammation and apoptosis are unknown. Trikas [35] examined the effects of levosimendan on markers of inflammation and apoptosis, over a period of 30 days following a 24-h infusion, in patients with heart failure. Their findings indicated that levosimendan decreases the expression of proinflammatory cytokines, tumor necrosis factor (TNF)-α receptors and sFAS, immediately after infusion, an effect which persists for 7–30 days.

The clinical application of gold nanoparticles

Plasmonic (noble metal) nanoparticles distinguish themselves from other nanoplatforms such as semiconductor quantum dots, magnetic and polymeric nanoparticle by their unique surface plasmon resonance

[36, 37, 38, 39, 40, 41, 42]. Nanogold (also called gold nanoparticle or colloidal gold) has been actively investigated in a wide variety of biomedical applications due to its biocompatibility and ease of conjugation to biomolecules [43, 44] and thus offering multiple modalities for biological and medical applications [45]. The non-cytotoxicity, non-immunogenicity and biocompatibility of many AuNPs make us relatively optimistic concerning their future essential applications in nanomedicine [43, 46].

Diagnostics

Gold nanoparticles are also used to detect biomarkers in the diagnosis of heart diseases, cancers, infectious agents (e.g., home pregnancy test) [46], and Alzheimer's disease [47, 48]. Multivalent AuNPs were found to inhibit HIV fusion [49], and AuNPs-hepatitis B virus (HBV) DNA was successfully prepared and could potentially apply to multi-gene detection chips [50]. A successful application of the AuNP-nanoprobe was the sensitive detection in clinical samples of*Mycobacterium tuberculosis*[51]. Diabetes was characterized as a multifactorial disease using the AuNP-nanoprobe method mentioned above and involving the capture of the analyte with a magnetic particle featuring recognition elements followed by binding of a AuNP with a second-recognition agent and marker DNA strands for cancer detection [52].

Therapeutic agent delivery

The study on drug delivery by nanoparticles is highly perspective of personalized medicine in the future [53]. Over the past decade, several delivery vehicles have been designed based on different nanomaterials, such as polymers [54], dendrimers [55], liposomes [56], nanotubes [57], and nanorods [58]. Therapeutic agents can also be coated onto the surface of gold nanoparticles. The large surface area-to-volume ratio of gold nanoparticles enables their surface to be coated with hundreds of molecules (including therapeutics, targeting agents, and anti-fouling polymers) [59].

Therapeutic vectors carry drugs, genes, and imaging agents into living cells and tissues [38, 60]. The drug vectors should also be stable in the circulatory system yet can also become labile under appropriate conditions when the targeted organ is reached. The drug vectors carry the drug by encapsulation or more or less strong binding (covalent, coordination, or supramolecular bond) [61]. Different routes of administration can result in various effects on the biodistribution of drug carriers.

Sonoporation

Vibration caused by ultrasonic waves can change the structure of the cell membrane and enhance its permeation. A new ultrasound-aided method, sonoporation, has been proposed and utilized to transmit target molecules (such as drugs and DNA) into cells for therapy [61]. Yu Hsin et al. [62] showed approximately 60% improvement in terms of fluorescence signals from the cellular uptake of gold nanoparticles after sonoporation treatment. Therefore, we conclude that the controlled release is feasible and can further improve the therapeutic effects of the nanoparticles [63]. Our recent results demonstrated that polyplex gene transfer by US exposure is effective. It illustrated the potential of ultrasound-triggered gene delivery technology for gene therapy [64]. Therefore, we conclude that the controlled release is feasible and can further improve the therapeutic effects of the nanoparticles.

Treatment

Gold nanoparticles are being investigated as carriers for drugs [36]. Kogan et al. utilized AuNPs in weak microwave fields in order to dissolve amyloid aggregates [37]. It was reported that gold nanoparticles were utilized for diagnostics [38] and cancer treatment [39].

The application of nanoparticles allows the combination of therapy and diagnosis, known as*theranostics*, which has received increasing attention in biomedicine [65].

Bioeffects of AuNPs

Oxidative stress is one of the main factors in cellular aging and other cellular disorders [66]. While therapeutic treatments cannot be based exclusively on the abatement of the oxidative stress, a neutralization of this cellular disorder could minimize collateral damages associated to the transformation of biomolecules in the cytosol. Traditionally, reactive oxygen intermediates were considered to be toxic by-products of aerobic metabolism, which were disposed of using antioxidants. Superoxide radicals and hydrogen peroxide [67] balance, together with the sequestering of metal ions, is thought to be important to prevent the formation of the highly toxic hydroxyl radical via the metal-dependent Haber–Weiss or the Fenton reactions.

Gold nanoparticles have been showing an antioxidant effect in a model of diabetes [68]. The use of Au/CeO_2 composites allows a large extent from the ability of gold to trap carbon-centered radicals as well as to decompose hydroperoxides [69, 70] and also has a strong antioxidant activity against cellular oxidative stress.

Assessment of risk of nanomaterials

The great expectations of gold colloid use for therapeutic purposes suggests that AuNPs should be biocompatible [43]. There is considerable potential use of AuNPs in nanomedicine, especially for imaging, diagnostics, and therapy, however, toxicity needs to be thoroughly examined with maximum care and accuracy. Because of their surface properties and very small size, nanotubes may bind and transport toxic chemical compounds as well as being toxic themselves by generating free radicals [71], inducing oxidative stress, and thus becomes a disadvantage for their application in medicine [35]. Seaton et al. established potential factors of toxicity of nanoparticles [71], which include length (greater than 15 μm, below it the fiber can be removed by pulmonary macrophages), diameter (less than 3 μm, allows fibers to be inhaled into the gas-exchanging part of the lung), insolubility, resistance to dissolution in the lung environment, and sufficient dose of delivery to the target organ. Particular attention in the context of medical use should be paid to the toxicity nanogold.

A number of studies indicate that AuNPs have low *cytotoxicity* and high *biocompatibility*[36, 72,73, 74, 75, 76]. Despite this lack of research on the nanogold toxicity in vivo, a necessary step is needed before the clinical re-dwelling drugs from AuNPs [74, 75]. The cytotoxicity of AuNPs, i.e., their cellular toxicity, has been examined by our research groups [36, 73, 74]. Since everything is toxic at high dose, the important question is whether AuNPs are toxic at the concentration at which they will be used (believed to be in the range of 1–100 AuNPs per cell). Also, *in vivo*conditions are different from *in vitro* results, and in particular, more *in vivo* studies are called for. Thus, no general conclusion can be drawn at present. It has been suggested, however, that it could be applicable to use AuNPs as reference nanoparticles for low toxicity in the set-up of a nanoparticle toxicity scale, given the higher toxicity of carbon nanotubes and quantum dots compared to non-cationic AuNPs. Finally, AuNPs are redox active and reduce the production of reactive oxygen and nitrite species [75].

Thus to the toxicity survey, it appears that AuNPs usually show rather little toxicity, if any, because many cytotoxicity studies report negative cytotoxicity results.

Cardioprotective properties of gold nanoparticles, particularly for heart failure as well as in drug delivery, were still not conclusively confirmed that a call for study using a reliable model is needed.

We suggest to increase the clinical efficacy of treatment to patients with heart failure using nanoconstructions based on gold nanoparticles due to their promising biological properties, as well as antioxidative activity and potentials for drug delivery.

The aim of the study is to develop new evidence-based approaches in the synthesis of biologically safe and biocompatible gold nanoparticles and gold-based nanoconstructions with cardiotropic drugs to improve their delivery addressed to cardiovascular pathologies.

The purposes of the study:

1. to assess biosafety, biocompatibility, and biological effectiveness of gold nanoparticles and AuNPs-Simdax conjugate created from gold nanoparticles and cardiotropic drug Simdax,
2. to conduct comparative preclinical testing of proved medication Simdax, gold nanoparticles, and AuNPs-Simdax nanoconstruction on suggested heart failure rat model, and
3. *3.* to test the sonoporation effect to increase nanoparticle delivery into myocardial cell.

METHODS

The first stage: biosafety and biocompatibility tests of gold nanoparticles and conjugate with Simdax [36, 60, 73, 74]

We developed and implemented original protocols for colloid-chemical synthesis of spherical gold nanoparticles of discrete sizes 10, 20, 30, and 45 nm; developed, designed, and optimized conjugate based on the cardiotropic agent Simdax and AuNP size of 30 nm, (AuNPs-Simdax). Conjugation was performed at component ratio 1:1 by volume. The final concentration of the active substance conjugate were Simdax 1.25 mg/ml, AuNPs of 30 nm, 19.3 mg/ml by metal. Gold nanoparticles were obtained by chemical condensation, by restoring a gold-hydrochloric acid, sodium citrate in the presence of potassium carbonate. The working solution of gold nanoparticles of size 30 nm were prepared using a 5% glucose solution so that the concentration of gold nanoparticles in solution was 1.17 mg/kg.

We received the colloid gold nanoparticles according to the following reactions:

$$2HAuCl_4 + 5K_2CO_3 \rightarrow 2KAuO_2 + 5CO_2 + 8KCl + H_2O \quad (1)$$

$$2KAuO_2 + 2CH_3COCH_3 + K_2CO_3 \rightarrow 2Au^0 + 3CH_3COOK + KHCO_3 + H_2 \quad (2)$$

The structure of gold nanoparticles synthesized by reaction (1) may be represented by the formula:

$$\{m[Au^0]nAuO_2^- : (n\text{-}x)K^+\}^{-x}xK^+, \quad (3)$$

where *m* is the number of molecules Au^0 and *n* is the number of excess ions AuO_2^- firmly absorbed on the surface of the unit (usually $m > n$) which are potential forming. *x* is the number of ions within the diffusion layer, and (*n*-*x*) is the number of counterions K^+ absorbed at the layer. The number of potassium ions (*n*-*x*) less than the number of absorbed ions AuO_2^- (*n*) results in the nanoparticle having a negative charge (*s*). The method used to obtain gold nanoparticles allows stable aqueous dispersions of nanoparticles of a certain size to be obtained.

The method used allows to obtain gold nanoparticles and stable aqueous dispersions of nanoparticles of a certain size.

Tests for biosafety and biocompatibility of gold nanoparticles and conjugate were performed according to standard requirements, assessing the appearance (color, size, and shape) of nanoparticles, contamination by extraneous bacterial and fungal microflora, and mycoplasma contamination. Biosafety *in vitro* was performed:

genotoxicity in terms of H^+-ATP-ase activity, Na^+, K^+-ATP-ase activity, lactatedehydrohenase activity, mutagenicity, impact on the gastrointestinal tract normal flora, biosafety *in vivo* in terms of genotoxicity test, micronucleus test, immunotoxicity, harmlessness *in vivo* in injecting white mice, and stability in model systems of blood.

For *in vitro* experiments, U937 (human leukemic monocyte lymphoma) cell line has been used. The AuNPs DNA-damaging activity *in vivo* has been estimated by the 'comet assay' method (alkaline gel electrophoresis of isolated eukaryotic cells). The working solution was injected into the tail vein of rats, and after 1 h, conducted the sampling of material for research.

We performed complex studies aimed at assessing the nature of the influence of gold nanoparticles on Ca^{2+}, Mg^{2+}-ATP-ase activity in myofibrils. Myofibrils from the cardiac muscles were isolated according to the Solaro method modifications. The concentrations of active ingredients in conjugate were calculated based on the therapeutic dose of Simdax and biosafety concentration of AuNPs, in which they observed minimal inhibitory effect on the amount of Ca^{2+}, Mg^{2+}-ATP-ase activity in myofibrils.

Assessment of cardioprotective properties and route of delivery of gold nanoparticles

We used 48 2-month-old laboratory Wistar rats weighing 180–200 g (n = 54) of each sex selected on the basis of analogies for the second stage and four rats for the third stage of experiment. Within 2 weeks after intravenous injection of doxorubicin Sigma solution in a cumulative dose of 12.0 mg/kg to simulate heart failure according to experimentally established scheme [34], animals showed an advanced heart failure, registered by US.

For US scanning, 3–12-MHz frequency for linear and microconvex transducers were used. The rats were examined while sedated in a supine position (Figure 1), with the chest closed and the transducer placed gently in the left parasternal position for echocardiography.

Multi-planar approaches were utilized for abdominal and pleural cavity examination. Soft fixation of animals was provided. General anesthesia was carried out by approved methods. Echocardiography was performed in longitudinal and transverse axes using the M-mode and color/pulse Doppler at the level of the left ventricular outflow tract. The heart function was evaluated from the left parasternal long axis with the beams directed 25° cranially. The focus area was set at 10–15 mm. 2D images of the liver, kidneys, chest, and abdominal cavities were obtained. Doppler techniques were applied for blood flow analysis in the portal vein, inferior vena cava, and renal vessels with a 60° angle of insonation. The rat organs were characterized by US using similar criteria and patterns as those used in humans according to the suggested model [8, 13, 34]. We considered the US criteria of CHF as follows: liver enlargement, expanding of inferior vena cava, decrease of ejection fraction, and presence of ascites and hydrothorax.

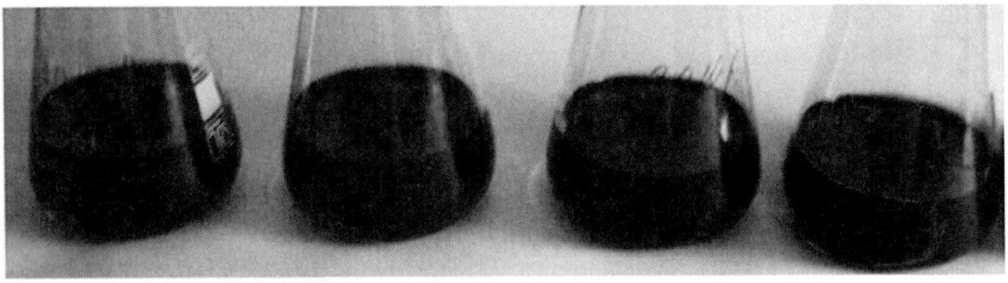

Figure 1. General view if AuNPs of discrete sizes 10, 20, 30, and 45 nm.

Two invasive interventions (pleural cavity) for drug testing were used under US guidance. Fine needles, 29–31 G, were used. US was performed three times: on the same day and on the first and second day after the administration, in order to verify the CHF regression. Percutaneous intervention performed at adequate visualization of a target was carried out in the transverse axis (out of plane) following the general principles of interventional sonography.

The second stage (comparative assessment the cardioprotective efficacy)

For comparative assessment, the cardioprotective efficacy of injection gold nanoparticle, gold nanoparticle conjugated with Simdax and Simdax only intrapleurally and intravenously. The laboratory Wistar rats (*N* = 48) were used for this stage within 2 weeks after intravenous injection of doxorubicin Sigma solution in cumulative dose of 12.0 mg/kg to simulate the heart failure according to experimentally established scheme. Animals showed an advanced heart failure that was caused by intravenously introduced doxorubicin (cumulative dose 12.0 mg/kg), as described in stages 1 and 2 of the study. Afterward, at the 14th day, animals with severe heart failure were assessed by ultrasound and were administered the following agents: (1) gold nanoparticles (2) Simdax (levosimendan), an inotropic and vasodilator agent, (3) gold nanoparticles and Simdax conjugate. Three kinds of solutions were administered in two different routes: into the pleural cavity (intrapleural injection under US guidance) or intravenously.

We formed six groups with eight rats in each (Table 2): the first three groups of animals received levosimendan (Simdax, Finland), gold nanoparticles, and conjugate (Simdax, gold), respectively, into pleural cavities in a dose of 0.06 ml per animal. The fourth, fifth, and sixth groups of animals received Simdax, gold nanoparticles, and conjugate (Simdax, gold), respectively, intravenously in same dose. We considered hydrothorax as the most representative sign for effective dynamic assessment of heart failure regression. The seventh group of animals (controls) received saline. Animals were observed until *natural death*, and afterward dissected and studied with light optical microscopy, laser correlation spectroscopy, and scanning electron microscopy (SEM).

Table 2. Comparative assessment of cardioprotective efficacy of AuNP injection, AuNPs-Simdax, and Simdax only intrapleurally and intravenously

Group ($n = 8$)	Medication, route of injection	Hydrothorax		
		First examination	Second examination	Third examination
1	AuNPs intrapleural	Right 1.8 ± 0.11 mm; left 2.1 ± 0.13 mm	No hydrothorax	No hydrothorax
2	AuNPs intravenous	Right 1.5 ± 0.09 mm; left 3 ± 0.16 mm	Right 0.5 ± 0.1 mm; left no hydrothorax	No hydrothorax
3	AuNPs-Simdax intrapleural	Right 0; left 1.8 ± 0.15 mm	No Hydrothorax	No hydrothorax
4	AuNPs-Simdax intravenous	right 0; left 0	Right no hydrothorax; left 1 ± 0.2 mm	No hydrothorax
5	Simdax intrapleural	Right 3 ± 0.12 mm; left 4.6 ± 0.26 mm	No hydrothorax	No hydrothorax
6	Simdax intravenous	Right 4 ± 0.16 mm; left 5.5 ± 0.21 mm	Right no hydrothorax; left 1.4 ± 0.21 mm	No hydrothorax
7	Controls	Hydrothorax: right 6 ± 0.46 mm; left 7 ± 0.35 mm	Severe ascites, hydrothorax, liver enlargement	Decrease of liver, nephropathy, severe ascites, hydrothorax, pericardial effusion

The third stage (sonoporation cardioprotective efficacy)

Consequently, we performed the interventional procedures under US guidance for four rats after modeling of heart failure (cumulative dose of doxorubicin 'Sigma' at 3.04 mg per animal or 15 mg/kg): two rats were injected with AuNPs into the pleural cavity with minimal insonation, and the other two were injected with AuNPs into the pleural cavity, which is connected to the pericardial cavity. After identification of spread near the heart muscle, the targeted locus of myocardium in depth of 1 cm during 180 s was insonated by 130 Db ultrasound using multifrequency 3–8 MHz probe.

We performed a dynamic assessment of heart failure regression measuring hydrothorax *in vivo*. After necropsy on the seventh day, we performed pathomorphological and histological analyses of experimental study.

Light optical microscopy of myocardium samples were stained with hematoxylin-eosin. Semi-fine sections were stained with methylene blue. Using the light microscope Docuval Carl Zeiss (Jena, Oberkochen, Germany), images of the investigated object were captured.

For SEM, pieces of myocardium were fixed in 2.5% glutaraldehyde solution, then co-fixated by 1% solution osmic acid. Further dehydration and pouring in resin (Epone 812 or a mixture of the eponym aralditom) was carried out by the conventional method. Cutting blocks was held by ultratome LKB-III (Sweden) using glass knives on the device Knife Maker 7801B (LKB, Sweden). Ultrathin sections of thickness 50–60 nm with 2% solution of uranila acetate and lead citrate were used thus achieved the best contrasting sections. Some samples of infarction rats were examined without staining. Ultrathin sections were examined with an electron microscope TEM - 125 K (Ukraine).

Visualization of gold nanoparticles and their interaction with cells was performed using laser correlation spectroscopy (Zetasizer-3, Malvern Instruments Ltd, UK), transmission electron microscopy (JEM-1230, JEOL, Tokyo, Japan), scanning electron microscopy (JSM-35C JEOL, Japan), and confocal microscopy (LSM510 META, Carl Zeiss, Oberkochen, Germany).

Evaluation of activity of the drug was carried out by comparing the morphological changes of internal organs according to US and echocardiography and mortality of animals in research groups.

US criteria were documented according to the following parameters: the size of the liver, liver parenchyma density, large diameter vein circulation (inferior vena cava), hepatic veins, renal veins, the renal portal system blood flow, the presence of ascites and hydrothorax, etc. The system hemodynamics was complexly evaluated assessing the target internal organs.

All animals were kept in a vivarium (plastic cages, in separate rooms) at constant temperature (20–25°C), and inversed cycle of light–dark (12–12 h), with free access to food and water. Condition was observed daily for 21 days. The animals were fed by standard granulated food, according to the guidelines on Pets in the vivarium (Kyiv, 1976), and approved by the Ministry of Health of Ukraine.

The medical ethics commissions of Zabolotny Institute of Microbiology and Virology of National Academy of Sciences of Ukraine approved the study.

Statistical method of Mann–Whitney U test was applied to perform comparison between groups.

RESULTS

Synthesis of gold nanoparticles of different sizes and their physico-chemical characteristics (performed in Ovcharenko Institute of Biocolloidal Chemistry of National Academy of Sciences of Ukraine)

The concentration of obtained gold nanoparticles was 38.6 μg/ml by metal, respectively, for each size. Samples of aqueous dispersions of gold nanoparticles of different sizes, synthesized using the condensation method of Davis, are presented in Figure 1.

Interaction of gold nanoparticles with eukaryotic cells

To carry this out, cell line U937 (human leukemic monocyte lymphoma) was used; electron microscopy images are presented in Figure 2. These cells demonstrated their ability to actively accumulate gold nanoparticles, which were studied in all sizes on the surface and inside cells.

The most efficient cells accumulate gold nanoparticles of 20 and 30 nm. Figure 3 presents confocal microscopy images of layered scan cell line U937 after their interaction with gold nanoparticles, confirming the high level of accumulation, as evidenced by changes in the intensity of color in the pictures (from red (maximum) to blue (least)).

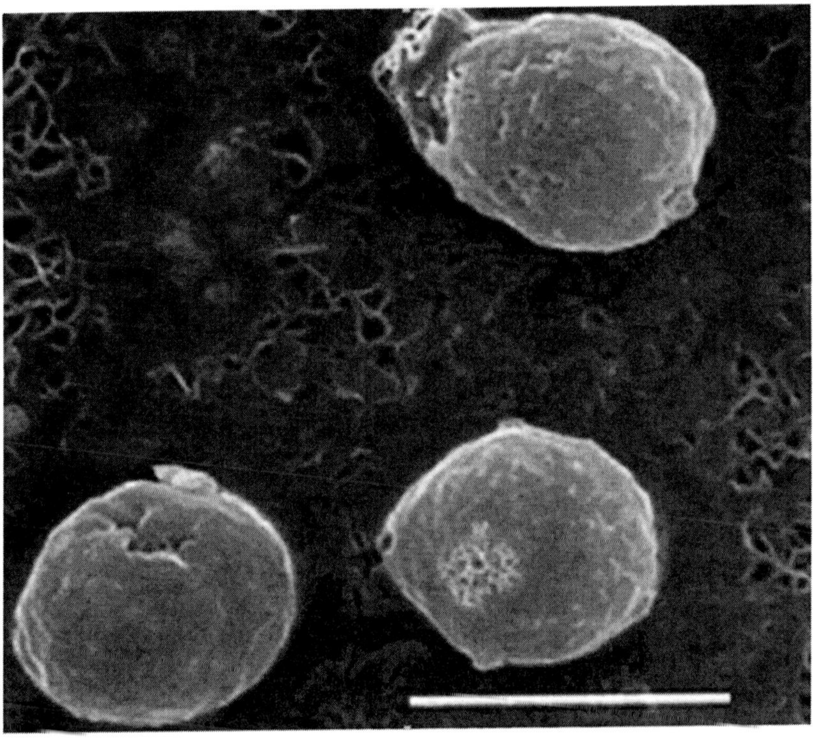

Figure 2. SEM image of cell line U937 (×3600).

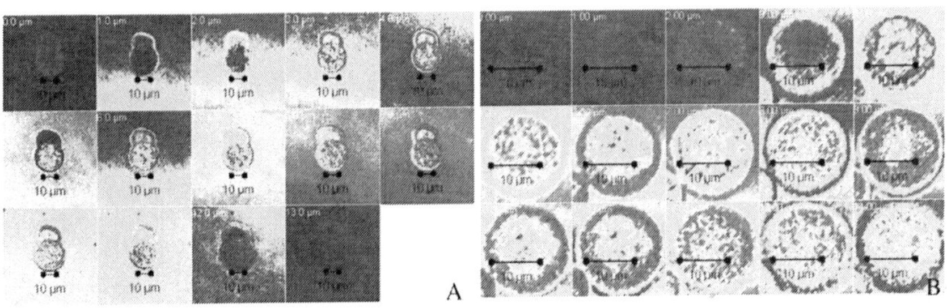

Figure 3. Confocal microscopy image cell line U937 (final concentration of 106 cells/ml) after incubation for 3 min. With gold nanoparticles of 20 nm **(A)** and 30 nm **(B)** in a final concentration of 12.7 μg/ml by metal. Scanning on the *z*-axis at intervals of 1 mm.

Experimentally, the interaction between cell line U937 with gold nanoparticles characterized by pronounced concentration dependence in the concentration range of 101–106 cells/ml for all studied nanoparticle sizes. Thus, the maximum binding concentration of nanoparticles of sizes 10 and 20 nm is 103 cells/ml (Figures 4 and 5).

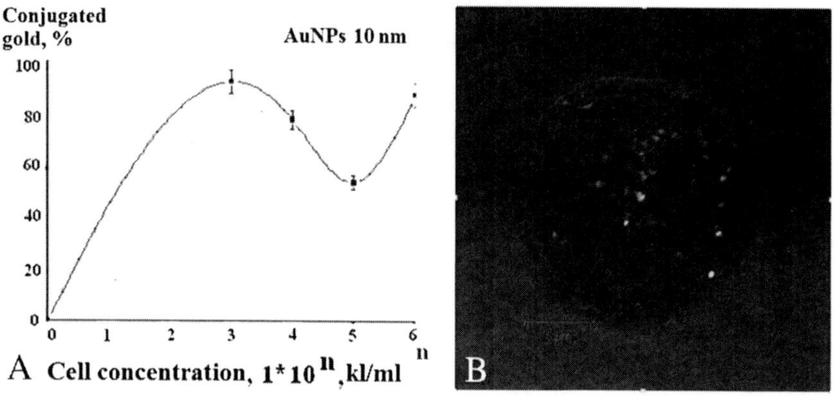

Figure 4. Interaction of AuNPs measuring 10 nm with cell line U937 (final concentration 12.7 μg/ml by metal). (A) Concentration curve of binding ($M \pm m$; $n = 5$, $P < 0.05$), **(B)** Confocal SEM image.

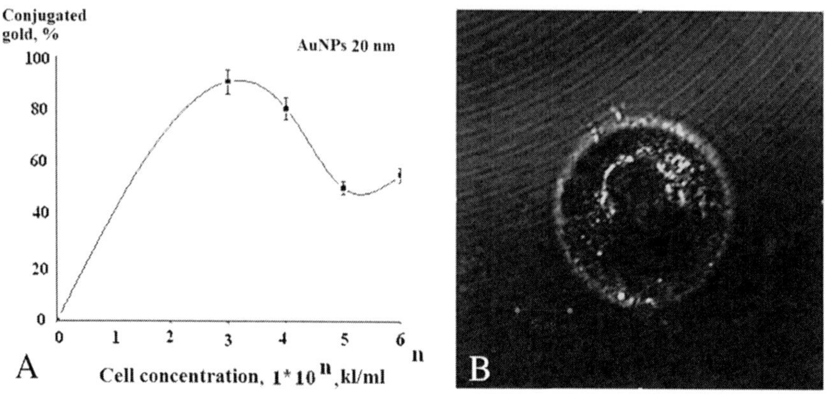

Figure 5. Interaction of AuNPs of 20 nm with cell line U937 (final concentration 12.7 μg/ml by metal). (A) Concentration curve binding ($M \pm m$; $n = 5$, $P < 0.05$), **(B)** Confocal SEM image.

It should be noted that the curve of binding for 10 nm gold nanoparticles measuring passes through a minimum at a concentration of 105 cells cells/ml, which may be due to reduction of active cell surface as a result of flocculation. This further increases the concentration of cells and leads to increased accumulation of gold nanoparticles to the maximum level by increasing the active surface area. That is, in the cells with nanoparticles, 10-nm concentration of 105 cells /ml is critical for cell-cell interactions.

Concentration curve of binding 30-nm nanoparticles differs from the previous two extended maximum, which is in the concentration range of 103–105 cells/ml (Figure 6).

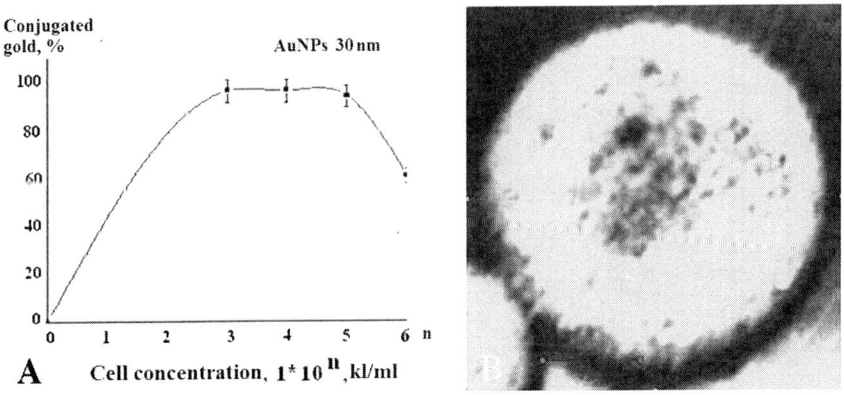

Figure 6. Interaction of 30-nm gold nanoparticles with cell line U937 (final concentration 12.7 μg/ml by metal). (A) Concentration curve of binding ($M \pm m$; $n = 5$, $P < 0.05$). **(B)** Confocal SEM image.

Regarding the 45-nm gold nanoparticles, the binding curve almost reaches a plateau in the concentration range of 103–106 cells/ml and is characterized by a weakly pronounced maximum at a concentration of 104 cells/ml (Figure 7).

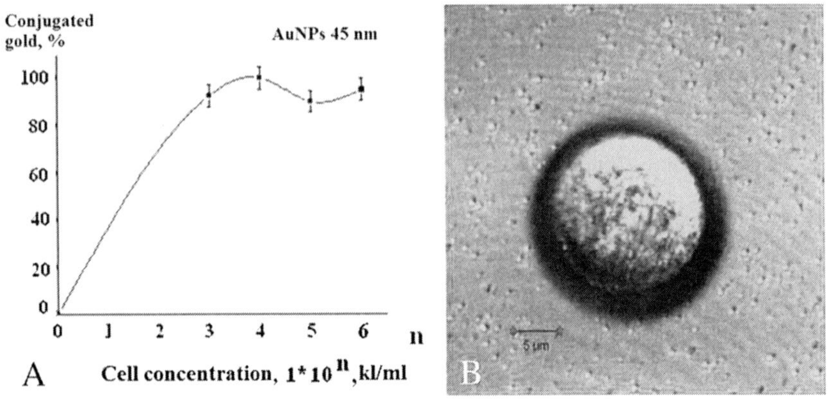

Figure 7. Interaction of 45-nm gold nanoparticles with cell line U937 (final concentration 2.7 mg/ml by metal). (A) Concentration curve of binding ($M \pm m$; $n = 5$, $P < 0.05$). **(B)** Confocal SEM image.

Changes in interaction efficiency of cell line U937 gold nanoparticles are most likely related to low concentrations of cells (from toxic effects of gold nanoparticles in the field of high concentrations of cells, a decrease in the area of the active surface contact of cells with nanoparticles due to the overwhelming intercellular interactions, that is, there are certain optimum ratio of cells and gold nanoparticles that determine the efficiency of binding.

In terms of a single-cell concentration, optimum interaction of gold nanoparticles with cell line U937 is in the range of approximately 0.1–1.0 ng metal nanoparticles for all studied sizes. Kinetics of this process shows that the process is characterized by its high speed; its maximum binding of gold nanoparticles by cells is achieved within 3–5 min (Figure 8).

It should be noted that for 10-nm nanoparticles, after reaching the maximum level of accumulation, a reverse effect was observed (*reducing binding time*). This may be due to the ability of cells to the active 'release' nanoparticles of this size (Figure 8, curve 1).

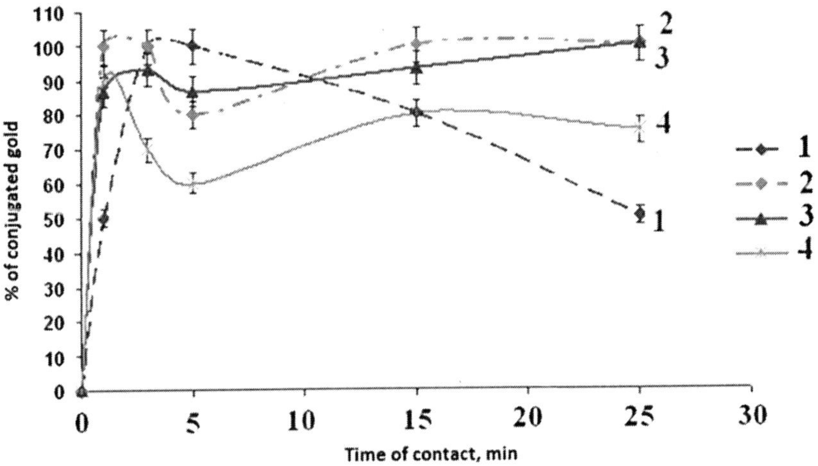

Figure 8. Kinetics of binding cell line U937 gold nanoparticles. With sizes 1–10, 2–20, 3–30, and 4–45 nm (*M*± *m*; *n* = 5, *P* < 0.05). The final concentration (106 cells/ml) with gold nanoparticles (12.7 μg/ml by metal).

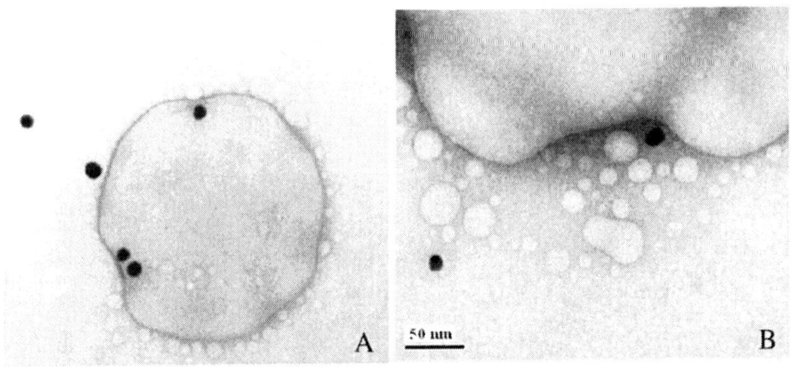

Figure 9. SEM image of the intracellular localization of gold nanoparticles in vacuoles cell line U937. Sizes of 20 nm **(A)** and 10 nm **(B)**. Cells at a final concentration of 106 cells/ml were incubated in the FSB buffer for 3–5 min with gold nanoparticles (final concentration of 12.7 μg/ml by metal).

After entry into the cell, gold nanoparticles have a different localization, depending on the size. Judging from electron microscopic analysis, we can speak about preferential accumulation of gold nanoparticles measuring 10 and 20 nm in the vacuoles (Figure 9).

As can be seen in places likely hit, nanoparticles in vacuoles observed protrusion of their membranes, which may indicate the penetration of gold nanoparticle average size 10 and 20 nm inside vacuoles. For gold nanoparticles of 30 and 45 nm, their vast accumulation of lysosomes were observed (Figure 10).

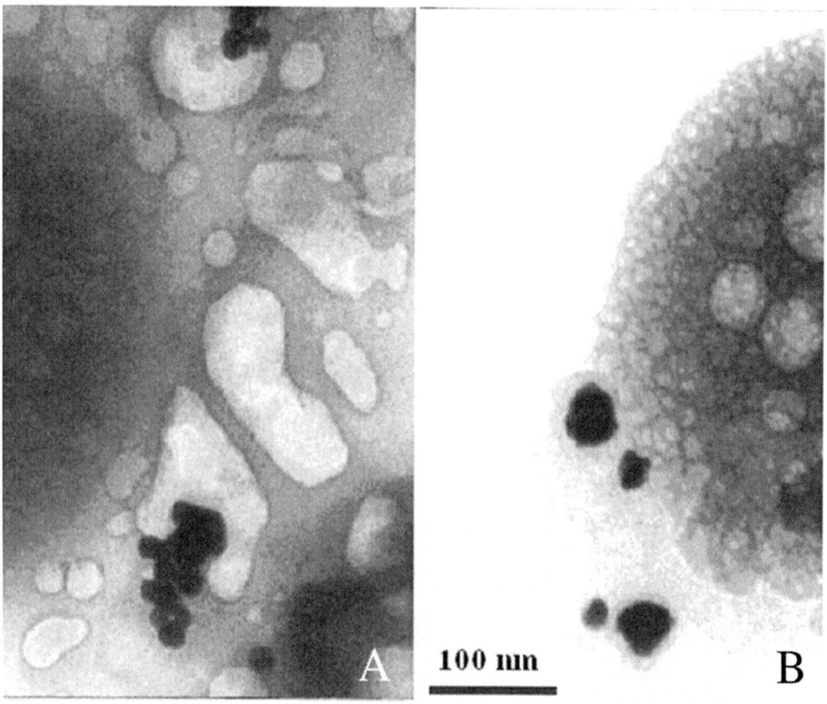

Figure 10. SEM of the intracellular localization of 30-nm gold nanoparticles in lysosomes cell line U937. Cells at a final concentration of 106 cells/ml were incubated in the FSB buffer for 3–5 min with gold nanoparticles (final concentration of 12.7 µg/ml by metal). Gold nanoparticles are observed on the lysosomes surface **(A)** and penetrated into the membrane protrusions **(B)**.

Effects of gold nanoparticles on the enzymatic activity of cell line U937

We found the significant changes in the presence of gold nanoparticles in the incubation medium size observed in Na^+, K^+-ATP-ase activity of the membrane fraction of cells (Figure 11, curves 1–4).

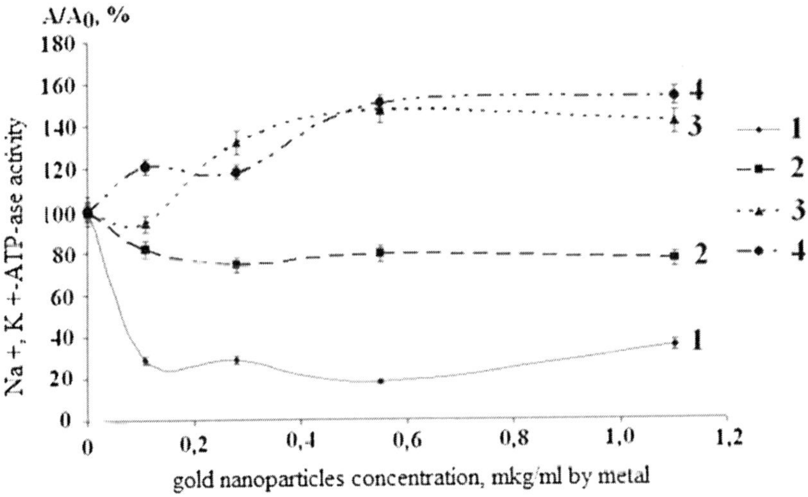

Figure 11. Change in value of Na^+, K^+ ATP-ase activity (A/A_0%) of membrane fraction from cell line U937 under AuNP influence. Sizes of 1–10, 2–20, 3–30, and 4–45 nm. ($M \pm m$; $n = 5$, $P < 0.05$ relative to control A_0). For 100% (control) adopted the value Na^+, K^+-ATP-ase activity in the absence of gold nanoparticles. Gold nanoparticles in the environment made fiber membrane fraction (150–200 mg) and the mixture was incubated for 3 min. Incubation medium for determination of enzyme activity (volume 1 ml) is 50 mM Tris–HCl, 5 mM $MgCl_2$, 100 mM NaCl, 20 mM KCl, 3 mM ATP (pH = 7.5). Incubation period is 10 min, and temperature is 37°C. The amount of membrane protein is 15–20 mg.

Thus, 10 nm gold nanoparticles in the concentration range of 0.11–1.1 mg/ml inhibit enzyme activity by 70% compared with the control (curve 1). Inhibition of Na^+, K^+-ATP-ase activity in the presence of gold nanoparticles of 20 nm is 20% (curve 2). Gold nanoparticles of 30 nm in the concentration range of 0.11–1.10 mg/ml stimulated the Na^+, K^+-ATP-ase activity; the value index, with increasing concentration of nanoparticles, increases and reaches 30%–40% in the concentration range of 0.28–1.10 mg/ml (curve 3). Under the influence of gold nanoparticles of 45 nm, an increase in Na^+, K^+-ATP-ase activity by 20%–40% was observed (curve 4). Thus, within the concentrations, 0.11–0.28 mg/ml for stimulation of metal is 20%. In the concentration range of 0.28–0.55 mg/ml by metal, enzymatic activity increases from 20% to 40% and averaged at 40% for the concentration range of 0.55–1.10 mg/ml by metal. Mg^{2+}-ATP-ase activity of membrane fraction of cell line U937 under the influence of gold nanoparticles of average sizes 10, 20, 30, and 45 nm were not significantly changed. Features of gold nanoparticles on Na^+, K^+-ATP-ase activity membrane fraction cell line U937 can be caused by the interaction of nanoparticles of a certain size with SH-groups of the enzyme molecule responsible for its conformational state.

The second stage

In all animals of the six groups, after the third day of post-medication injection, no ascites and no liver enlargement were registered (compared to controls $P < 0.001$). The linear cranio-caudal measurements of fluid level in the pleural cavities were as follows: for gold nanoparticles intrapleural right 1.8 ± 0.11 mm, left 2.1 ± 0.13 mm, compared to hydrothorax in controls right 6 ± 0.46 mm, left 7 ± 0.35 mm. Conjugate injection showed significantly higher hydrothorax reduction than that using Simdax injection only ($P < 0.01$); gold nanoparticle injection showed significantly higher than that using Simdax injection ($P < 0.05$). Gold nanoparticles and conjugate showed no significant difference in rat recovery.

We obtained sufficient ultrasound visualization of the affected organs (Figures 12, 13, 14, 15, 16, and 17); the evolution of symptoms in chosen groups with polar outcomes (controls and intrapleural conjugate) is presented in Tables 3 and 4.

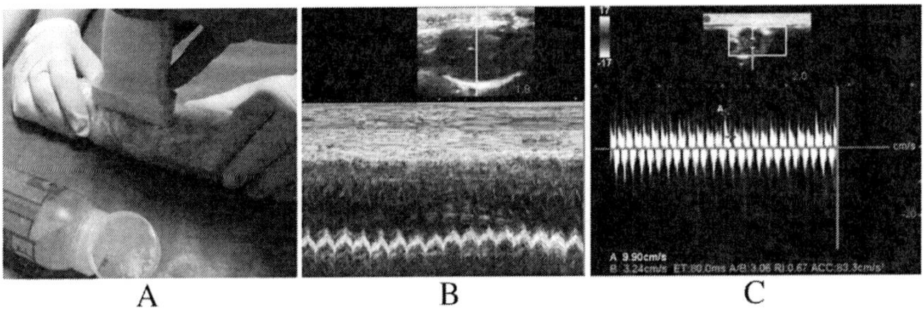

Figure 12. Rat ultrasound visualizations. (A) US survey. **(B)** echocardiography. **(C)** Doppler assessment of LV outflow tract [34].

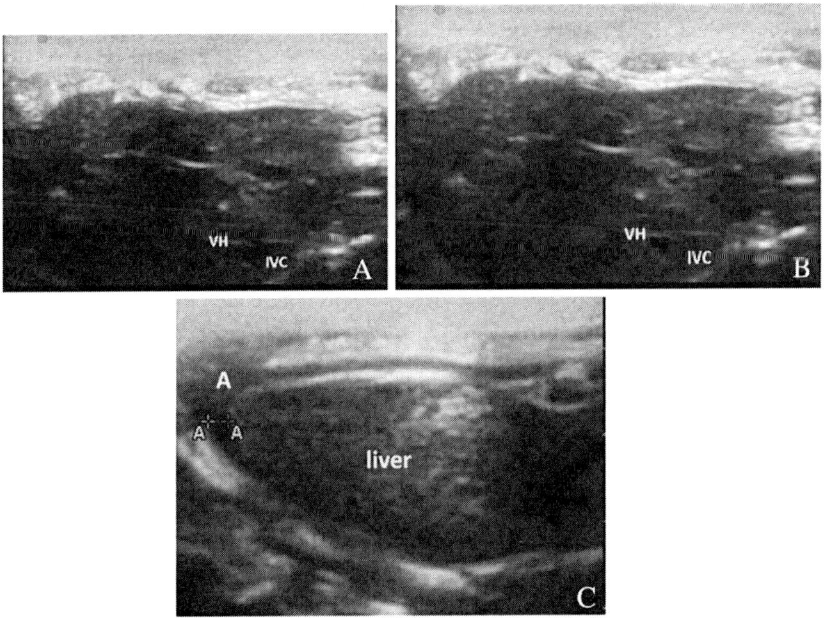

Figure 13. Liver sonogram. (A) Inferior vena cava (IVC) expanded to 4.5 mm, **(B)** dilated hepatic veins (HV), indirect sign of venous congestion in large circulation, and **(C)** mild ascites in rat. Near liver strip of liquid is revealed in **(A)**, an indirect sign of venous congestion in large circulation.

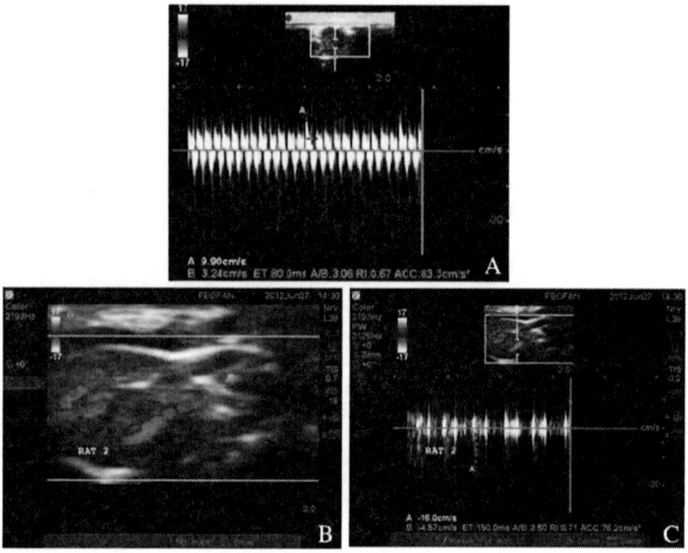

Figure 14. US scans. (A) an indirect sign of kidney venous congestion. IR in renal segmental artery is 0.67 (normal), **(B)** sonogram demonstrates kidney blood perfusion and ascites, **(C)** sign of nephropathy, IR in renal segmental artery is 0.71.

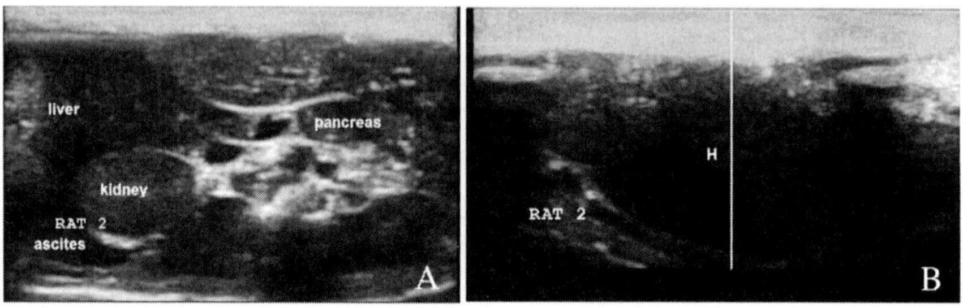

Figure 15: US scans severe venous congestion. (A) Severe ascites on cross-section abdominal scan. **(B)** Severe hydrothorax (H) on sagittal thoracic scan.

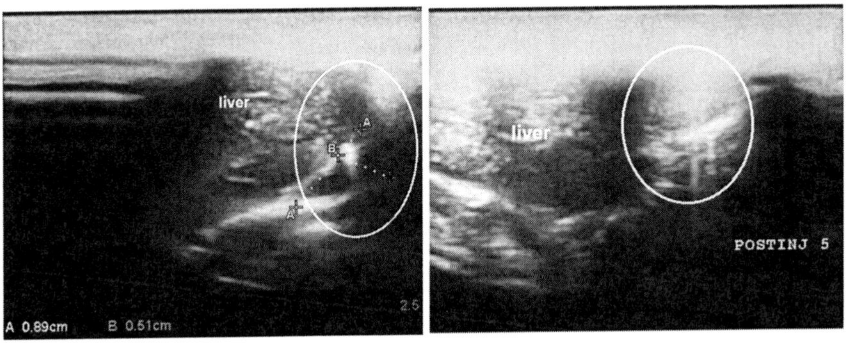

Figure 16. Pleural effusion assessment in rat (sagittal US scans). (A) Free fluid revealed in the pleural cavity.**(B)** No hydrothorax revealed 3 days after intrapleural injection of gold nanoparticle.

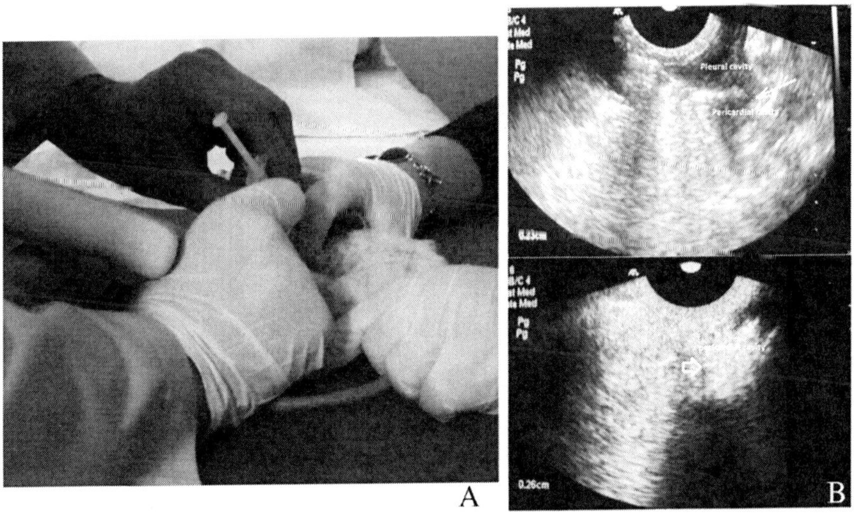

Figure 17. Injection into pleural cavity. (A) Procedure view and **(B)** spreading to the pericardial cavity through the pore (thin arrow), liquid in the pericardial cavity (arrow) [34].

Table 3. Heart failure rats, which received intrapleural conjugate of gold nanoparticles and Simdax, n = 7

Animal	First examination	Second examination	Third examination
Rat 1	Mild ascites (Figure 3), IVC expanded (Figure 4), liver enlargement	Mild ascites, liver enlargement	No symptoms
Rat 2	Mild ascites, IVC expanded, liver enlargement, mild hydrothorax	Mild ascites, IVC expanded, liver enlargement	Reduction of pericardial and pericardial effusion
Rat 3	IVC expanded, liver enlargement	Mild ascites, mild hydrothorax (Figure 5A), IVC expanded, liver enlargement	Reduction of pericardial and pericardial effusion
Rat 4	IVC expanded, liver enlargement	IVC expanded, liver enlargement	IVC expanded
Rat 5	Mild ascites IVC expanded, liver enlargement	Mild ascites, hydrothorax, pericaridial effusion	Reduction of pericardial and pericardial effusion
Rat 6	Mild ascites IVC expanded, liver enlargement	Ascites, hydrothorax, pericaridial effusion	Reduction of pericardial and pericardial effusion
Rat 7	IVC expanded, liver enlargement	Mild ascites, hydrothorax, IVC expanded, liver enlargement	IVC expanded, liver enlargement

Table 4. Rat controls (heart failure rats), ***n*** = 7

Animal	First examination	Second examination	Third examination
Rat 1	Ascites, hydrothorax, liver enlargement	Decrease of ejection fraction, severe ascites, hydrothorax, pericardial effusion	Decrease of liver, nephropathy, severe ascites, hydrothorax, pericardial effusion
Rat 2	Ascites, hydrothorax, liver enlargement	Severe ascites, hydrothorax, pericardial effusion.	Decrease of liver, nephropathy (Figure 5), severe ascites (Figure 6), hydrothorax, pericardial effusion
Rat 3	Ascites, liver enlargement	Severe ascites, hydrothorax, liver enlargement	Decrease of ejection fraction, severe ascites, hydrothorax, pericardial effusion
Rat 4	Ascites, hydrothorax, liver enlargement	Severe ascites, hydrothorax, pericardial effusion.	Decrease of liver, nephropathy, severe ascites, hydrothorax, pericardial effusion
Rat 5	Ascites, hydrothorax, liver enlargement	Severe ascites, hydrothorax, liver enlargement, pericardial effusion	Decrease of ejection fraction, severe ascites, hydrothorax, pericardial effusion
Rat 6	Ascites, hydrothorax, liver enlargement	Severe ascites, hydrothorax, liver enlargement	Decrease of liver, nephropathy, severe ascites, hydrothorax, pericardial effusion
Rat 7	Ascites, hydrothorax, liver enlargement	Severe ascites, hydrothorax, liver enlargement, pericardial effusion	Decrease of liver, nephropathy, severe ascites, hydrothorax, pericardial effusion

After the third examination post-treatment, hydrothorax remained the only US symptom for observation.

In all animals of the six groups after the third day after medication injection, physical conditions were observed as good. No ascites and no liver enlargement were registered in all animals of first six groups compared to signs of heart failure in controls ($P < 0.001$). The linear cranio-caudal measurements of fluid level were as follows: for gold nanoparticles, intrapleural right is 1.8 ± 0.11 mm and left is 2.1 ± 0.13 mm compared to hydrothorax in controls wherein right is 6 ± 0.46 mm and left is 7 ± 0.35 mm. Conjugate injection showed significantly higher hydrothorax reduction than that using Simdax injection only ($P < 0.01$).

Gold nanoparticle injection showed significantly higher results than that using Simdax injection ($P < 0.05$). Gold nanoparticles and conjugate showed no significant difference in rat recovery. The study of route of injection indicated that intrapleural injection showed better and faster results in reducing hydrothorax on the second exam in all groups ($P < 0.05$).

Mean life continuity was as follows:

1) for gold nanoparticles, intravenous injection had 5.4 months while intrapleural injection had 6.2 months;

2) for Simdax, intravenous injection had 3 months while intrapleural injection had 3.4 months; and

3) for gold nanoparticle and Simdax conjugate, intravenous injection had 6.8 months while intrapleural injection had 6.3 months.

Difference was significant between Simdax vs nanogold ($P < 0.05$) and Simdax vs conjugate ($P < 0.05$)

Table 4 depicts cardioprotective effects of all three substances using the two routes.

Structural changes in the myocardium, defined by light optical morphological study of heart tissue samples of rats with doxorubicin-induced heart failure, revealed emergence of larger lesions with contraction-damaged appearance of small foci vacuole degeneration and lysis of myofibrils. The results of injuries after modeling CHF were necrobiosis and necrosis of cardiomyocytes (CMC), which was accompanied by focal proliferation of connective tissues around dead CMC and the formation of small scars on the background of the diffuse proliferation of connective tissues and hypertrophy of individual CMC. These findings were most expressed in controls (Figures 12, 13, 14, and 15). After injection, 30-nm gold nanoparticles were found to be accumulated in the endothelial cells of infarcted arterioles and capillaries. Necrobiosis and scarring was significantly decreased after all treatments.

The third stage

In the sonoporation of rats, CHF symptoms and hydrothorax were totally gone on the first day after injection vs reduction on the third day (Figure 16). Figure 17 demonstrates the spreading of medication from the pleural to the pericardial cavity to obtain contact with myocardium to targeted sonoporation performance. Sonoporation is able to enhance gold nanoparticle delivery to myocardial cells *in vivo*, and electron microscopy of the myocardium of experimental rats showed that ultrasound enhances AuNP transfer into the cell and mytochondria which were highly localized, and that result was superior to that of controls ($P < 0.01$ for both). US changes after CHF modeling and after conjugate injection are presented in Figure 18.

The obtained data showed that the effect of 20-nm gold nanoparticle average (initial drug concentration 193 mg/ml by metal) on the value of myofibrils Ca^{2+}, Mg^{2+}-ATP-ase activity marked the inhibition of enzyme activity in the whole investigated concentration range of nanoparticles on average (20%–30%) and under the concentration of nanoparticles in the incubation medium 0.051 mg/ml by metal (37%) compared with control (Figure 19).

AuNPs-Simdax conjugate unlike Simdax normalized Ca^{2+}, Mg^{2+}-ATP-ase activity of heart myofibrils (Figure 19). We assume that this will help avoid potential side effects of Simdax including tachycardia or development of congestive heart failure.

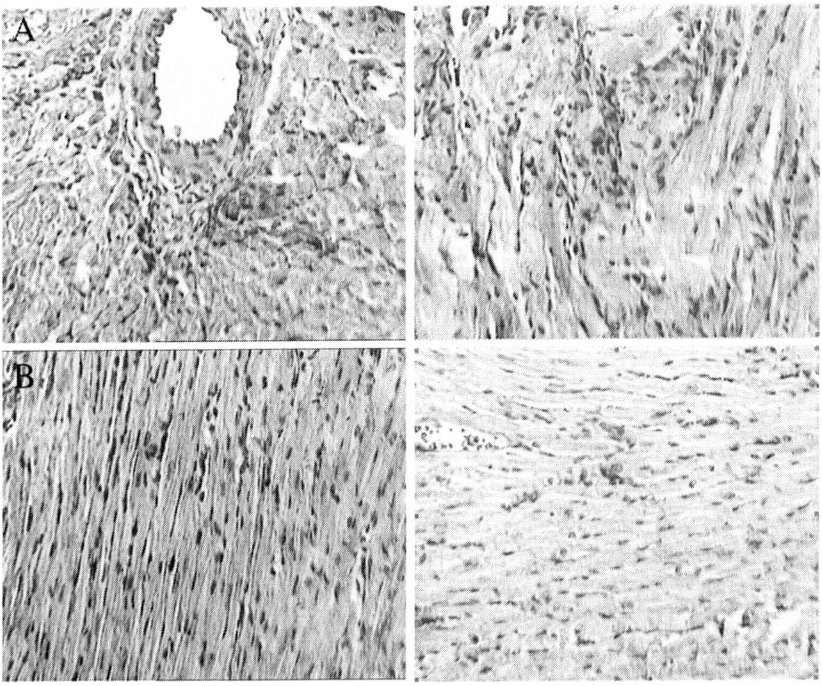

Figure 18. Light optical microscopy, painted by hematoxylin-eosin (×200). (A) CHF modeling in rat: CMC contraction damage, necrosis, nodular proliferation of connective tissue cells, and necrosis of nearby vessels; **(B)** after conjugate injection: slight nuclei hypertrophy of CMC, little amount of connective tissue.

Electron microscopic examination on AuNPs-Simdax conjugate samples revealed tropism of myofibrils and mitochondria of CMC for intravenous and intrapericardial injection. After 1 h, conjugate was detected in a small number of inclusions in the mitochondria myofibrils and CMC (Figure 20). Figures 21 and 22 demonstrate the difference of the accumulation of NPs in the myofibrils of CMC and mitochondria between regular injection and sonoporation groups. The conjugate was detected in a larger number of inclusions after myocardium insonation.

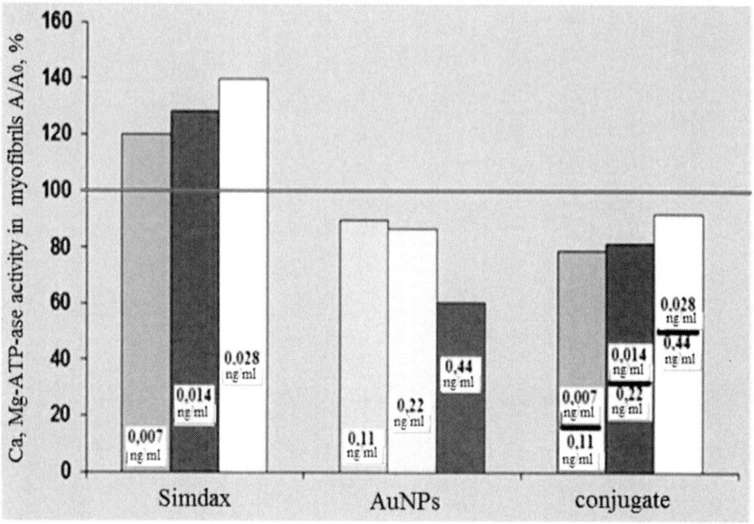

Figure 19. The Ca $^{2+}$, Mg $^{2+}$-ATP-ase activity in myofibrils of heart for Simdax, AuNPs, and conjugate.

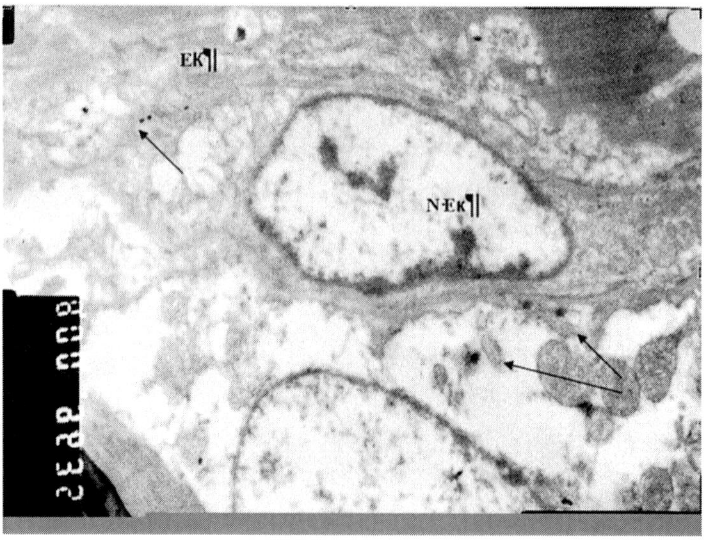

Figure 20. SEM (×16,000). Accumulation of 30-nm gold nanoparticles in arteriolar endothelium of left ventricular myocardium after intravenous injection. In the cytoplasm of endothelial cells, electron-dense inclusion of gold nanoparticles (indicated by arrows) was revealed. (EK) endothelial cells, (N-Ek) nucleus of endothelial cells, (arrows) NPs.

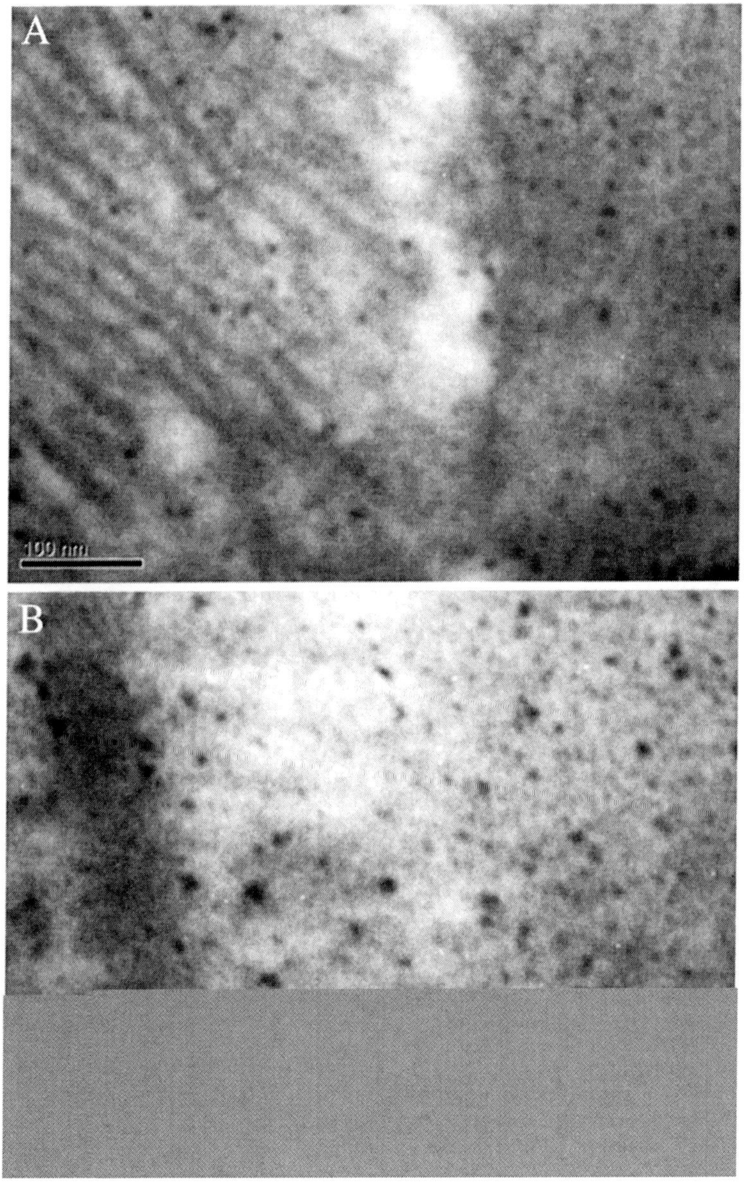

Figure 21. SEM (×250,000). Cardiomyocytes after NP injection to intact rats. **(A)** Myofibrils. **(B)** Mitochondria.

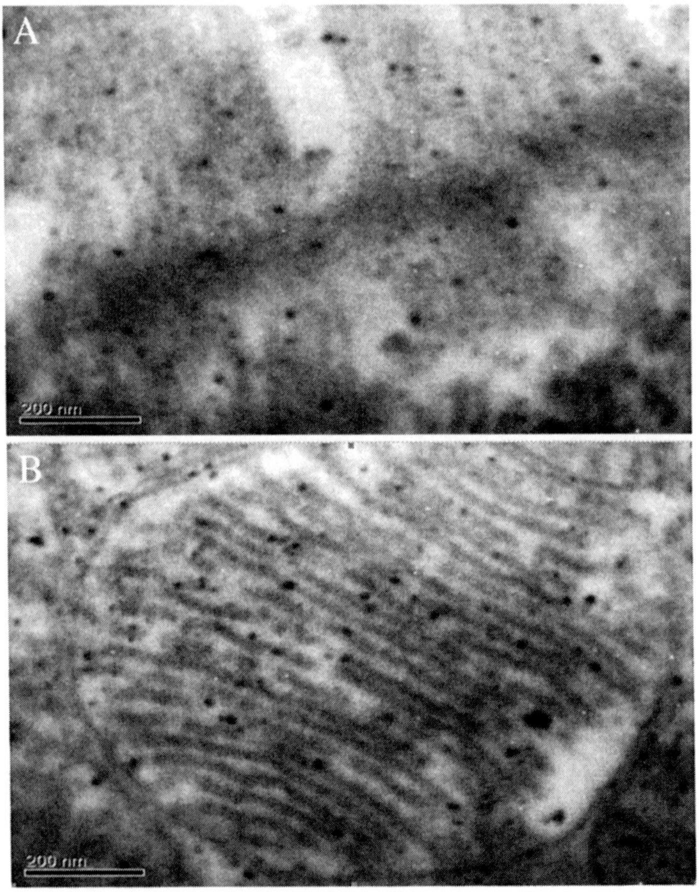

Figure 22. SEM (×250,000). Inclusion of NPs in **(A)** myofibrils and **(B)** mitohondrias. CMC after sonoporation (larger amount of particles is observed).

ENDNOTES

Findings of biosafety and biocompatibility tests of gold nanoparticles and conjugate with Simdax

- Genotoxicity: eukaryotic cells under the influence of gold nanoparticles and AuNPs-Simdax conjugate was at a negative control and did not exceed 0.3%;

- no mutagenic effect was found: gold nanoparticles and conjugate AuNPs-Simdax did not cause micronuclei in cell formation in laboratory animals (allows to predict the absence of such influence on the human body);
- no influence on intestinal microflora in intact rats (allow to predict the absence of such influence on the human body);
- no impact on immunoreactivity *in vivo* was registered (cytokine production, phagocytes, indicators of cellular immunity); and
- most gold nanoparticles of 30 nm are biologically safe and biocompatible *in vitro* and *in vivo*; based on 30-nm gold nanoparticles, AuNPs-Simdax conjugate was found the most biologically safe according to cytotoxicity, genotoxicity, and immunoreactivity.

Findings of assessment of cardioprotective properties and route of delivery of gold nanoparticles

- Ultrasonography is an effective modality for *in vivo* monitoring the condition of rat organs targeted for experiment for the study of cardiovascular function.
- The results of doxorubicin-induced injuries in myocardium on rat model are necrobiosis and necrosis of CMC, which was accompanied by focal proliferation of connective tissue around dead CMC and the formation of small scars on the background of diffuse proliferation of connective tissue and CMC hypertrophy.
- Intravenous injection of 30-nm gold nanoparticles were found to be accumulated in the endothelial cells of infarcted arterioles and capillaries. Necrobiosis and scarring was significantly decreased after all treatments.
- AuNPs-Simdax conjugate showed a positive effect on the cardiac contractile ability (level of energy costs) of conditionally healthy animals. Conjugate injection showed significantly higher

hydrothorax reduction than injection of Simdax only ($P < 0.01$); gold nanoparticle injection showed significantly higher than injection of Simdax ($P < 0.05$).

- Gold nanoparticles and conjugate showed no significant difference in rat recovery.
- In the study of the route of injection, intrapleural injection showed better and faster results in reducing hydrothorax on the second exam in all groups ($P < 0.05$).
- Preliminary results indicate higher mortality after Simdax administration and the longest survival after conjugate administration.
- Intrapleural (local delivery) route is preferred over intravenous (systemic) according to all tested parameters.

Theranostic potential

Sonoporation showed to enhance gold nanoparticle delivery to myocardial cells *in vivo*. Thus, after assessing relevant parameters as AuNPs demonstrated not only significant drug delivery properties but also discover strong inotropic cardioprotective activity that led to significant life extension compared with one of the most effective existing inotropic agents, being biosafe and biocompatible.

DISCUSSION

Considering the results of this study and literature data demonstrating strong antioxidative properties, biosafety of gold nanoparticles are promising for advanced therapy development and innovative drug delivery stratification and personalization of treatments in novel disciplines [6] such as nanocardiology [77, 78], nanoendocrinology [70], and nanoneurology [37, 71].

Nanocardiology

The rapid development of nanomedicine has not bypassed cardiovascular diseases. Although the publications in this sphere, with the use of nanomaterials, is still quite a bit few, there are already attempts to use the nanoparticles as vectors targeted delivery of cardioprotective drugs [43]. Nanoscale particles can be synthetically designed to potentially intervene in lipoprotein matrix retention and lipoprotein uptake in cells (processes central to atherosclerosis). Nanoengineered molecules called *nanolipoblockers* can be used to attack atherosclerotic plaques due to raised levels of low-density lipoproteins [79]. An experimental study in rats using injectable self-assembling peptide nanofiber bound to platelet-derived growth factor demonstrated sustained delivery to the myocardium resulting in decreased cardiomyocyte death and preserved systolic function after myocardial infarction [80]. In studies on rats, cell therapy with insulin-like growth factor 1 delivery by biotinylated nanofibers improved systolic function after experimental myocardial infarction [81]. As various mechanisms enabling cardiac regeneration are becoming elucidated, novel technologies using degradable microspheres for controlled release systems and self-assembling peptide nanofibers for cell and factor delivery were reported [82].

Cardiovascular diseases are strongly connected to immune response. Pathogenesis of cardiovascular diseases are associated with dysfunction of cytokine production. In most autoimmune diseases observed, stereotyped response in the form of a large subpopulation of activated Th1 lymphocytes [83], not rarely observed, decrease in the number of T-lymphocytes, impaired T helpers/suppressors ratio downward suppressor activity, weakening the response to the mitogens. In patients with autoimmune disease, often increased levels of proinflammatory cytokines (TNF-α, IL-1, IFN-γ) may result aberrant activation of the innate immune response [84]. During a persistent heart muscle damage, the exposure of the intracellular content to dead cells activates the innate immune response, such as the activation of Toll-like receptors (TLR). In the heart, TLR2 and TLR4 are perhaps involved in the host response to myocardial infarction [85]. The activation of TLR initiates the imbalance of TLR-induced cytokines.

We hypothesize that the AuNPs may affect the calcium channels and have an impact on the imbalance of cytokines.

Nanogold is known to impact on receptors and gene expression. AuNPs bind strongly to thiols and amines and thereby inhibit VEGF165-induced signalling [86]. Giljohann DA et al. described*gene regulation* with polyvalent RNA-gold nanoparticle conjugates (RNA-Au NPs) [87]. Patel PC et al. identified the pathway for DNA-AuNP entry in HeLa cells by a process involving receptor-mediated endocytosis, mediated by a class of pattern-recognition receptors [88, 89].

Nanoneurology

Kogan et al. reported the use of local heat delivered by metallic nanoparticles selectively attached to their target as a molecular surgery to safely remove toxic and clogging aggregates, particularly the amyloid beta protein involved in Alzheimer's disease, a neurodegenerative disease [37].

We hypothesize, that due to NP bioeffects against cellular oxidative stress, targeted teranostic treatment for neuromuscular diseases (myopathy, neuropathy, latent trigger points) may be applied in the near future after approval from evidentiary studies [77]. Combination with targeted biology therapies as growth factor of platelet rich plasma [78] gives new opportunities for neuromuscular disease management.

Nanoneurosurgery is a conceptual leap necessary for neuroscientists as well as neurosurgeons in developing and applying nanotechniques to neurosurgery at the nano level. According to Andrews [70], nanoscaffolds offer mechanical enhancement of neurorepair; carbon nanotube electrode arrays can provide nanolevel electrical and chemical enhancement. Even the traditional 'cut-and-sew' surgery is being taken down to the micron, if not nano, level for single-axon repair, and the technology can use capillaries to deliver therapeutics to virtually any portion of the nervous system with greater-than-pinpoint accuracy.

Future calls for upcoming PPPM-related studies with particular applications of AuNPs for therapeutic drug delivery properties in multifunctional nanomedical solutions related to genetics and cell biology are required in the following fields:

- Nanohepatology
- Nanonephrology
- Nanoallergology
- Nanogastroenterology

Consolidation of the PPPM concept

Personalized medical approach

Imaging/sonoporation combined with direct visualization of target tissues and optoacoustic phenomena to detect nanoparticles *in vivo* and its potential to be a contrast agent for US/MRI imaging is a significant opportunity for personalized theranostics.

Predictive medical approach

Optoacoustic phenomenon is a relevant basis for contrast imaging with biomarker registration with high predictive value potential. Extensive application of sensor based on AuNPs allows us to think about developing novel technologies for minimally invasive diagnostic/treatment procedures.

Preventive medical approach

Strong antioxidative effects potential to impact on cellular receptors and gene expression combined with high biosafety is a crucial challenge in anti-aging strategy. Further studies are necessary to clarify the molecular mechanisms of AuNP effects and its relevant dosage.

Study limitation

Although this research was carefully prepared with sufficient number of observations, we are still aware of its limitations. First of all, the research was conducted as part of a large study, concerning the creation of a rat model for testing new medications based on nanoparticles and drug delivery with the assistance of US. That is why some parameters were not presented in this paper. Secondly, our study was methodologically limited by use of general, not special US equipment for precise assessment of the heart tissue. The opticoacoustic phenomenon was not applied to detect nanoparticles *in vivo*. As CHF occurs in elderly humans, age-related comparative studies on rat models have to be relevant.

Future outlooks and recommendations

Further studies dedicated to the mechanism of the cardioprotective effects of gold nanoparticles for delivering drugs and testing on different animal heart failure models, especially with relation to the age of the animal, are required. Molecular mechanisms are still not clear, and further studies are required. Different approaches for drug delivery may be suggested and should be tested, based on the combination of expressions by different physical properties, e.g., sonoporation or colloid conjugation, liposomes, etc.

A study on interactions with other nanomaterials (e.g., cerium dioxide, carbon nanomaterials) and combination with other biological (gene, regenerative) therapies are recommended. After approval, agent safety development medications with future clinical testing should be initiated to implement theranostic approach for routine practice.

With the concluding points, we can formulate the following proposals (expert recommendations):

1) For the European Union (EU): create an international project to study gold nanoparticles for the development of nanoconstructions

to treat patients with heart failure. Extend studies to nanoparticle application in neurodegenerative, heart, liver, and kidney diseases and muscle dystrophy, combining with biological therapies to achieve sustainable effects from theranostic approach.

2) For Ukraine: participate in project in partnership with EU to follow up experimental and clinical trials and involve related institutions and centers to the study.

CONCLUSIONS

Based on the results, we have concluded the following:

1. We developed and implemented original protocols for colloid-chemical synthesis of spherical gold nanoparticles of discrete sizes 10, 20, 30, and 45 nm and designed and constructed AuNPs-Simdax conjugate, and both were found to be biologically safe (in cytotoxicity, genotoxicity, and immunoreactivity).

2. Most gold nanoparticles of 30 nm and its AuNPs-Simdax conjugate are biologically safe and biocompatible *in vitro* and *in vivo*.

3. Conjugate AuNPs-Simdax showed a positive effect on the cardiac contractile ability of conditionally healthy animals (have significant cardioprotective effects for doxorubicin-induced heart failure rats, higher than Simdax only).

4. Gold nanoparticle injection itself showed effects similar to the AuNPs-Simdax conjugate injection.

5. Intrapleural (local) delivery is more effective over intravenous (systemic) according to all tested parameters.

6. Sonoporation is able to enhance gold nanoparticle delivery to myocardial cells *in vivo*.

AUTHORS' INFORMATION

Professor MYS, Ph.D., D.Sci., is a corresponding member of the National Academy of Sciences of Ukraine and the director of the Inteferon Department of Zabolotny Institute of Microbiology and Virology, NAS of Ukraine, Kyiv, Ukraine. RVB, M.D., Ph.D., is a medical doctor in the Clinical Hospital 'Pheophania' of the State Affairs Department, National Representative of the European Association for Predictive, Preventive and Personalized Medicine (EPMA) in Ukraine. Professor IMY, M.D., D.Sci., is the director of the Scientific-Practical Centre of Pediatric Cardiology and Cardiac Health of Ukraine, Kyiv, Ukraine, and was a Minister of Health in Ukraine (2010–2011). Professor LLM, Ph.D., D.Sci. and TNO, Ph.D., a researcher, are members of the Inteferon Department of Zabolotny Institute of Microbiology and Virology, National Academy of Sciences of Ukraine group. Professor UZR, Ph.D., D.Sci., is the director of the Ovcharenko Institute of Biocolloidal Chemistry, National Academy of Sciences of Ukraine, Kyiv, Ukraine.

ACKNOWLEDGMENT

The study was conducted with the support of the State Agency on Science, Innovations and Informatization of Ukraine (Grant D3/490-2011). We acknowledge the contributions of Liudmyla Rieznichenko, Tamara Gruzina and Svitlana Dybkova from Ovcharenko Institute of Biocolloidal Chemistry, National Academy of Sciences of Ukraine in the synthesis and testing of gold nanoparticles and the kind help of the EPMA journal editorial team and BioMed Central team in improving the text of the article.

COMPETING INTERESTS

The authors declare to have no competing interests.

AUTHORS' CONTRIBUTIONS

MYS did the organization and analysis of the study. RVB developed the model and did the ultrasound survey, literature search, analysis of the study, and article preparation. IMY, LLM, and TNO developed the model and performed the biosafety tests. UZR synthesized the AuNPs and prepared the Simdax conjugate and performed the biosafety tests. IMY performed the analysis and SEM tests. All authors read and approved the final manuscript.

REFERENCES

1. Golubnitschaja O, Costigliola V, EPMA: General report & recommendations in predictive, preventive and personalised medicine 2012: white paper of the European association for predictive, preventive and personalised medicine. EPMA J. 2012, 3: 14

2. Juenger J, Schellberg D, Kraemer S, Haunstetter A, Zugck C, Herzog W, Haass M: Health related quality of life in patients with congestive heart failure: comparison with other chronic diseases and relation to functional variables. Heart. 2002, 87 (3): 235-241.

3. Hobbs FD, Kenkre JE, Roalfe AK, Davis RC, Hare R, Davies MK: Impact of heart failure and left ventricular systolic dysfunction on quality of life: a cross-sectional study comparing common chronic cardiac and medical disorders and a representative adult population. Eur Heart J. 2002, 23 (23): 1867-1876.

4. Neubauer S: The failing heart — an engine out of fuel. N Engl J Med. 2007, 356 (11): 1140-1151.

5. National Research Council: Guide for the Care and Use of Laboratory Animals. 2011, Washington: The National Academies, 246-Eighth

6. Doggrell SA, Brown L: Rat models of hypertension, cardiac hypertrophy and failure. Cardiovasc Res. 1998, 39 (1): 89-105.

7. Kannel WB: Hypertension as a risk for cardiac events – epidemiological results of long-term studies. J Cardiovasc Pharmacol. 1993, 21 (Suppl 2): S27-S37.

8. Bubnov RV, Spivak MY, Zholobak NM: Method for experimental modeling of biological processes. Patent Ukraine. 2013, 78: 082-IPC A61B

9. Colin KL, Turnbull DH: Ultrasound biomicroscopy-Doppler in mouse cardiovascular development. Physiol Genomics. 2003, 14: 3-15.

10. Kiessling F, Pichler Bernd J: Small Animal Imaging: Basics and Practical Guide. 2011, Heidelberg: Springer, 1

11. Bubnov RV, Spivak MY, Zholobak NM: The use the ultrasound equipment of general use for in vivo study of cerium dioxide nanoparticles introduction in mice. Proceedings of scientific conference with international participation on Innovative Technologies in Ultrasonic Diagnosis. 2011, Kyiv: Pheophania, 25-28.

12. Bubnov RV: The use of ultrasound equipment of general use for in vivo study of cerium dioxide nanoparticles introduction in mice. Ultrasound Med Biol. 2011, 37 (8): 1-S162.

13. Spivak MY, Yemets IM, Bubnov RV: Method modeling of heart failure. Patent Ukraine. 2013, 78: 105-IPC A61B

14. Bjornerheim R, Kiil Grogaard H, Kjekshus H, Attramadal H, Smiseth OA: High frame rate doppler echocardiography in the rat: an evaluation of the method. Eur J Echocardiogr. 2001, 2: 78-87.

15. Holinski S, Knebel F, Heinze G, Konertz W, Baumann G, Borges AC: Noninvasive monitoring of cardiac function in a chronic

ischemic heart failure model in the rat: assessment with tissue Doppler and non-Doppler 2D strain echocardiography. Cardiovasc Ultrasound. 2011, 26 (9): 15-

16. Pollick C, Hale SL, Kloner RA: Echocardiographic and cardiac Doppler assessment of mice. J Am Soc Echocardiogr. 1995, 8 (5 Pt 1): 602-610.

17. Lu L, Ko E, Schwartz GG, Chou TM: Transesophageal echocardiography in rats using an intravascular ultrasound catheter. Am J Physiol. 1997, 273 (4 Pt 2): H2078-H2082.

18. Cingolani OH, Yang XP, Cavasin MA, Carretero OA: Increased systolic performance with diastolic dysfunction in adult spontaneously hypertensive rats. Hypertension. 2003, 41: 249-254.

19. Sjaastad I, Sejersted OM, Ilebekk A, Bjørnerheim R: Echocardiographic criteria for detection of post infarction congestive heart failure in rats. J Appl Physiol. 2000, 89: 1445-1454.

20. Saraiva RM, Kanashiro-Takeuchi RM, Antonio EL, Campos OPJFT, Moisés VA: Rats with high left ventricular end-diastolic pressure can be identified by Doppler echocardiography one week after myocardial infarction. Braz J Med Biol Res. 2007, 40 (11): 1557-1565.

21. Kokubo M, Uemura A, Matsubara T, Murohara T: Noninvasive evaluation of the time course of change in cardiac function in spontaneously hypertensive rats by echocardiography. Hypertens Res. 2005, 28 (7): 601-609.

22. de Simone G, Wallerson DC, Volpe M, Devereux RB: Echocardiographic measurement of left ventricular mass and volume in normotensive and hypertensive rats. Necropsy validation Am J Hypertens. 1990, 3: 688-696.

23. Martinez PF, Okoshi K, Zornoff LA, Oliveira SA, Campos DH, Lima AR, Damatto RL, Cezar MD, Bonomo C, Guizoni DM, Padovani CR, Cicogna AC, Okoshi MP: Echocardiographic detection of congestive heart failure in postinfarction rats. J Appl Physiol. 2011, 111 (2): 543-551.

24. Miller DL: Induction of pulmonary hemorrhage in rats during diagnostic ultrasound. Ultrasound Med Biol. 2012, 38 (8): 1476-1482.

25. Lee RM, Triggle CR, Cheung DW, Coughlin MD: Structural and functional consequence of neonatal sympathectomy on the blood vessels of spontaneously hypertensive rats. Hypertension. 1987, 10: 328-338.

26. Hayward R, Hydock DS: Doxorubicin cardiotoxicity in the rat: an in vivo characterization. J Am Assoc Lab Anim Sci. 2007, 46 (4): 20-32.

27. Kharin S, Krandycheva V, Tsvetkova A, Strelkova M, Shmakov D: Remodeling of ventricular repolarization in a chronic doxorubicin cardiotoxicity rat model. Fundam Clin Pharmacol. 2012, 27 (4): 364-372.

28. Singal PK, Iliskovic N: Doxorubicin-induced cardiomyopathy. N Engl J Med. 1998, 339: 900-905.

29. Steinherz LJ, Graham T, Hurwitz R, Sondheimer HM, Schwartz RG, Shaffer EM, Sandor G, Benson L, Williams R: Guidelines for cardiac monitoring of children during and after anthracycline therapy: report of the cardiology committee of the childrens cancer study group. Pediatrics. 1992, 89: 942-949.

30. Dimitrakis P, Romay-Ogando MI, Timolati F, Suter TM, Zuppinger C: Effects of doxorubicin cancer therapy on autophagy and the ubiquitin-proteasome system in long-term cultured adult rat cardiomyocytes. Cell Tissue Res. 2012, 350 (2): 361-372.

31. Al Shabanah OA, Aleisa AM, Hafez MM, Al Rejaie SS, Al Yahya AA, Bakheet SA, Al Harbi MM, Sayed Ahmed MM: Desferrioxamine attenuates doxorubicin-induced acute cardiotoxicity through TFG-β/Smad p53 pathway in rat model. Oxid Med Cell Longev. 2012, 2012: 619185-

32. Fukuo Y, Nakatani T, Shinohara H, Matsuda T: The mouse pericardium: it allows passage of particulate matter from the pleural to the pericardial cavity. Anat Rec. 1988, 222 (1): 1-5.

33. Nakatani T, Shinohara H, Fukuo Y, Morisawa S, Matsuda T: Pericardium of rodents: pores connect the pericardial and pleural cavities. Anat Rec. 1988, 220 (2): 132-137.

34. Spivak M, Bubnov R, Yemets I, Lazarenko L, Timoshok N, Vorobieva A, Mohnatyy S, Ulberg Z, Reznichenko L, Grusina I, Zhovnir V, Zholobak N: Doxorubicin dose for congestive heart failure modeling and the use of general ultrasound equipment for evaluation in rats. longitudinal in vivo study. Med Ultrason. 2013, 15 (1): 23-28.

35. Trikas A, Antoniades C, Latsios G, Vasiliadou K, Karamitros I, Tousoulis D, Tentolouris C, Stefanadis C: Long-term effects of levosimendan infusion on inflammatory processes and sFas in patients with severe heart failure. Eur J Heart Fail. 2006, 8 (8): 804-809.

36. Rieznichenko LS, Dybkova SM, Gruzina TG, Ulberg ZR, Todor IN, Lukyanova NY, Shpyleva SI: Chekhun VF:Gold nanoparticles synthesis and biological activity estimation in vitro and in vivo. Exp Oncol. 2012, 34 (1): 25-28.

37. Kogan MJ, Bastus NG, Amigo R, Grillo-Bosch D, Araya E, Turiel A, Labarta A, Giralt E, Puntes VF: Nanoparticle-mediated local and remote manipulation of protein aggregation. Nano Lett. 2006, 6 (1): 110-115.

38. Boisselier E, Astruc D: Gold nanoparticles in nanomedicine: preparations, imaging, diagnostics, therapies and toxicity. Chem Soc Rev. 2009, 38:

39. Shukla R, Chanda N, Zambre A, Upendran A, Katti K, Kulkarni RR, Nune SK, Casteel SW, Smith CJ, Vimal J, Boote E, Robertson JD, Kan P, Engelbrecht H, Watkinson LD, Carmack TL, Lever JR, Cutler CS, Caldwell C, Kannan R, Katti KV: Laminin receptor specific therapeutic gold nanoparticles (198AuNP-EGCg) show efficacy in treating prostate cancer. Proc Natl Acad Sci USA. 2012, 31 (31): 109-12426–31

40. Link S, El-Sayed MA: Spectral properties and relaxation dynamics of surface plasmon electronic oscillations in gold and silver nanodots and nanorods. J Phys Chem B. 1999, 103 (40): 8410-8426.

41. Link S, El-Sayed MA: Shape and size dependence of radiative, non-radiative and photothermal properties of gold nanocrystals. Int Rev Phys Chem. 2000, 19 (3): 409-453.

42. Link S, El-Sayed MA: Optical properties and ultrafast dynamics of metallic nanocrystals. Annu Rev Phys Chem. 2003, 54: 331-366.

43. Spivak MY, Bubnov RV, Yemets IM, Lazarenko LM, Timoshok NO, Ulberg ZR: Gold nanoparticles - the theranostic challenge for PPPM: nanocardiology application. EPMA J. 2013, 4: 18.

44. Huang X, El-Sayed MA: Gold nanoparticles optical properties and implementations in cancer diagnosis and photothermal therapy. J Ad Res. 2010, 1: 13-28.

45. Thompson DT: Using gold nanoparticles for catalysis. Nano Today. 2007, 2: 40-43.

46. Sperling RA, Gil PRF, Zhang M: Zanella biological applications of gold nanoparticles Chem. Soc Rev. 2008, 37: 1896-1908.

47. Haes AJ, Hall WP, Chang L, Klein WL, Van Duyne RP: A localized surface plasmon resonance biosensor: first steps toward an Alzheimer's disease. Assa Nano Lett. 2004, 4: 1029-1034.

48. Haes AJ, Chang L, Klein WL, Van Duyne RP: Detection of a biomarker for Alzheimer's disease from synthetic and clinical samples using a nanoscale optical biosensor. J Am Chem Soc. 2005, 127: 2264-2271.

49. Bowman M-C, Ballard TE, Ackerson CJ, Feldheim DL, Margolis DM, Melander C: Inhibition of HIV fusion with multivalent gold nanoparticles. J Am Chem Soc. 2008, 130: 6896-6897.

50. Xi D, Luo X, Ning Q, Lu Q, Yao K, Liu Z: The detection of HBV DNA with gold nanoparticle gene probes. J Nanjing Med Univ. 2007, 21 (4): 207-212.

51. Baptista PV, Koziol-Montewka M, Paluch-Oles J, Doria G, Franco R: Gold-nanoparticle-probe–based assay for rapid and direct detection of *Mycobacterium tuberculosis* DNA in clinical samples. Clin Chem. 2006, 52: 1433-1434.

52. Baptista P, Pereira E, Eaton P, Doria G, Miranda A, Gomes I, Quaresma P, Franco R: Gold nanoparticles for the development of clinical diagnosis methods. Anal Bioanal Chem. 2008, 391 (3): 943-950.

53. Coelho J, Ferreira P, Alves P, Cordeiro R, Fonseca A, Góis J, Gil M: Drug delivery systems: advanced technologies potentially applicable in personalized treatments. EPMA J. 2010, 1: 164-209.

54. Xu PS, Van EA, Kirk YH, Zhan WJ, Murdoch M, Radosz YQ: Shen targeted charge-reversal nanoparticles for nuclear drug delivery Angew. Chem Int. 2007, 46: 4999-5002.

55. Paleos CM, Tsiourvas D, Sideratou Z, Tziveleka L: Acid- and salt-triggered multifunctional poly(propylene imine) dendrimer as a

prospective drug delivery system. Biomacromolecules. 2004, 5: 524-529.

56. Wu W, Wieckowski S, Pastorin G, Benincasa M, Klumpp C, Briand JP, Gennaro R, Prato M, Bianco A: Targeted delivery of amphotericin B to cells by using functionalized carbon nanotubes. Angew Chem Int. 2005, 44: 6358-6362.

57. Salem AK, Searson PC, Leong KW: Multifunctional nanorods for gene delivery. Nat Mater. 2003, 2: 668-671.

58. Brown SD, Nativo P, Smith J-A, Stirling D, Edwards PR, Venugopal B, Flint DJ, Plumb JA, Graham D, Wheate NJ: Gold nanoparticles for the improved anticancer drug delivery of the active component of oxaliplatin. J Am Chem Soc. 2010, 132: 4678-4684.

59. Ghosh P, Han G, De M, Kim CH, Rotello VM: Gold nanoparticles in delivery applications. Adv Drug Delivery Rev. 2008, 60: 1307-1315.

60. Chekman IS, Ulberg ZR, Gorchakova NO, Nebesna TY, Gruzina TG, Priskoka AO, Doroshenko AM, Simonov PV: The prospects of medical application of metal-based nanoparticles and nanomaterials. Lik Sprava. 2011, 1–2: 3-21.

61. Mo R, Lin S, Wang G, Wang Y, Wu EX: Preliminary in vitro study of ultrasound sonoporation cell labeling with superparamagnetic iron oxide particles for MRI cell tracking. In Conference Proceedings of IEEE Eng Med Biol Soc. 2008, 2008: 367-370.

62. Yu Hsin W, Ai Ho L, Jia Yu L, Cheng Ru L, Cheng Ham W, Tzu Min L, Churng Ren W, Pai Chi L: Enhanced delivery of gold nanoparticles by acoustic cavitation for photoacoustic imaging and photothermal therapy. 2013, San Francisco: SPIE Proceedings 8581, Photons Plus Ultrasound: Imaging and Sensing, 858123-

63. Toporova OK, Irodov DM, Bubnov RV, Kholodkova OL, Gulko TP, Ruban TP, Morgunov PV, Kordium VA: Intrahepatic ultrasound-mediated gene delivery. J Hepatol. 2013, 58: S119

64. Kim K, Kim JH, Park H, Kim YS, Park K, Nam H, Lee S, Park JH, Park RW, Kim IS, Choi K, Kim SY, Park K, Kwon IC: Tumor-homing multifunctional nanoparticles for cancer theragnosis: Simultaneous diagnosis, drug delivery, and therapeutic monitoring *J*. Control Release. 2010, 146 (2): 219-227.

65. Mittler R: Oxidative stress, antioxidants and stress tolerance. Trends Plant Sci. 2002, 7 (9): 405-410.

66. Asada K, Takahashi M: Production and scavenging of active oxygen in photosynthesis. Photoinhibition. Edited by: Kyle DJ, Osmond CB, Arntzen CJ. 1987, Amsterdam: Elsevier, 227-287.

67. Barath Mani Kanth S, Kalishwaralal K, Sriram M, Pandian SRK, Youn HS, Eom S, Gurunathan S: Anti-oxidant effect of gold nanoparticles restrains hyperglycemic conditions in diabetic mice. J Nanobiotechnol. 2010, 8: 16-

68. Alvaro M, Aprile C, Corma A, Ferrer B, Garcia H: Influence of radical initiators in gold catalysis: evidence supporting trapping of radicals derived from azobis(isobutyronitrile) by gold halides. J Catal. 2006, 245: 249-252.

69. Navalon S, Martin R, Alvaro M, Garcia H: Gold on diamond nanoparticles as a highly efficient Fenton catalyst. Angew Chem Int Ed Engl. 2001, 2 (45): 8403-8407. 49

70. Andrews RJ: Neuroprotection at the nanolevel – Part I: Introduction to nanoneurosurgery. Ann NY Acad Sci. 2007, 1122: 169-184.

71. Seaton A, Tran L, Aitken R, Donaldson K: Nanoparticles, human health hazard and regulation. J R Soc Interface. 2010, 7: 119-129.

72. Freese C, Uboldi C, Gibson MI, Unger RE, Weksler BB, Romero IA, Couraud PO, Kirkpatrick CJ: Uptake and cytotoxicity of citrate-coated gold nanospheres: Comparative studies on human endothelial and epithelial cells. Part Fibre Toxicol. 2012, 9: 23-

73. Roman'ko MIe, Rieznichenko LS, Hruzina TH, Dybkova SM, Ul'berh ZR, Ushkalov VO, Holovko AM: Influence of gold and silver nanoparticles on ATPase activity of native and rehydrated cells of Escherichia coli. Ukr Biokhim Zh. 2009, 81 (6): 70-76. Ukrainian

74. Ulberg ZR, Gruzina TG, Rieznichenko LS, Dybkova SM: Biological systems at various levels of the organization and the gold nanoparticles. Nanosciences, Nanobiology, nanopharmacology. Edited by: Chekman IS, Ulberg ZR, Malanchuk VA. 2012, Kyiv: Polygraph Plus, 327

75. Shukla R, Bansal V, Chaudhary M, Basu A, Bhonde RR, Sastry M: Biocompatibility of gold nanoparticles and their endocytotic fate inside the cellular compartment: a microscopic overview. Langmuir. 2005, 21: 10644-

76. Zhang Q, Hitchins VM, Schrand AM, Hussain SM, Goering PL: Uptake of gold nanoparticles in murine macrophage cells without cytotoxicity or production of pro-inflammatory mediators. Nanotoxicology. 2011, 5 (3): 284-295.

77. Bubnov RV: Evidence-based pain management: is the concept of integrative medicine applicable. EPMA J. 2012, 3 (1): 13.

78. Bubnov R, Yevseenko V, Semeniv I: Ultrasound guided injections of Platelets Rich Plasma for muscle injury in professional athletes. Comparative study. Med Ultrason. 2013, 15 (2): 101-105.

79. Chnari E, Nikitczuk JS, Uhrich KE, Moghe PV: Nanoscale anionic macromolecules can inhibit cellular uptake of differentially oxidized LDL. Biomacromolecules. 2006, 7: 597-603.

80. Hsieh PC, Davis ME, Gannon J, MacGillivray C, Lee RT: Controlled delivery of PDGFBB for myocardial protection using injectable self-assembling peptide nanofibers. J Clin Invest. 2006, 116: 237-248.

81. Davis ME, Hsieh PC, Takahashi T, Song Q, Zhang S, Kamm RD, Grodzinsky AJ, Anversa P, Lee RT: Local myocardial insulin-like growth factor 1 (IGF-1) delivery with biotinylated peptide nanofibers improves cell therapy for myocardial infarction. Proc Natl Acad Sci USA. 2006, 103: 8155-8160.

82. Sy JC, Davis ME: Delivering regenerative cues to the heart: cardiac drug delivery by microspheres and peptide nanofibers. J Cardiovasc Transl Res. 2010, 3 (5): 461-468.

83. Powrie F, Coffman RL: Cytokine regulation of T-cell function: potential for therapeutic intervention. Trends Pharmacol Sci. 1993, 14 (5): 164-168.

84. Astry B, Harberts E, Moudgil KD: A cytokine-centric view of the pathogenesis and treatment of autoimmune arthritis. J Interferon Cytokine Res. 2011, 31 (12): 927-940.

85. Mill JG, Stefanon I, dos Santos L, Baldo MP: Remodeling in the ischemic heart: the stepwise progression for heart failure. Braz J Med Biol Res September. 2011, 44 (9): 890-898.

86. Bhattacharya R, Mukherjee P, Xiong Z, Atala A, Soker S, Mukhopadhyay D: Gold nanoparticles inhibit VEGF165-induced proliferation of HUVEC cells. Nano Lett. 2004, 4: 2479-2481.

87. Giljohann DA, Seferos DS, Prigodich AE, Patel PC, Mirkin CA: Gene regulation with polyvalent siRNA-nanoparticle conjugates. J Am Chem Soc. 2009, 131 (6): 2072-2073.

88. Patel PC, Giljohann DA, Daniel WL, Zheng D, Prigodich AE, Mirkin CA: Scavenger receptors mediate cellular uptake of polyvalent oligonucleotide-functionalized gold nanoparticles. Bioconjug Chem. 2010, 21 (12): 2250-2256.

89. Kisak ET, Coldren B, Evans CA, Boyer C, Zasadzinski JA: The vesosome — a multicompartment drug delivery vehicle. Curr Med Chem. 2004, 11: 199-219.

Chapter 12

Nanoscale Delivery of Resveratrol towards Enhancement of Supplements and Nutraceuticals

Ana Rute Neves [1], Susana Martins [2], Marcela A. Segundo [1] and Salette Reis [1,*]

[1]*UCIBIO, REQUIMTE, Department of Chemical Sciences, Faculty of Pharmacy, University of Porto, Rua de Jorge Viterbo Ferreira, 228, 4050-313 Porto, Portugal*

[2]*Laboratory for Pharmaceutical Technology/Research Centre in Pharmaceutical Sciences, Faculty of Pharmacy, University of Porto, Rua de Jorge Viterbo Ferreira, 228, 4050-313 Porto, Portugal*

ABSTRACT

Resveratrol was investigated in terms of its stability, biocompatibility and intestinal permeability across Caco-2 cell monolayers in its free form or encapsulated in solid lipid nanoparticles (SLNs) and nanostructured lipid carriers (NLCs). SLNs and NLCs presented a mean diameter between 160 and 190 nm, high negative zeta potential of −30 mV and resveratrol entrapment efficiency of 80%, suggesting they are suitable for resveratrol oral delivery. Nanoencapsulation effectively protected resveratrol from photodegradation, and MTT assays demonstrated that neither resveratrol nor lipid nanoparticles adversely affected cell viability and integrity of Caco-2 cell monolayers. The *in vitro*intestinal permeability of resveratrol was significantly increased by NLCs, and SLNs did not impair the absorption of resveratrol. Resveratrol oral absorption can be enhanced during meals, since the intestinal permeability was increased in the presence of fed-state intestinal juices. SLNs and NLCs constitute carrier systems for resveratrol oral administration, for further use as supplements or nutraceuticals.

Keywords: resveratrol; biocompatibility; oral bioavailability; nanodelivery systems; lipid nanoparticles; intestinal permeability

1. INTRODUCTION

Resveratrol has been one of the most extensively studied naturally occurring compounds due to its great therapeutic potential in cancer therapy, cardio- and neuroprotection, anti-inflammatory action, antioxidant activity, antiaging effects and diabetes treatment [1,2,3]. However, resveratrol pharmacokinetic properties must be considered since this compound demonstrated low solubility, rapid degradation and extensive metabolism, resulting in poor oral bioavailability [4,5,6,7]. Moreover, *trans*-resveratrol, the biologically active isomer, is highly photosensitive, being rapidly converted to *cis*-resveratrol when exposed to light [8]. Different strategies have been implemented to overcome the above-mentioned problems, such as the co-administration with metabolism inhibitors, use of analogs, and the design of new delivery systems [9,10,11,12,13,14]. In the past decade, several nanoformulations focused on enhancing therapeutic potential of resveratrol [3,9,15], namely polymeric nanoparticles such as poly(lactide) (PLA) nanoparticles [16,17], poly-(lactic-co-glycolic) acid (PLGA) [18,19,20] and poly(epsilon-caprolactone) (PCL) nanoparticles [18,19], polymeric micelles [21], nanoparticles based on zein, an amphiphilic protein [22], lecithin-based nanoemulsions [23], cyclodextrins [24,25,26], and liposomes [27,28,29,30,31], or on dual nanoencapsulation approaches, such as the inclusion of cyclodextrin complexes inside liposomes [32]. In the present study, we have developed resveratrol nanodelivery systems based on lipid nanoparticles to increase its oral bioavailability for further use as supplements or nutraceuticals. So far, lipid nanoparticles for resveratrol encapsulation have been developed for dermal and brain delivery [33,34,35], and only two studies have used it for oral administration [36,37]. Solid lipid nanoparticles (SLNs) and nanostructured lipid carriers (NLCs) have proven to be suitable vehicles for resveratrol encapsulation [36]. While SLNs are made solely by solid lipids at room and body temperature, NLCs are composed by a mixture of both solid and liquid lipids [38,39]. The incorporation of a liquid lipid to the solid matrix of the nanoparticles seems to create an imperfect matrix with an increased number of cavities, facilitating the accommodation of the encapsulated compound, while preventing early crystallization and drug release [40,41]. Therefore, resveratrol stability, biocompatibility, and intestinal permeability studies were conducted in a solution or encapsulated in SLNs and NLCs. Intestinal apparent permeability was assessed using Caco-2 cell monolayers grown on permeable filter transwell devices, simulating the intestinal membrane barrier. Caco-2 cell monolayers are the most commonly used intestinal models to evaluate the effect of delivery systems on drug permeation because Caco-2 cells form differentiated monolayers with microvilli, tight junctions, enzymes and transport systems, after 21 days of growth [42,43]. In addition, the influence of physiological fluids that mimic gastrointestinal conditions on the apparent permeability of resveratrol and resveratrol-loaded nanoparticles was also tested. Fasted-state simulated intestinal fluid (FaSSIF) and fed-state simulated intestinal fluid (FeSSIF), besides the control medium Hanks' balanced salt solution (HBSS), were used. The first two media mimic fasted and fed digestive conditions because they contain natural surfactants (bile salts and lecithin) that form micelles that are present in the gastrointestinal fluids [44,45].

2. MATERIALS AND METHODS

2.1. Materials

trans-Resveratrol (>99% purity) was purchased from Sigma-Aldrich (St. Louis, MO, USA), cetyl palmitate was provided by Gattefossé SAS (Nanterre, France), polysorbate 60 (tween 60) was supplied by Merck (Darmstadt, Germany), and miglyol-812 from Acofarma (Madrid, Spain). For the preparation of buffer solutions, sodium hydroxide was obtained from Riedel-de Haën AG (Seelze, Germany), sodium phosphate monobasic monohydrated was acquired from Fluka (Seelze, Germany), sodium chloride was purchased from Panreac (Barcelona, Spain), and acetic acid (≥99.8%) was obtained from Sigma-Aldrich. The transport media HBSS was purchased from Gibco (Paisley, UK), while FaSSIF and FeSSIF were prepared by using simulated intestinal fluid (SIF) instant powder (Phares Drug Delivery AG, Muttenz, Switzerland) according to the manufacturer's instructions. The HPLC mobile phase was composed of acetonitrile and acetic acid (LiChrosolv HPLC grade) obtained from Merck. Caco-2 cell line was purchased from the American Type Culture Collection (ATCC, Wesel, Germany) between passage numbers 35 and 55, and maintained in Dulbecco's Modified Eagle Medium (DMEM) supplemented with 10% fetal bovine serum (South America origin), 1% fungizone (amphotericin B, 250 $\mu g \cdot mL^{-1}$), and 1% Pen Strep (penicillin, streptomycin), all obtained from Gibco. Trypsin-EDTA was also purchased from Gibco. Trypan blue and thiazolyl blue tetrazolium bromide (MTT) were both provided by Sigma-Aldrich.

2.2. Preparation of SLNs and NLCs

SLNs and NLCs were produced by a high shear homogenization technique followed by the ultrasound method to reduce the microparticles to the nanometer range, as described before [36,46]. SLNs were composed of 10% of the solid lipid cetyl palmitate, while NLCs were constituted by 7% of cetyl palmitate and 3% of the liquid lipid miglyol-812. Both types of lipid nanoparticles were dispersed in aqueous medium by the presence of 2% surfactant polysorbate 60. Resveratrol (5 mg) was added to the lipid phase and melted above the lipid's melting point, which was followed by dispersion in the aqueous phase. The oil/water (o/w) emulsion was then submitted to high-speed stirring (SLNs—30 s at 12,000 rpm and NLCs—2 min at 12,000 rpm) in Ultra-Turrax T25 (Janke and Kunkel IKA-Labortechnik, Staufen, Germany) and sonicated (SLNs—5 min at 80% intensity and NLCs—15 min at 70% intensity) in a Sonics and Materials Vibra-Cell™ CV18 (Newtown, CT, USA). After cooling at room temperature, lipid nanoparticles were formed and the formulations were stored for characterization and application.

2.3. Resveratrol Entrapment Efficiency

Resveratrol entrapment efficiency was measured indirectly by quantifying the amount of compound that was not internalized by the nanoscale particles, as dissolved compound in the aqueous phase of the formulation [38,47]. Amicon Ultra 4 centrifugal Filter Devices (Millipore, Billerica, MA, USA) were used to separate lipid nanoparticles from the aqueous medium after 15 min of 3300 *g* centrifugation in a Jouan BR4i multifunction centrifuge (Thermo Electron, Waltham, MA, USA). The non-entrapped resveratrol was quantified in the supernatant after absorbance spectral analysis using a V-660 spectrophotometer (Jasco, Easton, MD, USA) at 200–600 nm and the entrapment efficiency calculated according to the equation (1):

$$EE = \frac{\text{total resveratrol} - \text{non entrapped resveratrol}}{\text{total resveratrol}} \times 100 \quad (1)$$

2.4. Particle Size and Zeta Potential Measurements

Particle size and zeta potential analysis were performed by dynamic light scattering (DLS) and electrophoretic light scattering (ELS), respectively, in a Brookhaven Instrument (Holtsville, NY, USA). The samples were first diluted (1:400) in order to get a suitable scattering intensity. The mean hydrodynamic diameter (Z-average) and the polydispersity index were determined as a measure of the width of particles size distribution, while zeta potential was measured according to the electrophoretic mobility of nanoparticles, which is influenced by their charge. The measurements were performed in triplicate in cycles of 10 runs each.

2.5. Resveratrol Photostability Study

Photostability studies were performed to investigate the protection effect of lipid nanoparticles against photodegradation of *trans*-resveratrol over time. Aqueous solutions of free resveratrol and resveratrol encapsulated in SLNs and NLCs at the same concentration of 1 $mg{\cdot}mL^{-1}$ were exposed for 4 h to UV light (HPW125W-T E27, Philips) in a chamber with reflecting walls. The UV lamp had an emission spectrum between 320 and 400 nm, with an irradiation intensity of 5.5×10^{-3} $kJ{\cdot}s^{-1}{\cdot}m^{-2}$. Aliquots were withdrawn from each sample at 0, 0.5, 1, 2, 3 and 4 h, and a 20%-volume of ACN was added to promote the disruption of lipid matrix, allowing the quantification of *trans*-resveratrol in a solution by spectrophotometric detection at 306 nm in a V-660 spectrophotometer (Jasco, Easton, MD, USA). Resveratrol photodegradation was calculated as a percentage by comparing the absorbance of *trans*-resveratrol at each time to the maximum absorbance at the beginning of each experiment.

2.6. Caco-2 Cell Culture

Caco-2 cells were grown in DMEM supplemented with 10% fetal bovine serum, 1% fungizone, 1% Pen Strep at 37 °C, and 5% CO_2. Cells were supplied with a fresh medium every 2 days and subcultured by treatment with 0.25% trypsin–EDTA when they reached 80%–90% confluency, followed by counting in a Neubauer chamber with a trypan blue solution (0.4%, w/v). Cells were then seeded at a density of 10^4 cells per cm^2.

2.7. MTT Cell Viability Assay

Cell viability in the presence of nanoparticles was assessed by MTT assay. This assay detects living cells via mitochondrial dehydrogenases activity [48]. Cells were seeded in 96-well plates (10^4 cells per well) and grown for 20 h at 37 °C, 5% CO_2. Cells were then incubated with different concentrations of free resveratrol and resveratrol-loaded SLNs and NLCs, as well as with the respective placebo formulations for 4 h. After that, cells were treated with 0.5 mg/ml MTT for 4 h. Finally, DMSO was added to dissolve MTT formazan and incubated for 15 min, followed by absorbance measurement at 550 and 690 nm in a microplate reader (Synergy HT; Bio-Tek Instruments, Winooski, VT, USA).

2.8. Caco-2 Cell Permeability Study

Cells were seeded on transwell polycarbonate inserts (12 wells, pore diameter of 3 µm, 1.12 cm^2) in a density of 1×10^5 cells per insert and grown for 21 days, at 37 °C and 5% CO_2, until a confluent monolayer was achieved. In fact, Caco-2 cells present an absorptive polarized monolayer and an apical brush border after 21 days from seeding [49,50]. The integrity of the monolayers was monitored by measuring trans-epithelial electrical resistance (TEER) with an epithelial voltohmmeter (EVOM) from World Precision Instruments (Sarasota, FL, USA). Only monolayers with TEER values higher than 200 Ω cm^2 were used. Permeability assay was performed by incubating free-resveratrol and resveratrol-loaded SLNs and NLCs (10 µM) on the apical side for 4 h at 37 °C and 5% CO_2. Three different transport media were used to mimic intestinal fluids: HBSS was used as control, FaSSIF as the fasted state medium, and FeSSIF as the fed state medium. Aliquots from the basolateral side were collected at regular intervals of 30 min and treated with 20% acetonitrile/acetic acid (92:8, v/v) to promote the disruption of lipid nanoparticles and the release of resveratrol to be quantified. The quantification was performed by HPLC separation in a C18 monolithic column with isocratic elution in a 2% acetic acid solution/acetonitrile (80:20), followed by fluorimetric detection (330/374 nm), according to a validated method [51]. TEER values were rechecked at the end to confirm the quality of the monolayer after the experiment. The apparent permeability coefficients (P_{app}) in the three media tested were calculated after 4-h assay by the Equation (2):

$$P_{app}\,(cm/s) = \frac{Q}{A \times C \times t} \quad (2)$$

where *Q* represents the total amount of permeated resveratrol (μg), *A* is the surface area of the insert (cm^2), *C* is the initial resveratrol concentration ($\mu g/cm^3$) and *t* is the experiment time (s).

2.9. Statistical Analysis

Statistical analysis was performed using SPSS software (version 20.0; IBM, Armonk, NY, USA). The measurements were repeated at least three times and data were expressed as mean ± SD. Data were analyzed using one-way analysis of variance (one-way ANOVA), followed by Bonferroni, Tukey and Dunnett *post-hoc* tests. A *p* value less than 0.05 was considered statistically significant.

3. RESULTS

3.1. Characterization of Nanoparticles

The physicochemical characterization of nanoparticles is depicted in Table 1. All formulations presented a size between 160 and 190 nm, polydispersity index of 0.2 and high negative zeta potential around −30 mV, regardless of resveratrol incorporation. The results indicate that there is no statistically significant difference in the size and charge of both types of lipid nanoparticles (SLNs and NLCs) and that resveratrol did not significantly change these parameters. Resveratrol entrapment efficiency in both SLNs and NLCs was found to be very high (around 80%), suggesting its preferential partition into the nanoparticles lipid matrix. The developed nanoparticles can be considered physically stable because the absolute value of zeta potential is around 30 mV, and the electrostatic repulsions between particles can therefore avoid flocculation and aggregation of nanoparticles [52,53]. Moreover, polydispersity index of 0.2 suggests an acceptable monodispersity distribution, with low variability. The mean size of these nanosystems (<200 nm) confirmed that they are appropriated for oral administration and gastrointestinal absorption [54,55], and the negatively charged nanoparticles can interact with enterocytes, being prone for permeation across the intestinal barrier [56,57].

Table 1. Characterization of resveratrol-loaded solid lipid nanoparticles (SLNs) and nanostructured lipid carriers (NLCs).

	Z-Average (nm)	Polydispersity Index	Zeta Potential (mV)	Entrapment Efficiency (%)
SLN Placebo	189.2 ± 15.1	0.205 ± 0.045	-30.8 ± 7.3	-
SLN RSV	171.5 ± 17.1	0.215 ± 0.033	-32.1 ± 6.9	80.5 ± 3.4
NLC Placebo	172.9 ± 19.8	0.203 ± 0.030	-29.6 ± 7.4	-
NLC RSV	163.8 ± 21.7	0.198 ± 0.027	-29.9 ± 5.8	78.9 ± 2.5

Note: All values represent the mean ± standard deviation (n = 3).

3.2. Photostability Study of Resveratrol

Resveratrol is found in nature as both *trans* and *cis* isomers, *trans*-resveratrol being the biologically active form [58]. However, it is well-known that *trans*-resveratrol easily isomerizes into the *cis* form under UV irradiation [8,59].

Figure 1A displays the absorption intensity spectra of resveratrol before (*trans*-resveratrol) and after UV light exposure during 4 h. The result is in agreement with previous studies which show a decrease of 50% in the *trans*-resveratrol absorption intensity at 306 nm and a 20 nm shift from 306 nm to 286 nm for the maximum absorption intensity, typical of *cis*-resveratrol spectra [60,61]. The ability of lipid nanoparticles to protect the compound against isomerization was also investigated and the absorption spectra for resveratrol-loaded SLNs and NLCs before and after UV irradiation are represented in Figure 1B and Figure 1C, respectively. Resveratrol photostability after 4 h of UV light exposure was verified by comparing the

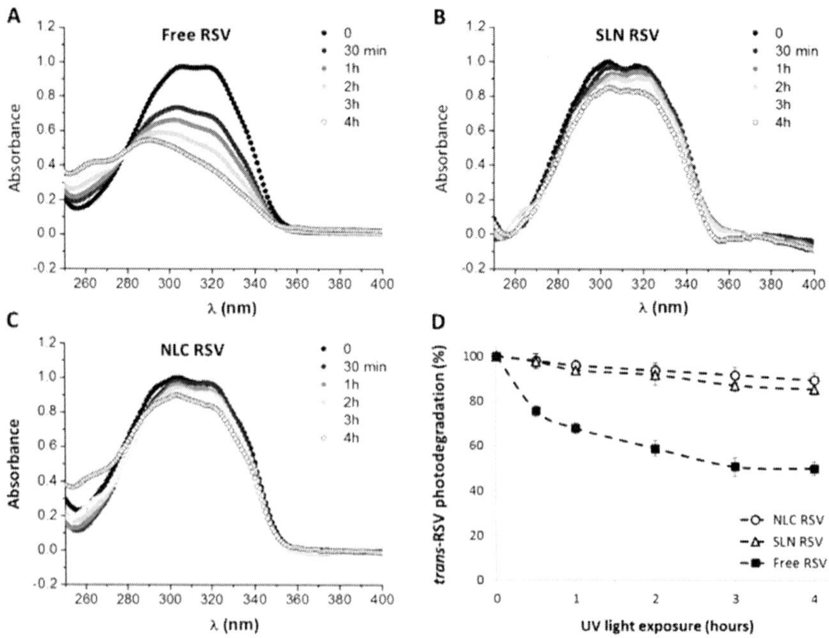

Figure 1. Photostability study of *trans*-resveratrol exposed to 312 nm UV light for four hours. (**A**) free resveratrol; (**B**) resveratrol loaded in SLNs; (**C**) resveratrol loaded in NLCs; (**D**) Photodegradation profile of *trans*-resveratrol in aqueous solution (■) compared to the compound encapsulated in SLNs (Δ) and NLCs (○).

percentage of photodegradation inside lipid nanoparticles with that of the pure compound in an aqueous solution at the same concentration. The results suggest that both types of lipid nanoparticles (SLNs and NLCs) enhance photostability of resveratrol (Figure 1D). In fact, around 50% of *trans*-resveratrol in solution was converted to the *cis* isomer after 4h of UV exposure and the entrapment of the compound inside lipid nanoparticles decreased this value for less than 10%. This result is consistent with previous studies using either SLNs or liposome delivery systems [28,37,62].

3.3. Caco-2 Cell Viability Study

Caco-2 cell viability studies were performed to assess the cytotoxicity of resveratrol and resveratrol-loaded lipid nanoparticles in the intestinal barrier. MTT assay evaluates the activity of cellular oxidoreductase enzymes inside mitochondria by converting the MTT tetrazolium dye into its insoluble formazan, which has a purple color. The quantitative measure of purple that is produced (550 nm) is directly proportional to the number of viable cells, allowing the determination of the biocompatibility of formulations. Observing Figure 2, it is possible to conclude that 10 μM concentration of resveratrol, resveratrol-loaded nanoparticles and the equivalent solid amount of placebo nanoparticles did not produce any cytotoxic effect after 4 h of incubation at 37 °C, when compared to cells in DMEM medium. Only at concentrations higher than 50 μM was there a significant reduction of cell metabolic activity. However, even for the highest concentration tested (100 μM), a cell toxicity below 50% was produced, indicating that resveratrol-loaded nanoparticles are biocompatible and well tolerated by the intestinal mucosa. This study also allowed us to choose the appropriate, non-toxic concentration (10 μM) for the intestinal permeability studies, without compromising Caco-2 cell monolayer.

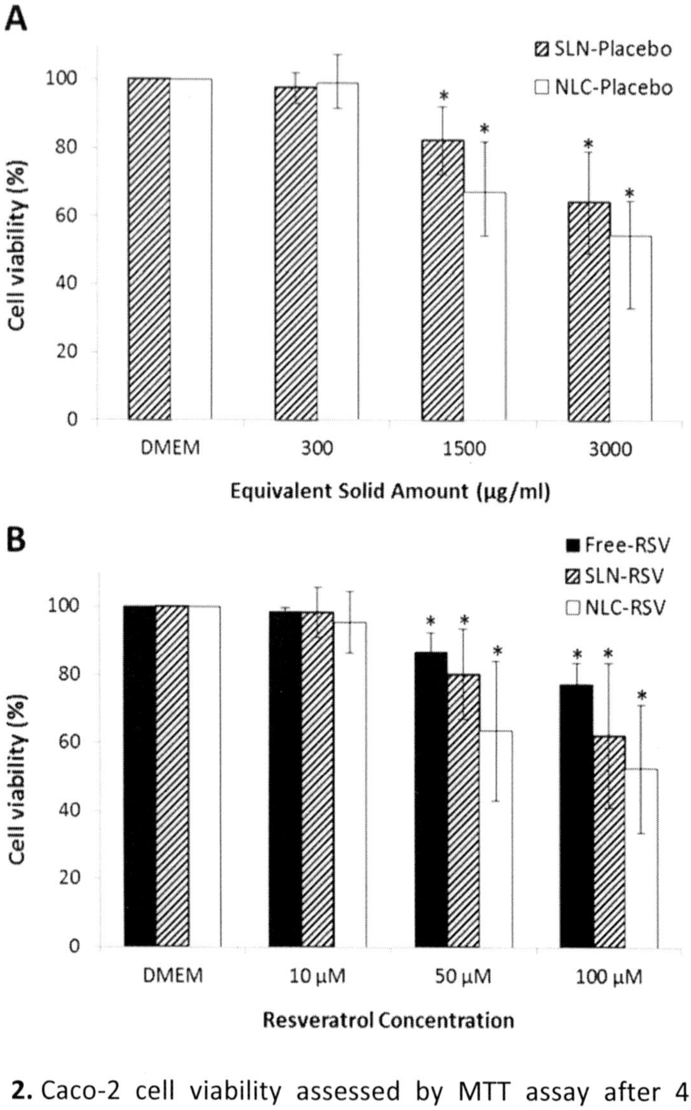

Figure 2. Caco-2 cell viability assessed by MTT assay after 4 h of incubation with increasing concentrations of samples. (**A**) Placebo SLNs (▨) and placebo NLCs (□) formulations; (**B**) free resveratrol (■) and resveratrol-loaded SLNs (▨) or NLCs (□). **Note:** All values represent the mean ± standard deviation (n = 3). Results were analyzed and compared with a DMEM medium, which represents the maximum of cell viability. (*) denotes statistically significant differences ($p < 0.05$) from DMEM.

3.4. Intestinal Permeability Study

In vitro intestinal permeability assays were performed in transwell devices using Caco-2 cell monolayers that mimic the intestinal barrier. Figure 3 shows Caco-2 cells photographs immediately after seeding and after forming a confluent monolayer. Confluent Caco-2 cells have been used as the standard model for the *in vitro* investigation of intestinal absorption due to their similarities to the small intestinal epithelium [63,64].

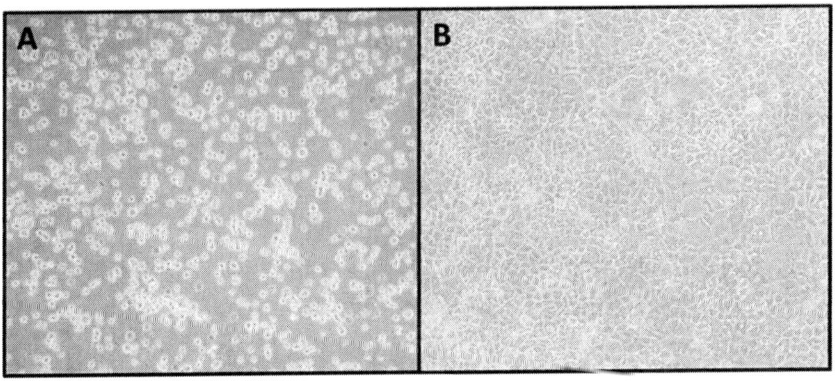

Figure 3. Unstained photographs of Caco-2 cells. (**A**) Immediately after seeding and (**B**) with 100% of confluence. Magnification: 100×.

In order to mimic the intestinal fluids, three transport media were applied: HBSS, FaSSIF and FeSSIF. HBSS was used as the control medium, while the last two media mimic the fasted- and fed-state intestinal juices, respectively, because they contain natural surfactants (bile salts and lecithin) that generate micelles that are present during the digestive process [44,45]. The HPLC quantification method was firstly developed and validated for resveratrol in the three different matrices [51]. The permeation of free resveratrol and resveratrol-loaded lipid nanoparticles across the intestinal barrier is presented as cumulative transport over 4 h in Figure 4. The results are also reported as P_{app} (Table 2), which provides independent values that can be compared between different studies. Figure 4 shows that resveratrol rapidly starts to cross Caco-2 monolayer, since the compound is detected on the basolateral side after only 30 min. This initial burst permeability has already been reported in previous studies where P_{app} of free resveratrol is in agreement with our value of 1.6×10^{-5} cm/s in HBSS medium [65,66]. The comparison between different transport media indicates that resveratrol P_{app} is 1.7-fold higher in FaSSIF and 2.1-fold higher in FeSSIF when compared to HBSS control medium. This fact can be related to the micellarization of resveratrol and lipid nanoparticles [45]. On the other hand, FaSSIF and FeSSIF protection against *trans*-resveratrol degradation is also reported [51], which can explain the increased resveratrol absorption when taken with meals. We have performed identical studies to ensure the integrity and stability of the nanoparticles in the different media used, in order to ensure the validity of the intestinal permeability assay. At regular intervals, when aliquots were collected from the basolateral side of Caco-2 monolayer, the size and zeta potential parameters of these aliquots were analyzed, and no statistically significant changes were detected compared to the size and zeta potential values of the fresh nanoparticles reported before (Table 1). This information indicates that the permeability results are justified by the permeation of the SLNs and NLCs themselves through the intestinal barrier and not to the diffusion of the free compound.

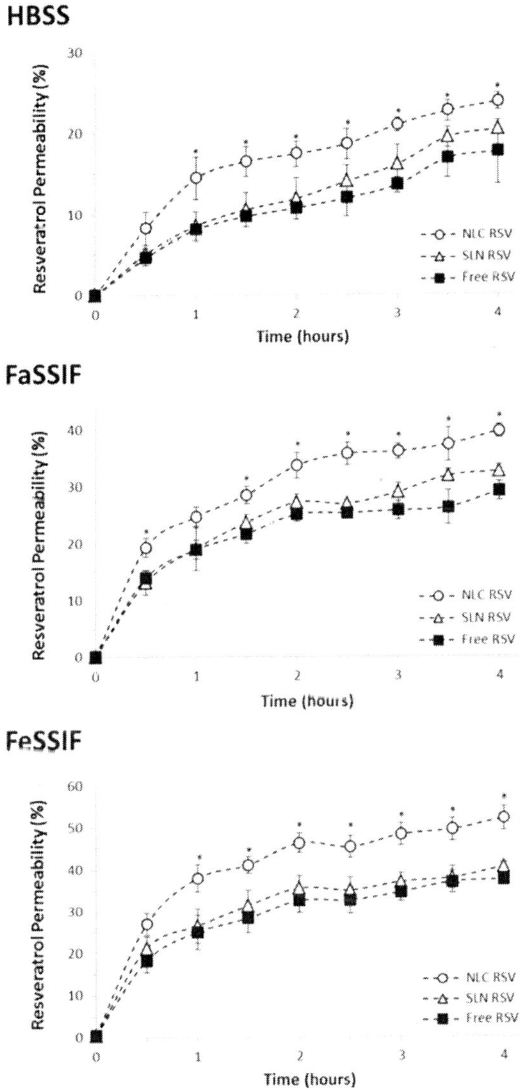

Figure 4. Resveratrol permeability over 4 hours of cumulative transport across Caco-2 cell monolayer mimicking intestinal permeability conditions, on free-form (■) and encapsulated in SLNs (Δ) or NLCs (○) in 3 different transport media. (**A**) HBSS; (**B**) FaSSIF and (**C**) FeSSIF. Note: All values represent the mean ± standard deviation (n = 3). Results were analyzed and compared with the free form of resveratrol. (*) denotes statistically significant differences ($p < 0.05$).

Table 2. Apparent permeability (P_{app}) of free resveratrol and resveratrol-loaded SLN or NLC for 4 h of transport across Caco-2 cell monolayer mimicking intestinal permeability conditions.

	P_{app} ($\times 10^{-5}$ cm/s)		
	HBSS	FaSSIF	FeSSIF
NLC RSV	2.2 ± 0.1 *	3.7 ± 0.1 *	4.8 ± 0.3 *
SLN RSV	1.9 ± 0.2	3.0 ± 0.1	3.8 ± 0.1
Free RSV	1.6 ± 0.4	2.7 ± 0.2	3.5 ± 0.4

Note: All values represent the mean ± standard deviation ($n = 3$). (*) denotes statistically significant differences compared with the free form of resveratrol ($p < 0.05$).

When comparing the different formulations tested, resveratrol permeability through Caco-2 monolayers was significantly increased by NLCs encapsulation (up to 1.5-fold increment, $p < 0.05$). On the other hand, SLNs did not produce any significant effect on resveratrol permeation. The difference between both types of lipid nanoparticles may be related with their different lipid composition, because their size, charge and resveratrol entrapment efficiency were found to be similar. In a recent study, we have found that NLCs promoted a more sustained and controlled release of resveratrol when compared to SLNs in gastrointestinal studies, since SLNs release 10% of resveratrol after 4 h assay, while NLCs only release 5% of compound at the same conditions [36]. The difference observed can be attributed to the less ordered lipid matrix conferred by the liquid lipid present in the NLCs, allowing better accommodation of resveratrol and avoiding its premature release. Therefore, although the encapsulation efficiency was identical in both systems, the early loss of compound in SLNs may have led to a lower permeability across the intestinal barrier when compared to NLCs. Besides that, the presence of a liquid lipid in NLCs composition can influence the lipid matrix of those nanoparticles that become more flexible, thus allowing a greater physical deformation at the time of crossing the barrier, and perhaps leading to an increase of resveratrol permeation. Indeed, the higher permeability of NLCs could be related to the decrease of tight junctions stickiness, promoting an enhancement of the paracellular transport route with this particular system. Actually, TEER values in the presence of NLCs were slightly smaller (10%) than those for SLNs and free-resveratrol, indicating a partial opening of tight junctions between epithelial cells when NLCs were incubated. Nevertheless, the TEER values were reverted at the end of the assay by replacing the nanoparticles solution by fresh medium, indicating that the opening of tight junctions was reversible and did not completely disrupt and compromise the monolayer integrity [67]. These results are in agreement with a recent paper where the applicability of SLNs and NLCs as oral drug delivery nanosystems was tested [68]. In this study, the cellular uptake, internalization pathways and transcytosis routes through Caco-2 monolayers were assessed. Transmission electron microscopy and confocal laser scanning microscopy images revealed the ability of these nanosystems to cross the monolayer by a transcellular route. Indeed, cell internalization occurred mainly through a clathrin-mediated endocytosis mechanism. However, the higher cellular uptake of NLCs together with the contribution of a paracellular route also involved in this nanocarrier permeation would explain the higher permeability found for NLCs compared to SLNs. These results support the conclusions drawn in the present study.

Therefore, we conclude that NLCs exhibit greater efficiency in the transport across the intestinal barrier, promoting an increase in resveratrol permeability. Regarding SLNs, they do not produce any significant increase in resveratrol permeation, but still do not compromise its absorption when compared with the free compound. Thus, SLNs may also be used for resveratrol delivery into systemic circulation, since they also provide gastrointestinal protection and resistance to the early first-pass metabolism [37]. As a conclusion, both nanosystems might be used for oral administration of resveratrol.

4. DISCUSSION

In the present study, lipid nanoparticles were successfully developed, characterized and applied for oral administration of resveratrol. SLNs and NLCs presented a mean diameter of 160–190 nm, high negative zeta potential of −30 mV and a resveratrol entrapment efficiency around 80%, suggesting that they are suitable for resveratrol oral delivery, being prone for its permeation across the intestinal barrier [55,57]. The results also revealed that resveratrol encapsulation effectively protected it from photodegradation, and previous studies have already shown that these nanosystems conferred protection during its gastrointestinal transit avoiding premature release in simulated gastric and intestinal conditions [36]. Therefore, this study demonstrated the applicability of these nanoparticles, protecting resveratrol from degradation as well as allowing their permeability through the intestinal barrier in order to reach the systemic circulation. Indeed, SLNs did not impair the absorption of resveratrol, and NLCs further increased the permeability of the polyphenol compound across Caco-2 cell monolayer. Furthermore, it was observed that resveratrol oral absorption can be enhanced during meals, since the intestinal permeability was increased when fed-state intestinal juices were applied. At this point, the development of resveratrol-loaded nanoparticles may be important towards the production of novel food supplements or nutraceuticals. This can be achieved by improving products derived from food sources, such as juices, yogurts, milk, or cheese, with extra health benefits similar to those attributed exclusively to resveratrol-rich red wine consumption. A combination of several innovative formulation strategies have been applied in order to accomplish this great challenge [3,9,15], including the use of polymeric nanoparticles [16,17,18,19,20], polymeric micelles [21], zein-based nanoparticles [22], lecithin-based nanoemulsions [23], cyclodextrins [24,25,26], liposomes [27,28,29,30,31,32], and lipid nanoparticles [33,34,35,36,37]. The efforts in tuning these intelligent nanocarriers are based on improving the permeation across an epithelial cell monolayer, on preserving the physical integrity of the nanoparticles during the biodistribution process, and on enhancing the activity of the encapsulated resveratrol. Here, lipid nanoparticles not only meet these physical, chemical and biological requirements, as exploited before, but also represent the most suitable nanosystems for food industry application. In fact, SLNs and NLCs are composed of biodegradable and biocompatible lipids recognized as safe by Food and Drug Administration, which can be loaded with the lipophilic and poorly soluble resveratrol, for further use in food supplements [38,47]. Moreover, the preparation of lipid nanoparticles is very simple, rapid and economically affordable for food industry scale up [52].

5. CONCLUSIONS

As a conclusion, SLNs and NLCs were developed and validated for *trans*-resveratrol protection, stabilization and intestinal permeability. Both lipid nanoparticles seem to be compatible and adequate for resveratrol delivery after oral administration, representing a promising strategy for enhancing its *in vivo*efficacy.

ACKNOWLEDGMENTS

This work received financial support from the European Union (FEDER funds) and National Funds (FCT/MEC, Fundação para a Ciência e a Tecnologia and Ministério da Educação e Ciência) under the Partnership Agreement PT2020 UID/MULTI/04378/2013 - POCI/01/0145/FEDER/007728. ARN also thanks the FCT (Fundação para a Ciência e a Tecnologia) and POPH (Programa Operacional Potencial Humano) for her PhD grant SFRH/BD/73379/2010. The funders had no role in study design, data collection and analysis, decision to publish, or preparation of the manuscript.

AUTHOR CONTRIBUTIONS

Ana Rute Neves and Salette Reis conceived and designed the experiments; Ana Rute Neves performed the experiments; Ana Rute Neves, Susana Martins, Marcela A Segundo and Salette Reis analyzed the data; Marcela A Segundo and Salette Reis contributed reagents/materials/analysis tools; Ana Rute Neves wrote the paper.

CONFLICTS OF INTEREST

The authors declare no conflict of interest.

REFERENCES

1. Baur, J.A.; Sinclair, D.A. Therapeutic potential of resveratrol: The in vivo Evidence. Nat. Rev. Drug Discov. 2006, 5, 493–506.

2. Delmas, D.; Aires, V.; Limagne, E.; Dutartre, P.; Mazue, F.; Ghiringhelli, F.; Latruffe, N. Transport, stability, and biological activity of resveratrol. Ann. N. Y. Acad. Sci. 2011, 1215, 48–59.

3. Neves, A.R.; Lucio, M.; Lima, J.L.; Reis, S. Resveratrol in medicinal chemistry: A critical review of its pharmacokinetics, drug-delivery, and membrane interactions. Curr. Med. Chem. 2012, 19, 1663–1681.

4. Walle, T.; Hsieh, F.; DeLegge, M.H.; Oatis, J.E.; Walle, U.K. High absorption but very low bioavailability of oral resveratrol in humans. Drug Metab. Dispos. 2004, 32, 1377–1382.

5. Almeida, L.; Vaz-da-Silva, M.; Falcao, A.; Soares, E.; Costa, R.; Loureiro, A.I.; Fernandes-Lopes, C.; Rocha, J.F.; Nunes, T.; Wright, L.; et al. Pharmacokinetic and safety profile of trans-resveratrol in a rising multiple-dose study in healthy volunteers. Mol. Nutr. Food Res. 2009, 53, S7–S15.

6. Kapetanovic, I.M.; Muzzio, M.; Huang, Z.; Thompson, T.N.; McCormick, D.L. Pharmacokinetics, oral bioavailability, and metabolic profile of resveratrol and its dimethylether analog, pterostilbene, in rats. Cancer Chemother. Pharmacol. 2011, 68, 593–601.

7. Chen, X.; He, H.; Wang, G.; Yang, B.; Ren, W.; Ma, L.; Yu, Q. Stereospecific determination of cis- andtrans-resveratrol in rat plasma by HPLC: Application to pharmacokinetic studies. Biomed. Chromatogr.2007, 21, 257–265.

8. Trela, B.C.; Waterhouse, A.L. Resveratrol: Isomeric molar absorptivities and stability. J. Agric. Food Chem. 1996, 44, 1253–1257.

9. Amri, A.; Chaumeil, J.C.; Sfar, S.; Charrueau, C. Administration of resveratrol: What formulation solutions to bioavailability limitations? J. Control. Release 2012, 158, 182–193.

10. Johnson, J.J.; Nihal, M.; Siddiqui, I.A.; Scarlett, C.O.; Bailey, H.H.; Mukhtar, H.; Ahmad, N. Enhancing the bioavailability of resveratrol by combining it with piperine. Mol. Nutr. Food Res. 2011, 55, 1169–1176.

11. Amiot, M.J.; Romier, B.; Dao, T.M.; Fanciullino, R.; Ciccolini, J.; Burcelin, R.; Pechere, L.; Emond, C.; Savouret, J.F.; Seree, E. Optimization of trans-resveratrol bioavailability for human therapy. Biochimie2013, 95, 1233–1238.

12. Bonechi, C.; Martini, S.; Ciani, L.; Lamponi, S.; Rebmann, H.; Rossi, C.; Ristori, S. Using liposomes as carriers for polyphenolic compounds: The Case of Trans-Resveratrol. PLoS ONE 2012, 7, e41438.

13. Sun, Y.; Xia, Z.; Zheng, J.; Qiu, P.; Zhang, L.; Mc Clements, D.J.; Xiao, H. Nanoemulsion-based delivery systems for nutraceuticals: Influence of carrier oil type on bioavailability of pterostilbene. J. Funct. Foods 2015, 13, 61–70.

14. Augustin, M.A.; Abeywardena, M.Y.; Patten, G.; Head, R.; Lockett, T.; De Luca, A.; Sanguansri, L. Effects of microencapsulation on the gastrointestinal transit and tissue distribution of a bioactive mixture of fish oil, tributyrin and resveratrol. J. Funct. Foods 2011, 3, 25–37.

15. Summerlin, N.; Soo, E.; Thakur, S.; Qu, Z.; Jambhrunkar, S.; Popat, A. Resveratrol nanoformulations: Challenges and opportunities. Int. J. Pharm. 2015, 479, 282–290.

16. Da Rocha Lindner, G.; Bonfanti Santos, D.; Colle, D.; Gasnhar Moreira, E.L.; Daniel Prediger, R.; Farina, M.; Khalil, N.M.; Mara Mainardes, R. Improved neuroprotective effects of resveratrol-loaded polysorbate 80-coated poly(lactide) nanoparticles in MPTP-induced Parkinsonism. Nanomedicine (Lond.) 2015, 10, 1127–1138.

17. Guo, W.; Li, A.; Jia, Z.; Yuan, Y.; Dai, H.; Li, H. Transferrin modified PEG-PLA-resveratrol conjugates:in vitro and in vivo studies for glioma. Eur. J. Pharmacol. 2013, 718, 41–47.

18. Musazzi, U.M.; Youm, I.; Murowchick, J.B.; Ezoulin, M.J.; Youan, B.B. Resveratrol-loaded nanocarriers: Formulation, optimization, characterization and in vitro toxicity on cochlear cells. Colloids Surf. B Biointerfaces 2014, 118, 234–242.

19. Sanna, V.; Siddiqui, I.A.; Sechi, M.; Mukhtar, H. Resveratrol-loaded nanoparticles based on poly(epsilon-caprolactone) and poly(D,L-lactic-co-glycolic acid)-poly(ethylene glycol) blend for prostate cancer treatment. Mol. Pharm. 2013, 10, 3871–3881.

20. Singh, G.; Pai, R.S. Optimized PLGA nanoparticle platform for orally dosed trans-resveratrol with enhanced bioavailability potential. Expert Opin. Drug Deliv. 2014, 11, 647–659.

21. Lu, X.; Ji, C.; Xu, H.; Li, X.; Ding, H.; Ye, M.; Zhu, Z.; Ding, D.; Jiang, X.; Ding, X.; Guo, X. Resveratrol-loaded polymeric micelles

protect cells from Abeta-induced oxidative stress. Int. J. Pharm. 2009, 375, 89–96.

22. Penalva, R.; Esparza, I.; Larraneta, E.; Gonzalez-Navarro, C.J.; Gamazo, C.; Irache, J.M. Zein-based nanoparticles improve the oral bioavailability of resveratrol and its anti-inflammatory effects in a mouse model of endotoxic shock. J. Agric. Food Chem. 2015, 63, 5603–5611.

23. Sessa, M.; Balestrieri, M.L.; Ferrari, G.; Servillo, L.; Castaldo, D.; D'Onofrio, N.; Donsi, F.; Tsao, R. Bioavailability of encapsulated resveratrol into nanoemulsion-based delivery systems. Food Chem.2014, 147, 42–50.

24. Ansari, K.A.; Vavia, P.R.; Trotta, F.; Cavalli, R. Cyclodextrin-based nanosponges for delivery of resveratrol: in vitro characterisation, stability, cytotoxicity and permeation study. AAPS Pharm. Sci. Tech. 2011, 12, 279–286.

25. Silva, F.; Figueiras, A.; Gallardo, E.; Nerin, C.; Domingues, F.C. Strategies to improve the solubility and stability of stilbene antioxidants: A comparative study between cyclodextrins and bile acids. Food Chem. 2014, 145, 115–125.

26. Venuti, V.; Cannava, C.; Cristiano, M.C.; Fresta, M.; Majolino, D.; Paolino, D.; Stancanelli, R.; Tommasini, S.; Ventura, C.A. A characterization study of resveratrol/sulfobutyl ether-beta-cyclodextrin inclusion complex and in vitro anticancer activity. Colloids Surf. B Biointerfaces 2014, 115, 22–28.

27. Catania, A.; Barrajon-Catalan, E.; Nicolosi, S.; Cicirata, F.; Micol, V. Immunoliposome encapsulation increases cytotoxic activity and selectivity of curcumin and resveratrol against HER2 overexpressing human breast cancer cells. Breast Cancer Res. Treat. 2013, 141, 55–65.

28. Coimbra, M.; Isacchi, B.; van Bloois, L.; Torano, J.S.; Ket, A.; Wu, X.; Broere, F.; Metselaar, J.M.; Rijcken, C.J.; Storm, G.; et al.

Improving solubility and chemical stability of natural compounds for medicinal use by incorporation into liposomes. Int. J. Pharm. 2011, 416, 433–442.

29. Lu, X.Y.; Hu, S.; Jin, Y.; Qiu, L.Y. Application of liposome encapsulation technique to improve anti-carcinoma effect of resveratrol. Drug Dev. Ind. Pharm. 2012, 38, 314–322.

30. Narayanan, N.K.; Nargi, D.; Randolph, C.; Narayanan, B.A. Liposome encapsulation of curcumin and resveratrol in combination reduces prostate cancer incidence in PTEN knockout mice. Int. J. Cancer2009, 125, 1–8.

31. Wang, X.X.; Li, Y.B.; Yao, H.J.; Ju, R.J.; Zhang, Y.; Li, R.J.; Yu, Y.; Zhang, L.; Lu, W.L. The use of mitochondrial targeting resveratrol liposomes modified with a dequalinium polyethylene glycol-distearoylphosphatidyl ethanolamine conjugate to induce apoptosis in resistant lung cancer cells.Biomaterials 2011, 32, 5673–5687.

32. Soo, E.; Thakur, S.; Qu, Z.; Jambhrunkar, S.; Parekh, H.S.; Popat, A. Enhancing delivery and cytotoxicity of resveratrol through a dual nanoencapsulation approach. J. Colloid Interface Sci. 2016,462, 368–374.

33. Jose, S.; Anju, S.S.; Cinu, T.A.; Aleykutty, N.A.; Thomas, S.; Souto, E.B. In vivo pharmacokinetics and biodistribution of resveratrol-loaded solid lipid nanoparticles for brain delivery. Int. J. Pharm. 2014,474, 6–13.

34. Gokce, E.H.; Korkmaz, E.; Dellera, E.; Sandri, G.; Bonferoni, M.C.; Ozer, O. Resveratrol-loaded solid lipid nanoparticles versus nanostructured lipid carriers: Evaluation of antioxidant potential for dermal applications. Int. J. Nanomed. 2012, 7, 1841–1850.

35. Teskac, K.; Kristl, J. The evidence for solid lipid nanoparticles mediated cell uptake of resveratrol. Int. J. Pharm. 2010, 390, 61–69.

36. Neves, A.R.; Lucio, M.; Martins, S.; Lima, J.L.; Reis, S. Novel resveratrol nanodelivery systems based on lipid nanoparticles to enhance its oral bioavailability. Int. J. Nanomed. 2013, 8, 177–187.

37. Pandita, D.; Kumar, S.; Poonia, N.; Lather, V. Solid lipid nanoparticles enhance oral bioavailability of resveratrol, a natural polyphenol. Food Res. Int. 2014, 62, 1165–1174.

38. Muchow, M.; Maincent, P.; Muller, R.H. Lipid nanoparticles with a solid matrix (SLN, NLC, LDC) for oral drug delivery. Drug Dev. Ind. Pharm. 2008, 34, 1394–1405.

39. Shidhaye, S.S.; Vaidya, R.; Sutar, S.; Patwardhan, A.; Kadam, V.J. Solid lipid nanoparticles and nanostructured lipid carriers—Innovative generations of solid lipid carriers. Curr. Drug Deliv. 2008, 5, 324–331.

40. Beloqui, A.; Solinis, M.A.; Rodriguez-Gascon, A.; Almeida, A.J.; Preat, V. Nanostructured lipid carriers: Promising drug delivery systems for future clinics. Nanomedicine 2016, 12, 143–161.

41. Muller, R.H.; Radtke, M.; Wissing, S.A. Nanostructured lipid matrices for improved microencapsulation of drugs. Int. J. Pharm. 2002, 242, 121–128.

42. Artursson, P.; Palm, K.; Luthman, K. Caco-2 monolayers in experimental and theoretical predictions of drug transport. Adv. Drug Deliv. Rev. 2001, 46, 27–43.

43. Corti, G.; Maestrelli, F.; Cirri, M.; Zerrouk, N.; Mura, P. Development and evaluation of an in vitromethod for prediction of human drug absorption II. Demonstration of the method suitability. Eur. J. Pharm. Sci. 2006, 27, 354–362.

44. Schwebel, H.J.; van Hoogevest, P.; Leigh, M.L.; Kuentz, M. The apparent solubilizing capacity of simulated intestinal fluids for

poorly water-soluble drugs. Pharm. Dev. Technol. 2011, 16, 278–286.

45. Frank, K.J.; Westedt, U.; Rosenblatt, K.M.; Holig, P.; Rosenberg, J.; Magerlein, M.; Brandl, M.; Fricker, G. Impact of FaSSIF on the solubility and dissolution-/permeation rate of a poorly water-soluble compound. Eur. J. Pharm. Sci. 2012, 47, 16–20.

46. Neves, A.R.; Queiroz, J.F.; Weksler, B.; Romero, I.A.; Couraud, P.O.; Reis, S. Solid lipid nanoparticles as a vehicle for brain-targeted drug delivery: Two New Strategies of Functionalization with Apolipoprotein E. Nanotechnology 2015, 26, 495103.

47. Acosta, E. Bioavailability of nanoparticles in nutrient and nutraceutical delivery. Curr. Opin. Colloid Interface Sci. 2009, 14, 3–15.

48. Mosmann, T. Rapid colorimetric assay for cellular growth and survival: Application to Proliferation and Cytotoxicity Assays. J. Immunol. Methods 1983, 65, 55–63.

49. Delie, F.; Rubas, W. A human colonic cell line sharing similarities with enterocytes as a model to examine oral absorption: Advantages and Limitations of the Caco-2 Model. Crit. Rev. Ther. Drug Carrier Syst. 1997, 14, 221–286.

50. Behrens, I.; Kissel, T. Do cell culture conditions influence the carrier-mediated transport of peptides in Caco-2 cell monolayers? Eur. J. Pharm. Sci. 2003, 19, 433–442.

51. Neves, A.R.; Reis, S.; Segundo, M.A. Development and validation of a HPLC method using a monolithic column for quantification of trans-resveratrol in lipid nanoparticles for intestinal permeability studies. J. Agric. Food Chem. 2015, 63, 3114–3120.

52. Muller, R.H.; Mader, K.; Gohla, S. Solid lipid nanoparticles (SLN) for controlled drug delivery - a review of the state of the art. Eur. J. Pharm. Biopharm. 2000, 50, 161–177.

53. Müller, R.H.; Jacobs, C.; Kayser, O. Nanosuspensions as particulate drug formulations in therapy: Rationale for development and what we can expect for the future. Adv. Drug Deliv. Rev. 2001, 47, 3–19.

54. Des Rieux, A.; Fievez, V.; Momtaz, M.; Detrembleur, C.; Alonso-Sande, M.; van Gelder, J.; Cauvin, A.; Schneider, Y.J.; Preat, V. Helodermin-loaded nanoparticles: Characterization and transport across anin vitro model of the follicle-associated epithelium. J. Control. Release 2007, 118, 294–302.

55. Florence, A.T. Nanoparticle uptake by the oral route: Fulfilling its potential? Drug Discov. Today Technol. 2005, 2, 75–81.

56. Des Rieux, A.; Ragnarsson, E.G.; Gullberg, E.; Preat, V.; Schneider, Y.J.; Artursson, P. Transport of nanoparticles across an in vitro model of the human intestinal follicle associated epithelium. Eur. J. Pharm. Sci. 2005, 25, 455–465.

57. Yin Win, K.; Feng, S.-S. Effects of particle size and surface coating on cellular uptake of polymeric nanoparticles for oral delivery of anticancer drugs. Biomaterials 2005, 26, 2713–2722.

58. Stervbo, U.; Vang, O.; Bonnesen, C. A review of the content of the putative chemopreventive phytoalexin resveratrol in red wine. Food Chem. 2007, 101, 449–457.

59. Vian, M.A.; Tomao, V.; Gallet, S.; Coulomb, P.O.; Lacombe, J.M. Simple and rapid method for cis- andtrans-resveratrol and piceid isomers determination in wine by high-performance liquid chromatography using chromolith columns. J. Chromatogr. A 2005, 1085, 224–229.

60. Figueiras, T.S.; Neves-Petersen, M.T.; Petersen, S.B. Activation energy of light induced isomerization of resveratrol. J. Fluoresc. 2011, 21, 1897–1906.

61. Camont, L.; Cottart, C.H.; Rhayem, Y.; Nivet-Antoine, V.; Djelidi, R.; Collin, F.; Beaudeux, J.L.; Bonnefont-Rousselot, D. Simple spectrophotometric assessment of the trans-/cis-resveratrol ratio in aqueous solutions. Anal. Chim. Acta 2009, 634, 121–128.

62. Detoni, C.B.; Souto, G.D.; da Silva, A.L.; Pohlmann, A.R.; Guterres, S.S. Photostability and skin penetration of different E-resveratrol-loaded supramolecular structures. Photochem. Photobiol. 2012, 88, 913–921.

63. Hubatsch, I.; Ragnarsson, E.G.; Artursson, P. Determination of drug permeability and prediction of drug absorption in Caco-2 monolayers. Nat. Protoc. 2007, 2, 2111–2119.

64. Artursson, P.; Karlsson, J. Correlation between oral drug absorption in humans and apparent drug permeability coefficients in human intestinal epithelial (Caco-2) cells. Biochem. Biophys. Res. Commun.1991, 175, 880–885.

65. Willenberg, I.; Michael, M.; Wonik, J.; Bartel, L.C.; Empl, M.T.; Schebb, N.H. Investigation of the absorption of resveratrol oligomers in the Caco-2 cellular model of intestinal absorption. Food Chem.2015, 167, 245–250.

66. Teng, Z.; Yuan, C.; Zhang, F.; Huan, M.; Cao, W.; Li, K.; Yang, J.; Cao, D.; Zhou, S.; Mei, Q. Intestinal absorption and first-pass metabolism of polyphenol compounds in rat and their transport dynamics in Caco-2 cells. PLoS ONE 2012, 7, e29647.

67. Ward, P.D.; Tippin, T.K.; Thakker, D.R. Enhancing paracellular permeability by modulating epithelial tight junctions. Pharm. Sci. Technol. Today 2000, 3, 346–358.

68. Neves, A.R.; Queiroz, J.F.; Costa Lima, S.A.; Figueiredo, F.; Fernandes, R.; Reis, S. Cellular uptake and transcytosis of lipid-based nanoparticles across the intestinal barrier: Relevance for Oral Drug Delivery. J. Colloid Interface Sci. 2016, 463, 258–265.

Index

N

O

P

Q

R

S

T